Anonymous

Industrial History of Milwaukee

The Commercial, Manufacturing and Railway Metropolis of the North-West

Anonymous

Industrial History of Milwaukee
The Commercial, Manufacturing and Railway Metropolis of the North-West

ISBN/EAN: 9783337294656

Printed in Europe, USA, Canada, Australia, Japan

Cover: Foto ©ninafisch / pixelio.de

More available books at **www.hansebooks.com**

INDUSTRIAL
HISTORY OF MILWAUKEE

THE

COMMERCIAL, MANUFACTURING

AND

RAILWAY METROPOLIS OF THE NORTH-WEST.

Its Great Natural Resources and Advantageous Location as a Shipping Point, with a Review of its General Business Interests, including History of Milwaukee Chamber of Commerce, Statistical and Descriptive, to which is added a Series of Sketches of the Prominent Places and People of the Cream City, the Rise and Progress of Firms, Institutions and Corporations.

ILLUSTRATED.

MILWAUKEE:
E. E. BARTON, PUBLISHER.
1886.

Entered according to act of Congress, in the year 1885, by

ELMER E. BARTON,

In the office of the Librarian of Congress, at Washington.

CRAMER, AIKENS & CRAMER, PRINTERS, MILWAUKEE.

HISTORICAL SKETCH OF MILWAUKEE.

MILWAUKEE is the metropolis of Wisconsin, one of the chief commercial and manufacturing cities of the Northwest, and one of the most healthful and charming places of residence on the globe. It is situated on the west shore of Lake Michigan, 100 miles north of its southern end, 80 miles north of Chicago, and 1,000 miles northwest of New York by rail, in 43° 3' north latitude, 87° 55' west longitude (10° 54.5' west of Washington). The shore of the lake is 600 feet above the level of the sea. The Milwaukee and Menomonee rivers unite in the center of the business portion of the city, about half a mile from their debouchure into Lake Michigan, where they are joined by a third and smaller stream—the Kinnickinnic. A bay, 6 miles from cape to cape, and 3 miles broad, stretches in front of the city, which commands a fine water view, the ground rising along the shore 80 feet above the level of the lake, then gradually sloping westward to the Milwaukee river, and again rising on the west and north to a height of 125 feet. The ground also rises to a commanding elevation south of the valley of the Menomonee. Few cities present so many natural attractions of site, as indeed its Indian name indicates ("the beautiful hollow or bay"); and art has added to nature. In the residence parts of the city there are miles of avenues from 70 to 100 feet wide, lined on both sides with elms and maples, behind which stand handsome houses with spacious lawns, fountains and evergreens, giving the appearance of a continuous park. The material used for building is largely cream-colored brick made in the vicinity, from which Milwaukee-is sometimes called the "Cream City." The climate, tempered by the great lake, is remarkably pleasant and healthy. The mean temperature, as shown by the records of twenty years, is 46.7° Fahrenheit. The coldest month is January (average 22.37°), the hottest July (70.4°). During the last eleven years the average death rate has been but 20 per 1,000.

THE SETTLEMENT OF MILWAUKEE.

Milwaukee's first formal historian appears to have been Julius P. Bolivar MacCabe, who in 1847 published the first Directory of the city, to which was prefixed an epitomized history—"MacCabe's History of Milwaukee." From this work the following statement of the first settlement of the city is extracted: "On the 14th day of September, 1818, a large Michilimackinac bateau entered the Milwaukee river, and as it approached the shore it was hailed by numerous red men of the forest, who were then the only inhabitants of Eastern Wisconsin, and who recognized in this little craft two French Canadian traders, who were destined to be the first white settlers in Eastern Wisconsin. These were Solomon Juneau, Esq., and his father-in-law, Mr. Jacques Vieau. The latter had visited the country bordering on the Milwaukee river in the summer of the preceding year, and erected a log trading-house on the Menomonee river, about two miles from its mouth, and near what has since been known as Pettibone's lime-kiln. But no white settlement had ever been made here, although several fur traders, for some time previous, had occasionally visited this place, which was then an important point for Indian commerce. * * * * The only building erected on the site of Milwaukee was a rudely constructed log-house covered with cedar bark, which had been built by Mr. B. LeClair a short time previous, for the accommodation of traders during the winter months, and stood on a portion of the ground now occupied by the store of Messrs. Ludington & Co. Mr. Juneau was not only the first white settler in this place, but was actually the first white resident of Wisconsin, with the exception of the settlers at Green Bay and Prairie du Chien, who with the then few citizens of Chicago, were his nearest white neighbors. Neither Galena in Illinois, nor Dubuque in Iowa, were then commenced. The country for many miles around Milwaukee was inhabited by the Pottawattamies, and a few of the Ottawa, Chippewa and Menomonee tribes of Indians. * * * * * The land first occupied, and afterwards purchased by Mr. Juneau, was the northeast quarter of section 29, town 7, range 22. It extended from Division street to Wisconsin street, and embraced land on either side of the river, all of which measured about 132 acres. From the time Mr. Juneau landed here in 1818, up to the settlement of Capt. Saunders at this point in 1835, Mr. Juneau's was the only white family residing in Milwaukee. During the sanguinary Sauk war in July, 1832, those savage aborigines were encamped on the banks of Whitewater Creek, about 34 miles west of Milwaukee, and in con-

WASHINGTON MONUMENT.

sequence thereof Gen. Atkinson ordered all the friendly Indians to assemble at Milwaukee, and remain here until further orders, lest they should be mistaken for the Sauks, whom the army was then in pursuit of. Their whole number, which amounted to several thousand, erected their wigwams on either side of the river, where they remained until the war was terminated by the battle of Bad Axe, near Prairie du Chien, in September, 1832. The first frame building erected within the village of Milwaukee was put up by Mr. Juneau in the year 1824. It stood on the lot at the northwest corner of East Water and Wisconsin streets."

Byron Kilbourn, who came here in 1834, and Col. George H. Walker, who came here in the preceding year, form, with Solomon Juneau, the trinity of Milwaukee's founders. They were not, however, the first Anglo-Saxon settlers here, that honor being claimed for Albert Fowler, Rodney J. Currier, Andrew J. Lansing and Quartus G. Carley, who came here in November, 1833, just after the Indians ceded to the general government the land on which the western and southern divisions of the city stand. The Indian title to the eastern division of the city was extinguished in 1831. Byron Kilbourn purchased from the government a tract on the west side of the river, " with a mile and a half of water front, and an infinity of morass," as an early chronicler of Milwaukee describes it. As soon as he had secured his patent, he took steps to improve the land and laid off the plat in town lots. Col. Walker in 1834 built a log-house on a piece of land long known as Walker's Point, which at that time stretched into the river from the South Side. Col. Walker purchased from the government a large tract of land on that side of the river, and platted a portion of it into town lots. Solomon Juneau did the same with his land on the East Side. The East Side, Mr. Juneau's domain, was distinctively known as Milwaukee. The West Side was for a time called Kilbourntown, after Mr. Kilbourn, and the South Side was for years locally known as Walker's Point. The village of Milwaukee, comprising the territory which is now the East Side of the city, was organized February 27, 1837. Kilbourntown was annexed March 11, 1839. Walker's Point was not annexed until February 15, 1845. The date of Milwaukee's incorporation as a city was January 31, 1846. The first charter election, at which Solomon Juneau was elected mayor, was held in April, 1846. The population of the city at that time was 9,660. The state census taken in July, 1885, showed the population of the city to be over 158,000, and at this writing it is undoubtedly upward of 160,000.

THE FIRST ELECTION.

On the 19th of September, 1885, the citizens of Milwaukee celebrated the fiftieth anniversary of the organization of Milwaukee township. The members of the Milwaukee County Pioneer Association, the members of the Milwaukee Old Settlers' Club, and the city and county officials, formed in procession at Court House Park, and, preceded by a band, moved through the principal streets to

Schlitz Park, where a programme of music and oratory was carried out. The orator of the occasion on behalf of the old settlers was Winfield Smith. The following extract from his address is an interesting contribution to the history of early Milwaukee:

"On this day fifty years ago, then as now the last day of the week, the eighty or a hundred persons scattered through the vicinity of the residence of the Indian trader, Juneau, held by ballot the first election ever seen here. Thirty-nine persons voted, and thus organized a township government. The original record, now in my hand, opens thus:

"September 7th, 1835, Milwaukee. Met pursuant to an act of the Legislature of the territory of Michigan to organize the township of Milwaukee. First, chose Albert Fowler, moderator; second, James Heath, clerk, *pro tem.*; third, adjourned to Saturday, the 19th of September, inst., at 9 o'clock A. M.

"September 19th,. 1835. Met pursuant to notice. Elected George H. Walker moderator; James Heath clerk, *pro tem.*; B. H. Edgerton, inspector. On motion of B. H. Edgerton, resolved, that all actual settlers have the privilege of voting at this meeting, and that all our proceedings be referred to the legislative council for their approval, etc., etc. Elected the following township officers.

"Then follow the names of Supervisor Geo. H. Walker, Town Clerk Horace Chase, and twenty-two other officers. The meeting took place under the laws (it would probably, if the stories be true, be too much to claim that it was pursuant to the laws) of the territory of Michigan, of which this soil was then a part. The record is not very formal, and it was probably much more formal than the proceedings. The young men who voted were not fond of legal strictness, but this paper proves that among them were men of good education and much accuracy in written statements. The number of ballots cast for the several candidates does not appear, but in the list of those then chosen as township officers are the names of George H. Walker, James Sanderson, Albert Fowler, Solomon Juneau, Samuel Brown, James Heath, Brazillai Douglas, Horace Chase, and Dr. Enoch Chase, names familiar to many of our citizens, of whom the last two are yet often read by us in the newspaper accounts of the doings of the day. Our esteemed friend, Horace Chase, who would probably not yet wish to be called venerable, is still in the same way of active participation in municipal government on which he entered fifty years ago. * * We rejoice that Messrs. Horace and Enoch Chase, honored with the confidence of their fellows in 1835, still live to enjoy it, after fifty years of industry, of upright dealing, of bodily and mental activity, which have given them a right to rest which few can show, and which they seem in no haste to claim.

"Following the record of the election is the note, 'Voted, that the ballots be all received in one box at the next election.' Then the titles and signatures verifying the record: 'Officers of the meeting, George H. Walker, James Heath, B.

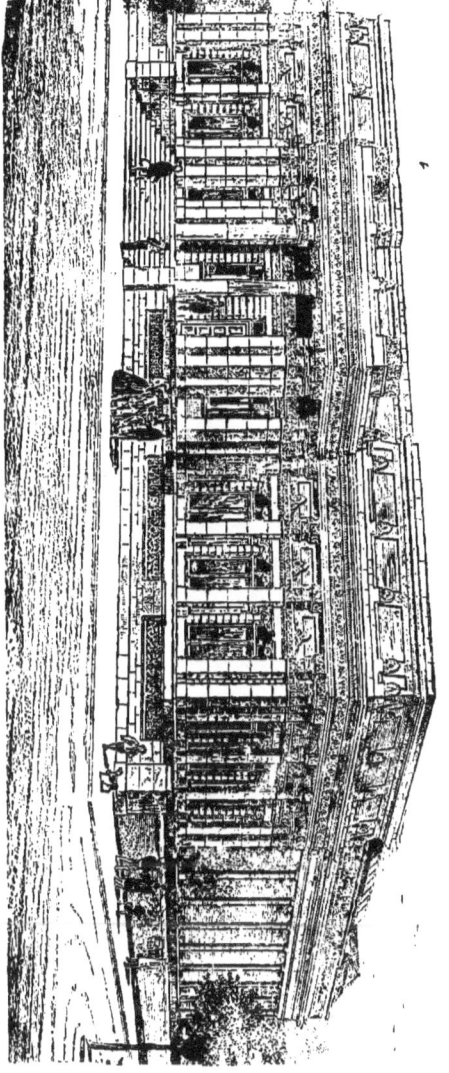

Layton Art Gallery.

INDUSTRIAL HISTORY OF MILWAUKEE. 13

H. Edgerton.' The oaths of office are next written and signed, George H. Walker as supervisor, and Horace Chase, town clerk, making oath before Albert Fowler, justice of the peace.

"The affidavit of Mr. Walker follows, signed and sworn to September 21, 1835. The oath of office of Mr. Chase was taken on the same day, as also those of Messrs. Finch, Juneau and Harman, commissioners of highways; and Messrs. Brown, Cole, and Bigelow, commissioners of common schools; and Messrs. Juneau and Finch, directors of the poor. Mr. Chase took his oath of office as assessor September 24, pledging himself thereby to assess honestly and impartially the several persons and estates within the township of Milwaukee, and to observe in such assessment, to the best of his knowledge and judgment, the laws of the territory directing such assessments to be made. Immediately following the last record, and without any break, come these words: 'A crop and slit in the left ear. September 31, 1835. B. W. Finch.' Then further oaths of office, and again the following: 'A crop on the right ear and a hole in the left. September 26, 1835. Joseph Porthier.' Next: 'A slope off the under side of the left ear. April 2, 1836. Clybourn & Chase.' I understand that these marvelous expressions relate, not to the election or the township organization, nor to any of the citizens who may be supposed to have undergone the punishments therein indicated, but rather to the pigs which were allowed to run at large in those times, and which were thus branded by their respective owners. There being, as I am told, no other blank book in the entire county than the one from which I am reading, the marks of cattle and swine were deemed important enough to be inserted therein, among those of the newly-elected officers, and the importance of the act so absorbed the attention of the writers that they quite forgot to indicate the purpose or character of their entries. In the record I have been reading the name of the new town is spelled 'Milwakee,' the last syllable having two e's and no i, upon which point there was strong dispute thirty-five years ago. Milwaukee was also spelled 'Milwalkie' and 'Milwalky.' The affidavits call the county 'Brown,' but speak of the duties as to be performed in 'Milwakee' county. The latter county was set off from Brown county September 6, 1834, but had not been organized. A poundmaster—Enoch Chase—pathmasters and road commissioners were elected, and the next spring, fence-viewers, although there were no pound, no roads, no fences in the county. It is difficult now to realize the scene which this place then presented. A plat of the town—now the Seventh Ward alone—had been prepared shortly before by Juneau and Martin, and recorded September 8, 1835, and some streets began to be known; while no plat was recorded of lots west of the river until October 8, and no streets were there to be seen. Water covered most of the land now the Third Ward, in which grew reeds and rushes, extending from the river to the sandy beach of the lake. On the West Side a like marsh covered the area between Fourth street and the river, south of Grand Avenue to the Menomonee. Of the

South Side, Dr. Lapham writes, in 1845: 'The city commences about a mile above the mouth of the river, at a place called Walker's Point, and extends about a mile and a half along the river. Below Walker's Point the river is bordered by impassable marshes.' Walker's Point, to which he refers, is a name meaningless to our young citizens. But it was a point of high ground running several hundred feet through the marsh northeasterly, to the south bank of the river, near the present East Water street bridge. On it was built the dwelling of George H. Walker, the first town supervisor, afterwards mayor, and he entered the land at the first government sale. That point, then conspicuous enough, was the only place where a house could stand within a quarter of a mile. Many years ago it disappeared, as it was cut down and the marshes on both sides were filled. Half a dozen houses, scattered along for a mile to the south, contained all the population of the South Side. The ground was high where the point extended back, widening toward the west. The forest grew heavy, except where it had been cut away in patches by the settlers, and stumps not yet uprooted indicated how recent had been the work of the pioneer. No other trace was seen of the hand of civilization. Upon the East Side, the marshes that covered the whole of the present Third Ward were varied by two islands of dryer land, one near the north end of East Water street bridge, and the other covering the corner of Jackson and Detroit streets, as now laid out, the latter of which bore the significant title of Duck Island. The land in which the present Seventh Ward lies was mostly high, running by a steep descent into the marshes of the Third Ward, and into the marsh which also lay along the river front from south to north. The western line of the bluff crossed Wisconsin street at the northeast corner of Broadway, and one of my own early recollections of the city is the digging down of the bluff preparatory to the removal from it of the three-story wooden hotel called the Milwaukee House, which had been previously kept by Caleb Wall. Some seven or eight houses, the furthest north of which was near Biddle street, were all that had yet been built. On the west side of the river Longstreet's and Dr. Graham's stores, the house of Byron Kilbourn, at Chestnut street, and the American House, near the site of the present Republican House, were all that were to be seen. The marsh covered the Fourth Ward, as now laid out, along the Menomonee river and the Milwaukee as far north as Spring street. Near Seventh street the ground suddenly rose to the west, and trees covered the bluffs and also the low land north of Spring street. The forest was dense and unbroken, penetrated by no roads except Indian trails. These were the white man's only guide on his way to Green Bay or to Fort Winnebago. Only three or four wagons were in the southeastern part of the territory, and most of the people were living in the so-called 'Cottage Inn,' and American House. The line of the river was margined by no wharfs, and was lost in the rushes which filled the marshes. The lake shore has remained with little change to the present time, but the mouth of the river

ALEXANDER MITCHELL'S RESIDENCE.

was nearly a mile south of the present harbor, and the channel meandered through the marshes, considerable portions of which yet indicate to the observer how the principal area of Milwaukee then appeared. There were some log houses and some frame houses, built without much reference to streets, or any other consideration, except rapidity and cheapness of construction. No brick was seen, and none had yet been made. The citizens at that time had no suspicion of the richness of the earth which was to furnish them a renowned article for the construction of their sightly buildings, and which should, in time to come, give name and wealth to the city."

An interesting fact in connection with Milwaukee's first election is that one of the electors who took part in it was a negro, who is said to have been the first negro voter in the United States.

Traveling was by no means the easy task during the early stage of Milwaukee's development that it is at the present day, and it requires an effort of imagination to realize how completely the people who came from the East, and helped to build up the city, were cut off from the rest of the world. The traveler in those days might, with ordinary fortune, be three weeks on the journey from Detroit to this place. News came no faster, because there was no mail route except by water. The telegraph was not in use. Three to five weeks might well be taken for the letter from New York to Milwaukee. The railroad was a light, flat rail track, running a few miles west from Albany, and all the journey besides to Chicago was performed in stages, unless the wayfarer was so happy as to get a boat; and from Chicago hither he walked, unless he rode his own horse. Despite the difficulty of the trip, and the isolation of the place, however, a stream of immigration poured steadily into Milwaukee. The population, which was 275 in 1836, had swelled to 1,810 in 1840, and when the census of 1850 was taken, Milwaukee was a city of close upon 20,000 inhabitants.

THE BRIDGE WAR.

Perhaps the most notable episode in the early history of Milwaukee was what is known as the Bridge War. E. D. Holton has given a succinct and picturesque account of this bloodless struggle, which is worthy of transcription here. Premising with a description of the three founders of the city, he plunges into his recital as follows:

"Behold the men! Juneau, Walker and Kilbourn, of nearly equal height and size! The first from Montreal, the second from Virginia, the third from Connecticut. The domain of the first lay north and east of the Milwaukee river; that of the second south of the Milwaukee and Menomonee rivers; that of the third north of the Menomonee and west of the Milwaukee—three grand divisions. Upon one point these men were agreed, and only one, and that was that neither of the others was to have a town on their lands. The Virginian

said, ' Behold the country at my rear, and the harbor at hand; certainly the town must be here.' The Connecticut man said, ' This river has two sides, and it's a meandered stream, and under the laws of Congress you cannot bridge it. The country is also behind me, and such a country! See the fine bluffs for residences, and the convenient valley for business, and the long line of docks along West Water street for shipping and other commercial purposes.' Mr. Juneau said, ' All very good, gentlemen, but the people come and buy lots of me, and I sell them.' Now, as I said, in the early days the two sides of the river were well-defined and there was no way of crossing it except by a ferry at Walker's Point, and one at Spring Street [now Grand Avenue]. Those who had come and bought the Frenchman's lots at length insisted upon a bridge, and the Chestnut Street Bridge was built somewhere about the year 1839. This led to a long contention in the courts. How it ever came out I never knew, only that the bridge continued to stand until it fell over by its own weight. The county repaired it again, and gave to Mr. James H. Rogers the broad sides of the clumsy superstructure which had fallen down. These sides were made of heavy pine plank, in a kind of lattice work. Mr. Rogers, in the summer of 1842, moved them down to Spring street, and made of them a kind of float bridge which was used for a while to cross upon by teams as well as by foot. It was so light that if a team did not move pretty lively it would sink. Several immersions were gained by this process. A freshet in the fall carried away the concern. In the spring of 1843, John Clifford, Jacob S. Bean, J. H. Rogers, Holton and Goodall and some few others, made a subscription and built the first frame bridge crossing from Spring to Wisconsin street. * * * * It passed the heaviest loads, and was in good condition when taken down after two years' service. Although allowed to stand for the time being, it was loudly denounced by many of the West Siders. In the summer of 1844, Daniel Wells and others secured the construction of the Oneida street bridge. This was a frame bridge with a draw sustained by floats. * *
* * * * Things ran on pretty smoothly until 1845. The municipal affairs of the town were conducted by two separate corporations, called the East and West Wards, until 1845, when the South Ward—Walker's Point—was added. To be sure, the trustees—five from each ward—met together in the same room, employing the same clerk and the same records, but their funds and all their legislation, so far as related to their own wards, were entirely separate. In other words, the doctrine of State rights prevailed in these little commonwealths. They of the East Ward could do what they pleased in matters which related to their own affairs, and *vice versa*. It so happened that the East Ward had assumed the support, mainly, of attending the bridges. But after the construction of the Oneida street bridge, it not only refused to support Spring street bridge, but, as was asserted, maliciously and wilfully ran a vessel against it and broke it down. The West Warders considered that they had just cause for wrath

THE ARMORY.

and retaliation, and thereupon arose a great controversy. The trustees of the West Ward claimed absolute jurisdiction, territorially, to the middle of Milwaukee river, and a resolution was brought forward in the Board of Trustees to that effect. But the trustees of the South Ward joined with those of the East Ward—and the decision of the majority was that the river was common ground—that although it had two banks, yet the water between was common territory, and to be held and occupied in common by all concerned. This was something of a damper to the valorous members of the West Ward. For, mind you, the object of gaining an agreement in council by the West Warders, that the center of the river was the boundary of each Ward, was that they might, under the right of absolute and undivided authority in their own dominions, and upon finding that the middle of the river was the boundary of the Ward, then proceed to remove exactly so much of all of the bridges as laid west of that line, out of the river. The proposition, however, after having been stoutly and ably argued, was lost. But under the old maxim, there is no great loss without some small gain, it was incidentally settled that the boundary of each Ward *did* actually go to the water's edge at low water mark, and here the West Warders took their stand—absolute authority and control in their own territory! The Chestnut street bridge was a huge structure, standing upon high, massive abutments, with an immensely heavy draw, running off upon the west side on a sort of railroad track. It was found that the entire abutment on the west end of the bridge stood considerably upon the undisputed territory of the West Ward. Whereupon the trustees of the West Ward ordered that so much of said bridge as rested upon and was located in said ward, be removed out of the ward as a nuisance. Accordingly workmen were directed to so remove the nuisance, and in the prosecution of their work commenced by sawing in two the huge draw, and as the East Warders supplied no support to the part which lay in their territory when that of the West Ward was removed, the part that belonged to the territory of the East Ward fell into the river. And now arose among these early inhabitants one of the greatest excitements ever witnessed in the town. Guns were fired, and flaming speeches made, but no lives were lost. The excitement passed away at length, and cooler and better counsels prevailed. Not long after, a convention was agreed upon between the belligerents, which settled the whole basis upon which bridges should be constructed and maintained, and since that auspicious time the two sides of the river have happily grown less and less distinct."

THE HARBOR IMPROVEMENT.

Another important struggle which was carried on in the early developmental period of the city had reference to the improvement of the harbor. In the summer of 1835 the United States War Department authorized Judge J. Duane Doty, then of Green Bay, to institute such proceedings as were necessary to secure a preliminary survey of the Milwaukee river, with a view of constructing a harbor. The first survey was made in 1836, by Lieuts. Center and Rose, of the United States Topographical Engineer Corps, who recommended the making of a straight cut from the river to the lake, 3,000 feet north of the natural outlet of the river. This was the plan favored by the citizens of Milwaukee, and was ultimately carried out, but not without a long struggle. The first government appropriation for the improvement of Milwaukee harbor was made in 1843. The act made no reference to the survey of Lieuts. Center and Rose, but provided for "the construction of a harbor at the most suitable situation at or near Milwaukee, in the territory of Wisconsin, to be made under the survey of an officer to be appointed by the Secretary of War." The Secretary appointed for the work Lieut. T. J. Cram, who decided adversely to the construction of the straight cut, and in favor of the improvement of the mouth of the river. Great public indignation was expressed at this decision, which was believed to be detrimental to the interests of the city. A party of citizens dug a ditch from the river to the lake, in the hope that the water rushing through would form a channel sufficiently wide and deep to permit of the passage of large vessels, but sandbars formed at its mouth, and prevented it from attaining the dimensions desired. The government meantime went on with the improvement of the mouth of the river, and in May, 1844, the work of dredging had been carried forward so far that the brig "Virginia," drawing seven feet of water, was enabled to proceed up the river without meeting any obstruction. The feeling against the natural channel of the river and in favor of the improvement of the straight cut continued, however, and in 1848 Byron Kilbourn, who was elected mayor, recommended in his first message to the Council, that the city should raise money by issuing bonds, and construct for itself an entrance to the river at the point proposed by Lieuts. Center and Rose. A committee was appointed by the Council to examine the site and estimate the cost of building piers and dredging a channel. There for a time the matter again rested. In 1852 Congress listened to the appeal of the citizens for the improvement of the straight cut, and appropriated $15,000 toward the work. The inadequacy of the amount was so palpable as to convince the citizens that if they wanted the improvement in their own generation they must make it themselves. Authority from the State legislature to levy a direct tax, not exceeding $50,000, for the purpose of making the improvement, was secured by the city authorities, and in 1855 the money was placed by the city at the disposal of the government. The straight cut was soon rendered navigable for vessels, and the old entrance to the harbor was abandoned. The work of improving the straight cut went on for years, and by a train of circumstances which it would be tedious to describe here the city became liable for a far greater expenditure on behalf of the work than had been originally contemplated. The contractors' claims which the city was eventually obliged to pay amounted to

$445,971. In addition to this, the general government, between the years 1855 and 1875, expended about $200,000 for the work. The government has lately reimbursed the city for a portion of its outlay on the improvement, the benefit of which is shared by all interested in the navigation of the lakes.

THE MILWAUKEE AND ROCK RIVER CANAL.

Another chapter in the history of early Milwaukee deserves to be adverted to, although it deals with an enterprise that was never fully carried out, and that therefore conferred upon the city only a tithe of the material benefits that were expected to be derived from it. Wheeler's " Chronicles of Milwaukee " summarizes the matter referred to as follows:

"As early as the summer of 1836, Byron Kilbourn, of Milwaukee, with the assistance of several other gentlemen, commenced a series of examinations of the country between Milwaukee and Rock river, with a view to the construction of a canal. Having satisfied himself as to the practicability of the works, Mr. Kilbourn attracted public attention to the scheme by a series of articles written by himself, and published in the *Advertiser* in '37. A bill was introduced in the first legislative assemby, at its session held at Belmont in 1836, praying for a charter of incorporation for a company, but no action was taken upon it at that time. The articles of Mr. Kilbourn aroused public attention, and again, in 1837, petitions were forwarded to the legislature—then in session at Burlington—for the passage of an act of incorporation. The company was incorporated in 1838. The capital stock was to be $100,000, with the privilege of increasing the amount to a sum not exceeding $1,000,000, should the same be found necessary to the completion of the works. In 1842 the dam was built just above Kilbourntown, by Capt. John Anderson, and in December of that year the water was let into so much of the canal as had been constructed, viz., from the dam to its present terminus in the Second Ward, just above the Chestnut street bridge. A celebration accompanied this event, and a very able oration was delivered by John Hustis. This finished portion of the canal was immediately invested with a great deal of interest to capitalists, and the next year a saw mill was built upon it by Samuel Brown and Benjamin Moffat, and Mr. Rathbone put up a large grist mill, which was shortly after followed by a woolen factory. The water power was looked upon as the most important element of the present and future prosperity of Milwaukee. The dam, 430 feet in length and 18 feet high, gave a water-way of 400 feet. The established rent for the water was $75 a year for 100 cubic feet per minute. The lots between the canal and the river, 60 feet front by an average of 130 feet deep, were worth from $400 to $800. The history of the Milwaukee and Rock River Canal is long and unsatisfactory. The company, after its incorporation, applied for and received from Congress a grant of land, commonly known as the canal grant, and subsequently, the legislature and the company becoming involved in a

The New Chicago, Milwaukee & St. Paul Railway Passenger Depot.

mesh of difficulties concerning the grant and the money accruing from the sale of the lands, the work stopped, and all that remains at this day of the Rock River Canal is the still substantial dam, the guard-lock, and one mile of canal, which empties itself into the river just above Chestnut street bridge. Byron Kilbourn, having been the originator of the enterprise and having been prominent in its prosecution from the first, much of the odium attending its failure attached to him, though there is no one, even at this day, who is not willing to admit that had the work been consummated according to Mr. Kilbourn's original views as then set forth, the town would have been incalculably benefited." Mr. Wheeler's account was published in 1861. Since he wrote, steam-power has largely supplanted water-power in the manufactories of the country. The Rock River Canal Company probably no longer has a legal representative. Within a very recent period the old canal has been filled up. The dam, which has been washed out several times, and rebuilt, is now valued partly because by holding back the water of the upper Milwaukee it makes that stream navigable for pleasure boats which carry parties to the attractive parks and other resorts a short distance north of the city, and partly because it affords a means of flushing and cleansing the lower portion of the stream, which else would become offensive in the summer time by reason of the burden of sewage which it is made to bear away—a task that is of necessity imposed upon all rivers flowing through the centers of great cities.

Thus much space has been devoted to a partially unsuccessful enterprise, because it is believed that notwithstanding its incompleteness it was an important factor in giving a manufacturing tendency to the city. The flour mills alone that stand along the site of the now dismantled canal, give employment to hundreds of operatives and contribute in no small degree to Milwaukee's prosperity. The establishment of the old water-power was the enterprise that brought them into being.

Before the era of railroads in Wisconsin, several plank-roads leading out of Milwaukee were constructed by stock companies composed of enterprising citizens. They became avenues of an important traffic between the city and its tributary territory.

THE BIRTH OF MILWAUKEE'S RAILWAY SYSTEM.

Alexander Mitchell, than whom no man is a better authority, has given it as his opinion that if, when railroads began to be built in the West, the citizens of Milwaukee had remained passive, and had done nothing to command the trade of the great region to the north and west of them, the city would have missed her opportunity, and would have been relegated to the position of a quiet country village.

The first railway train which ever ran out of Milwaukee took an excursion party from this city to Waukesha in February, 1851, over the Milwaukee &

Mississippi Railroad, one of the lines which subsequently coming under one management, form what is now known as the Chicago, Milwaukee & St. Paul Railway system. The first earth for this railroad had been moved in the fall of 1849 from a spur of high land near elevator "A", in the Menomonee valley. The energy, perseverance and courage required to construct a railway across Wisconsin at that early date, the first to touch "the Father of Waters," can hardly be understood now. The country was sparsely settled, and the inhabitants were poor. Money was difficult to borrow, and railroad supplies were costly and distant. To that pioneer railroad more than to any other one thing, except her location on Lake Michigan, Milwaukee is indebted for her steady growth and her present commercial prominence. The first directors of the enterprise were Byron Kilbourn, J. H. Tweedy, Dr. L. W. Weeks, Anson Eldred, James Kneeland, Alexander Mitchell, Dr. E. B. Wolcott, E. D. Clinton and E. D. Holton. Mr. Kilbourn was the first president. Mr. Holton, in an address on the occasion of the opening of the Milwaukee Chamber of Commerce, in 1858, which was subsequently published in the collections of the State Historical Society, gave the following interesting and picturesque account of the circumstances under which this important railway enterprise was undertaken and carried forward:

" It was a great undertaking for that day, under the circumstances. We were without money, as a people, either in city or country. Every man had come to the country with limited means, and each had his house, his store, his shop, his barn to build, his land to clear and fence, and how could he spare anything from his own individual necessities? Some wise men looked on and shook their heads, and there were many croakers. But in the minds of those who had assumed the undertaking, there was a sober, earnest purpose to do what they could for its accomplishment. It was demanded of our own people that they should lay aside all their feuds and personalities, and one and all join in the great work. To a very great extent this demand was complied with, and gentlemen were brought to work cordially and harmoniously together, who had stood aloof from each other for years. The spirit of union, harmony and concord, exhibited by the people of the city, was most cordially reciprocated by those of the country along the contemplated line of road. Subscription books were widely circulated, and the aggregate sum subscribed was very considerable. I said we had no money, but we had *things*, and subscriptions were received with the understanding that they could be paid in such commodities as could be turned into the work of constructing the road. This method of building a railroad would be smiled at now, and was, by some among us, then. But it was, after all, a great source of our strength and of our success; at any rate, for the time being. The work was commenced in the fall of 1849, and for one entire year the grading was prosecuted and paid for by orders drawn upon the merchants, payable in goods—by carts from wagon makers, by harnesses from harness makers, by cattle, horses, beef, pork, oats, corn, potatoes and flour from the farmers, all received on account of stock subscriptions, and turned over to the contractors in payment of work done upon the road. A large amount of the grading of the road from here to Waukesha was performed in this way. Upon seeing this work go on, the people began to say everywhere: 'Why, there is to be a railroad, surely,' and the work rose into consequence and public confidence. It having become settled in the minds of the directors that they could make headway against all difficulties in casting up the road-bed, the pressing inquiry was, 'How can the road be ironed? Iron costs money, and money we have not got.' In this emergency, a mass meeting of stockholders was called at Waukesha in the spring of 1850. About three hundred people assembled, mostly farmers. The question propounded was, 'How can $250,000 be obtained for the purchase of iron to reach from Milwaukee to Whitewater?' It was during this meeting, and after much discussion, that Major Joseph Goodrich, of Milton, said: 'See here; I can mortgage my farm for $3,000 and go to the East, where I came from, and get the money for it. Now, are there not one hundred men between Milwaukee and Rock River that can do the same? If so, here is your money. I will be one of them.' This was a new idea. It was turned over and over. It had serious objections, but after all it was the best thing that was presented, and the plan was accepted; and here arose, so far as I know, the plan of raising farm mortgages in aid of the construction of railroads. The one hundred men were found, who put up the required amount of mortgages, and an attempt was made to negotiate them. But this was found, at first, impossible. It was a class of security entirely unknown, and no market could be found for them. In the attempt to negotiate these securities, it was found that while they would not sell, the bonds of the city of Milwaukee would. Whereupon an application was made to the city to come forward and issue $234,000 of her bonds in aid of the road. The city promptly and cordially responded. The bonds sold for cash at par, the money was at once invested in iron, at very low prices, and the success of the Milwaukee & Mississippi Railroad was set down as fixed. I have dwelt thus long upon this road, because it was the great pioneer road of this city and of the State, and upon its success all the other roads built from the city have found both their origin and their success."

The city's experiences with railroad enterprises were not all of a happy character. Wheeler, in his Chronicles, after relating the history of the municipal encouragement of the Milwaukee & Mississippi, or as it was first called, Milwaukee & Waukesha Railroad Company, says: " Apparently the facility with which the city had been inveigled into the encouragement of railroads, received, as it merited, public attention; and invited a combined movement upon its quality of yieldingness by all those whose sagacity is ever awake to discern the means of their individual advancement in the complication of the embarrassments into which organized society may be plunged. This movement resulted in the act of the Legislature of the 2d of April, 1853, entitled 'An Act to authorize the city of Milwaukee to loan its credit in aid of certain railroads,' and the act in addition thereto passed July 12th, 1853, and the act of March 31st, 1854, amendatory thereof; by force of which acts the city was authorized to loan its credit, in the manner therein particularly specified, 'to any railroad company duly incorporated and organized for the purpose of constructing railroads leading from the city of Milwaukee into the interior of the State,' as well as 'railroads to intersect and connect with any other railroad having its terminus in said city,' which, in the opinion of the Common Council, might be entitled to aid from the city. A provision was also contained in said acts requiring the question of the issue of bonds to any such railroad company to be first submitted to the voters of the city, and their approval of the measure by the ordinary test of the ballot was a necessary preliminary to such issue. Pursuant to this legislation, elections were held from time to time —always resulting in favor of the issue—and ordinances passed by the Common Council, under which there were issued and delivered to the several companies deemed to come within the provisions of the acts, 7 per cent. bonds of the city amounting to $1,380,000, in addition to those before issued to the Milwaukee & Waukesha Railroad Company. * * * * * These latter bonds were to be merely loans of credit on the part of the city to the several companies, and the city was to be amply indemnified by said companies against all liability on said bonds, either for principal or interest. And at the times of the several issues to the companies, the city officers took to themselves the credit of assuming that the securities that the city received for such indemnification were sufficient. But partly from a misapprehension of the value of said railroad securities, and partly from too great compliance on their part—not to raise the question of connivance and rascality—those securities, or such of them as the city has not suffered itself to be wheedled out of, are now found lamentably inadequate. * * * * * Whatever of palliation there may have been for the encouragement originally given by the city corporation to the Milwaukee & Waukesha Railroad, when that enterprise was essaying those feeble steps that have since widened into the strides by which it reached the Mississippi, there was none for the wholesale system, which, with the connivance of the Legislature, the city afterward adopted, of extending a credit, to which it was by no means entitled itself, indiscriminately to all the roads projected to terminate in the city, as well as to all their branches and connections which did not come within many miles of the city." In March, 1861, a readjustment act was passed which contained a provision prohibiting the city from issuing any new bonds until its bonded debt should be reduced to $500,000. In 1871, when the city determined upon the construction of water works, the passage of a special enabling act by the Legislature was necessary before the city could issue bonds for the purpose, as even at that late date the city debt was above $700,000. While the city reaped a rich reward for the aid which it

St. Paul's Church.

extended to legitimate railway enterprises in their infancy, it had to suffer for many years for the indiscretion which prompted the indiscriminate extension of its credit. Still, he who looks calmly back over the history of the matter will be inclined to say that it was better that there should have been some waste along with Milwaukee's liberality to the early railroad enterprises, than that the city should have refrained from granting those which were legitimate the encouragement of financial aid. Alexander Mitchell, who has been before quoted on this subject, said what must command the assent of all clear-headed men, when he remarked: "The location of Chicago, at the head of Lake Michigan, forced greatness upon her. The citizens of Chicago, individually, or in their corporate capacity, did comparatively nothing for the first railroads which entered that city; while, if it had not been for the enterprise and public spirit and liberality of the citizens of Milwaukee, both individually and collectively, Milwaukee to-day might have been no larger than Manitowoc or Sheboygan."

THE MILWAUKEE OF TO-DAY.

THE MUNICIPALITY.

Milwaukee is governed by a Mayor and a Common Council of thirty-nine aldermen. The streets and public buildings are under the charge of the Board of Public Works, composed of three commissioners and the City Engineer, all subject to the Common Council. A bountiful supply of water is obtained from the lake, and the streets are well supplied with sewers. The value of the property assessed for taxation in 1885 was $78,861,366. The Tax Commissioner states that the churches and other untaxed property aggregate in value $8,000,000 more. The city debt is $2,561,000, mostly for the water works, which are city property. There is an efficient system of public schools under a superintendent and Board of School Commissioners, the value of the buildings with their sites being estimated at somewhere in the neighborhood of $1,000,000. For the higher education, there are a high school, a normal school and three commercial colleges, while the Roman Catholics and Lutherans have several excellent denominational seminaries and colleges. A public library belonging to the city contains upward of 32,000 volumes. The public museum, also the property of the city, is another educational institution of great value. The area of Milwaukee is about twenty square miles. At the end of 1884 the City Engineer reported the entire length of paved streets in the city to be 27.2 miles, and of streets otherwise improved, 137 miles. It is probable that the new streets opened since the making of the above report, are ten miles in length, which would make the present length of the city's improved streets about 175 miles. The length of the water mains was, at the date named,

111 miles, and is now probably 120 miles. There were then 118 miles of sewers, and there are now about 135 miles. There were 5,351,549,821 gallons of water pumped by the water works during the year 1884. The fire department has ten steam fire-engines, and other apparatus in proportion, and an elaborate fire and police telegraph alarm system is in vogue.

THE POPULATION.

The total population of the city, as returned by the enumerators who took the State census in July, 1885, is 158,509, a gain of 42,931, or 37 per cent. in five years. The comparison is made with the federal census of 1880. Classified according to nativity, the population of the city consists of 93,812 persons born in the United States; 48,306 born in Germany; 2,290 born in Great Britain; 2,790 born in Ireland; 211 born in France; 546 born in British America; 1,570 born in Scandinavia; 630 born in Holland, and 8,354 born in other countries. The census blanks made no provision for the separate classification of natives of Poland. It is probable that next to the Germans, the natives of Poland are more numerous than any other foreign-born residents of Milwaukee. The three wards in which the Polanders chiefly reside—the First, Eleventh and Twelfth—contain nearly two-thirds of the inhabitants classified in the census blanks under the heading, "all other countries." Of the white population of the city, 78,453 are males and 79,737 are females; of the colored population, 206 are males and 113 females. The following table shows the population of Milwaukee by divisions, with the increase during the five years from 1880 to 1885:

	1880.	1885.	Increase.
East Side	25,093	28,323	3,230
South Side	30,875	46,792	15,917
West Side	59,610	83,394	23,784
Total	115,578	158,509	42,931

Following is the per cent. of increase from 1880 to 1885:

East Side..nearly 13 per cent.
South Side..over 51 per cent.
West Side...nearly 40 per cent.
Total increase..nearly 38 per cent.

The per cent. of increase in the several divisions from 1870 to 1880, the preceding period of ten years, was about as follows:

East Side..18 per cent.
South Side..102 per cent.
West Side...78 per cent.

INDUSTRIAL HISTORY OF MILWAUKEE. 33

MILWAUKEE'S TRANSPORTATION FACILITIES.

The railway system of Milwaukee extends to every part of Wisconsin, to the mineral regions of Northern Michigan, to Iowa, to Minnesota and Dakota, to the West and Northwest, and through Northern Illinois and Central Iowa to the Missouri river in the Southwest, comprising upward of ten thousand miles of completed railroads having terminal facilities at this city. Extensive additions to the mileage of all of the roads have been made within the past few years, and the system is now rapidly approaching a stage of practical completion. The natural results of these stupendous works in the development of the country and the consequent growth of commerce and manufactures will be felt for generations to come, and will, from year to year, exercise an ever-increasing influence upon the prosperity of Milwaukee.

CHICAGO, MILWAUKEE & ST. PAUL RAILWAY.

The most important of the great railroads starting from Milwaukee, the Chicago, Milwaukee & St. Paul Railway, now comprises 4,804 miles of completed and fully equipped railway, all under one management, located here, and all owned by one company, of which a citizen of Milwaukee has been the efficient president from its first organization, beginning with but little more than 200 miles of road. The present Chicago, Milwaukee & St. Paul system includes four great east and west trunk lines, with numerous branches, extending from Lake Michigan westward to the Missouri river and Upper Missouri valley, and two north and south trunk lines running parallel with the Mississippi, extending from Rock Island, Ill., and Davenport, Ia., to St. Paul and Minneapolis. The most southerly of the east and west lines extends from both Chicago and Milwaukee to Council Bluffs, the respective distances being 487 and 506 miles from the two Lake Michigan depots. The most southerly point at present reached is Ottumwa, Ia., 95 miles southwest of Marion, on the Council Bluffs division, but an extension to Kansas City is now in contemplation, and will be built before long. All the other east and west lines radiate from Milwaukee. The next line extends directly westward from Milwaukee to the Missouri river at Chamberlain, D. T., 595 miles, with branches tapping the great river at three other points, viz., Sioux City, Yankton and Running Water. The third of the east and west trunk lines extends from Milwaukee via La Crosse and Southern Minnesota to Woonsocket, D. T., 584 miles from Lake Michigan. The fourth, including that portion of the last-named line between Milwaukee and La Crosse and that portion of the River division from La Crosse to Hastings, extending westward from the latter point to its present terminus in Dakota, constitutes a continuous northwesterly line from Milwaukee of 642 miles in length, exclusive of branches. The last three trunk lines are connected near their western termini by a north and south line 167 miles in length, extending through the famous James River valley, pointing toward a connection with the

(3)

Northern Pacific at no distant day. The Chicago and Milwaukee, together with the La Crosse and River divisions, constitute the principal route of through travel between the Northwest and the East, connecting with the Northern Pacific at St. Paul and Minneapolis. This is also the fast mail line.

CHICAGO & NORTHWESTERN RAILWAY.

The Chicago & Northwestern Railway system, including roads owned and operated or controlled by that corporation, consists of 6,000 miles of completed railway, in construction and equipment probably unsurpassed by any other railroad on the continent. About two-thirds of the whole system lies north of a line extending due west from Milwaukee, penetrating Northeastern Wisconsin and Northern Michigan and Northwestern Wisconsin to the shores of Lake Superior at Marquette, Ashland, Bayfield and Superior, and the central and southern portions of Minnesota and Central Dakota to the Missouri river, 725 miles west of Milwaukee. It is but a few years since Milwaukeeans regarded the growth of the Chicago & Northwestern Railway in the territory referred to with serious apprehension, since it then had no connection with Milwaukee except by an inconvenient and circuitous line. The construction of two connecting lines, however, the first from Milwaukee to Fond du Lac, and the second from Milwaukee to Madison, brought the whole system in Wisconsin, Northern Michigan, Minnesota and Dakota, into closer relations with Milwaukee than Chicago, so that it might now be more appropriately named the Chicago, Milwaukee & Northwestern. A liberal share of the trade of this city is derived from the Chicago & Northwestern Railway, now one of the main arteries of its commerce. The company has found it necessary to greatly enlarge its terminal facilities here from year to year, and is still engaged in this work.

The other three railroads terminating at Milwaukee, viz., the Wisconsin Central, the Milwaukee, Lake Shore & Western, and the Milwaukee & Northern, have been vigorously pushed toward completion during the past year. The first two may now be fairly classed among the trunk lines of the Northwest.

WISCONSIN CENTRAL RAILROAD.

The Wisconsin Central system consists of the Wisconsin Central Railroad proper, 354 miles in length; the Milwaukee & Lake Winnebago Railroad, 96 miles; the Wisconsin & Minnesota Railroad, 54 miles, and the Minnesota, St. Croix & Wisconsin Railroad, 116 miles. Total mileage Wisconsin Central Line, 620. The company is now engaged in building an extension of its line from Schleisingerville to Chicago, and will build another line from Milwaukee to Waukesha.

The distances from Milwaukee via the Wisconsin Central are: To Ashland, Lake Superior, 346 miles; to St. Paul, 372 miles; and to Portland, Oregon, via Ashland, 2,296 miles. The Northern Pacific has a track to Ashland, and Milwau-

INDUSTRIAL HISTORY OF MILWAUKEE.   35

kee enjoys communication via the Wisconsin Central to all points on its lines and connections on the Pacific slope.

MILWAUKEE, LAKE SHORE & WESTERN RAILROAD.

During the past summer the locomotives of the Milwaukee, Lake Shore & Western Railroad have for the first time awakened the echoes on the shore of Lake Superior at the rising young city of Ashland. The company has constructed at that point extensive ore docks and other terminal facilities at an outlay of about $400,000. Among the new railroad enterprises of the Northwest none has grown into substantial existence more rapidly or with better promise of success than the Milwaukee, Lake Shore & Western. The company has now in operation 527 miles of road, of which 150 miles have been built with reference to the development of the iron mines of the Lake Superior country. The docks at Ashland have a capacity of receiving from cars and loading into vessels 500,000 tons of ore in the season of navigation. The company acquired the ownership of the line known as the St. Paul Eastern Grand Trunk Railway, and completed the road during last year to a junction with the main line at Clintonville, from which point it extends in a northeasterly direction to Oconto, one of the most important lumber ports on Green Bay. In its early stages the road had to encounter sharp competition from competing roads, as well as from Lake Michigan. From the head of Lake Winnebago northward, following the divide from which the streams flow east into the lakes and west into the Mississippi, it occupies a territory without competition nearer than fifty miles on either side of the main line, hitherto uninhabited, but abounding in unlimited resources of business. At Ashland it forms very favorable connections with the Chicago, St. Paul, Minneapolis & Omaha Railroad and the Northern Pacific Railroad, extending to the timberless plains of Dakota, Iowa and Nebraska. Milwaukee was fortunate in becoming the southern terminus of this vigorous young railroad, which opens to her merchants and manufacturers a new and important avenue of trade, extending into a region in which the advantages of rates and distances are and must ever remain largely in their favor.

MILWAUKEE & NORTHERN RAILROAD.

The pioneer of Milwaukee's northern railway system, which terminated for several years at Green Bay, with a branch to Menasha, and thence along the water-power of the Fox River to Appleton, is steadily pushing its way through the pine forests north of Green Bay. The main line has reached a point 185 miles from Milwaukee and about twenty miles south of the iron district in which the celebrated Chapin mines are located. A branch about twenty-one miles in length, extends from a point on the main line near Lake Noquebay to the port of Menomonee, on Green Bay, where the company has lately been making extensive improvements to accommodate its lumber traffic and prospective iron ore business.

The projected extension of the main line extends through the center of the iron district of Northern Michigan, and when completed will furnish an almost air-line from Milwaukee to the great mines southwest of Marquette. Another branch, starting from a point about thirty miles from Menomonee, and extending in a northwesterly direction, will connect the main line with the Ontonagon section, tapping the well-developed mines of the Iron River district. When completed, this road will form much the shortest route from Milwaukee to Northern Michigan and Lake Superior. The company now has in operation 228 miles of road connected with Milwaukee, and twenty miles on the Lake Superior end extending southward from Ontonagon.

The systems of railroads thus briefly sketched radiating North, West and Southwest from Milwaukee, and having terminal facilities here, represent a total of not less than 10,000 miles of completed roads directly tributary to this city. Every mile of the vast territory traversed by these roads, abounding in numerous and inexhaustible resources of business, is accessible to the merchants and manufacturers of Milwaukee.

EASTWARD TRANSPORTATION LINES.

The facilities for the shipment of freight eastward from Milwaukee include a regular line of steamers plying between Milwaukee and Ludington in connection with the Flint & Pere Marquette Railway, which, with the Detroit & Milwaukee line of iron steamers, making daily trips throughout the year between Milwaukee and Grand Haven, and the two all-rail lines via Chicago, in addition to the great water-way of the lakes during the season of navigation, affords shippers a choice of routes, abundant facilities, and reasonable freights to all parts of the East and South and to Europe during the entire year.

MILWAUKEE HARBOR.

The harbor of Milwaukee is admitted to be the best inland harbor on the entire continent, and it is a fact the importance of which cannot be overestimated. The superiority of the harbor was enhanced by cutting through the narrow strip of land lying between the Milwaukee river and Lake Michigan, forming what is known as the "Straight Cut." This " cut " is 260 feet wide, 1,370 feet long, and has an average depth of 17 feet of water, thus affording, at all seasons, a perfectly safe entrance to vessels of the heaviest draught. The wharves on the rivers are numerous and commodious, both banks being docked for miles. No matter to what extent Milwaukee's shipping interests grow, there will always be wharf-room. As Lake Michigan is one of the chain of lakes connecting the East and West, and as, through the St. Lawrence river, access is had to the Atlantic, it follows that Milwaukee, through her shipping interests, even as with her thorough system of rail-

All Saints' Cathedral.

SUMMERFIELD M. E. CHURCH.

roads, can carry on uninterrupted communication with the outer world, being a port of entry. As far back as 1859 a Milwaukee merchant consigned the cargo of the "Hanover" of this city for Hamburg, Germany. The "G. C. Trumpf," the "Gold Hunter," the "M. S. Scott," the "Juniata Patten," and other ships have cleared from this port for Europe with wheat cargoes. Various lines of steamers ply between this city and other points upon the lake daily, during summer and winter.

The custom-house records show that the number of vessels which entered this port during 1884 was 5,176. Of these, 567, with a tonnage of 354,807 tons, were side-wheel steamers; 2,061, tonnage 1,796,594, were propellers; and 2,548, tonnage 486,424, were sailing vessels.

The first vessel that ever landed goods at Milwaukee was the "Chicago Packet," a schooner of 30 tons, commanded by Capt. Brittam. She was chartered by Solomon Juneau to take a cargo from Chicago to this place in 1823.

The value of the lake marine, as reported upon the register of the Treasury Department of the United States, is over $60,000,000, and it represents a commerce that exceeds the total foreign commerce of the United States. Milwaukee's share of the 3,087 vessels composing the lake navy in 1880 was 362, with an aggregate carrying capacity of 100,000 tons. Of these 269 were sailing vessels, and 93 steam vessels. The cash value of the fleet was estimated at $3,677,000. As a port of construction, Milwaukee has always ranked high, because of the excellence of its shipwrights. There are two large shipyards here, giving employment to 300 men. The ship chandlery establishments of Milwaukee do a large business.

With the view of converting Milwaukee bay into a harbor of refuge, the United States government is at present engaged in the construction of a breakwater some distance off shore, reaching from near the extremity of North Point three-quarters of the distance toward the entrance to the harbor proper. It is designed that under stress of weather ships shall run behind this sea-wall, into the haven, where the water will at all times be smooth. One of the government life-saving stations is located on Jones' Island, at the entrance to Milwaukee harbor. The crew has done good work on several occasions, during heavy storms, rescuing many imperiled seamen from a watery grave.

THE WATER WORKS SYSTEM.

The first water works in Milwaukee were those which supplied the old United States Hotel, at the corner of Huron and East Water streets, upward of thirty years ago. The source of supply was a spring just south of Wisconsin street, between Jackson and Van Buren streets. The pipes were of tamarack wood, bored and laid by James Brooks. The connecting pieces and taps were turned by the late Henry Bleyer. The main from the spring to the hotel went south under the alley to Michigan street, thence along the south side of that thoroughfare to the alley at present flanked by the Chamber of Commerce and the Mitchell building, and thence south to the hotel. Many residents along Michigan street, as well as the people of the hotel, were supplied with pure, cool water by this primitive system. Long after the burning of the hotel, in 1854, the water continued to pour into its basement through the tamarack pipes. Soon after the burning of the hotel, an agitation to secure water works was begun, which at length resulted in the passage by the Common Council, in June, 1857, of an ordinance authorizing the grant of seven acres of city property and the issuance of city bonds to the Milwaukee Hydraulic Company, to aid the latter in establishing a system of water supply. The plans of the company, however, were never carried out. In March, 1859, Hubbard & Converse, of Boston, proposed to build a water works system with 25 miles of pipe, completing the same before January 1, 1861, at a cost of $450,000. Their proposition was favorably received, and would doubtless have been accepted, but for the war cloud which loomed up while it was under consideration. In 1860, as heretofore noted in this work, a readjustment act was passed, prohibiting the city from running further into debt. Nothing of important result in the matter was undertaken until 1868, when the Common Council secured the services of E. Chesbrough, a noted Chicago engineer, to examine and report a plan for securing a water supply and improving the sewerage system of the city. His report was made to the Council in the following year, and by that body referred to a special committee. As, however, under the provisions of the readjustment act of 1860, the city could not add to its indebtedness for municipal improvements while its outstanding liabilities amounted to $500,000, the water works project continued to sleep until 1870, when the debt had been reduced to within $250,000 of that amount. A committee appointed by Mayor Phillips, of which John Black was chairman, reported in August, 1870, favorably upon taking immediate steps to secure water works. A bill for submission at the legislative session of 1871 was prepared, empowering the city to issue water bonds, and appointing a board of water commissioners, constituted as follows: Edward O'Neill, President; Matt. Keenan, Secretary; David Ferguson, Treasurer; E. H. Brodhead, George Burnham, Alexander Mitchell, John Plankinton, Fred. Pabst and Guido Pfister. The bill passed the Legislature, and the board organized in April, 1871, making its first report in the following December. The City Engineer, Moses Lane, in company with Matt. Keenan, had meantime made a tour of examination among the Eastern cities having water works systems, and in September, 1871, had commenced work on the Milwaukee system in conformity with one of the plans proposed by Mr. Chesbrough. Water was first pumped into the reservoir October 24, 1873, the length of pipe laid at that time being about 55 miles, and the supply being temporarily taken from the Milwaukee river, north of the dam. Water was first pumped from the lake into the reservoir through the force main across the aqueduct bridge, December 23, 1874. In 1875 the commissioners turned over the works to the Board of Public Works. The disbursements to that date aggregated $1,948,009.60. The West Side branch pumping works were constructed in 1878 at a cost of $165,000.

THE SEWERAGE SYSTEM.

Previous to the year 1869 about three miles of sewers had been built in Milwaukee, but no general plan of sewerage had been adopted. E. S. Chesbrough, the Chicago engineer who was employed by the city to furnish plans for systems of water works and sewers, recommended a system of sewers conveying the drainage of the city into the Milwaukee, Menomonee and Kinnickinnic rivers, to be carried by them into the lake. By the first of January, 1879, 93½ miles of sewers were in existence—partly small brick conduits, and partly pipe not exceeding 18 inches in diameter. The rivers being sluggish at most seasons of the year, the emptying of so much sewage into them was found to be attended with unpleasant results. In 1879 a committee of experts, which had been engaged to determine upon the best means for the abatement of the nuisance, reported in favor of the construction of a system of intercepting sewers, and the pumping of all the sewage directly into the lake. In 1880 the State Legislature passed a bill, introduced by Senator Paul, prohibiting the deposition of any obnoxious matter from any slaughter house or factory in any of the rivers, and making it the duty of the Board of Public Works to provide for the disposal of all the filth of the city. The intercepting sewer plan was adopted. It contemplates the interception and removal by gravitation to one or more pumping stations of the sewage proper and liquid refuse from an area of 8,700 acres included within the limits of the city, together with one-fourth of an inch of rainfall in 24 hours from the same area. The capacity of the works embraced in this plan is calculated for a prospective population of 280,000 inhabitants, within the present area of the city. A portion of these works is already built. The cost of the whole system will be $600,000. The pumping works for the South Side sewerage district are located on Jones' Island. The sewage passes from the mainland to the pumping works through an inverted syphon 520 feet long and 50 inches in diameter. The syphon is the largest in the world.

THE GAS COMPANY.

The darkness of the city was dispersed by the benignant rays of the Milwaukee Gas Light Company for the first time on the evening of November 23, 1852. The company at the outset consisted of John Lockwood, James Kneeland, W. P. Lynde, James Rogers, and D. P. Hull. On the evening of November 24 a banquet was held at Young's Hall to celebrate the event. Eighty guests were present, most of whom are now dead. Now there are about 6,000 meters, with 1,000 miles of pipe. The number of street lamps was 2,105 on September 30, 1885. The city's gas bill last year was for 36,000,000 feet. The price of gas has fluctuated very little, and since 1869 it has decreased invariably. Up to 1868 $3.75 and $2.50 per 1,000 feet were the prices charged the general public and the municipality respectively. In those days the meter rent was about 50 cents a month in addition to the price paid for gas. In 1868 the price of gas went to $4.50 to private persons, the highest figure that it has ever sold for in this city. In 1871 it went up to $3.75 and in 1872 to $3.50. The meter rent was abolished in 1872. Since then the decline of prices has been as follows: 1873, to $3.50 per 1,000 feet; 1875, to $3; 1876, to $2.50; 1878, to $2.25; 1882, to $2; 1883, to $1.80; 1884, to $1.60; 1885, to $1.40.

STREET RAILWAY LINES.

All the notable points in the city are easily accessible by means of the street car lines. There are three street railway companies in Milwaukee, which own and operate a total of fifty miles of double track, each having also several spurs of single track in various parts of the city. The Milwaukee City Railway Company, the pioneer street car line of Wisconsin, operates thirty-one miles, the West Side Company ten miles and the Cream City Line a trifle over nine miles of road—really, it is said, equal to eighteen miles, counting, as is generally done, by the length of the several lines which are run over the double track. The probability is that at least ten miles of additional street-car track will be built in Milwaukee during the year 1886. Each of the three old lines has applied for right of way on streets leading to the Chicago, Milwaukee & St. Paul Company's depot in the Fourth Ward, and one or two ordinances granting the right-of-way to proposed new companies are now in the hands of the Common Council.

Chamber of Commerce.

MILWAUKEE'S TRADE AND MANUFACTURES.

THE CHAMBER OF COMMERCE.

THE Milwaukee Chamber of Commerce was organized on the 22d of October, 1858, in a basement room of the Newhall House, on the northwest corner of Broadway and Michigan street. Previous to that date the dealers in grain met on the freight platform of the old Milwaukee & Mississippi Railroad, or at one or another of the warehouses. The wheat which came to Milwaukee was all received in bags, and carried from the depot to the river warehouses and the mills. Warehouse receipts, such as are now used, were unknown. There had been one or two attempts at organization by the grain dealers previous to the date named above, but for some reason they failed of success. On the 22d of November, 1858, the infant Chamber of Commerce met for the first time in a hall at No. 1 Spring street, now No. 1 Grand avenue, which had been secured as an exchange room. The room was formally dedicated to the use for which it had been secured, addresses appropriate to the occasion being delivered by E. D. Holton, Dr. L. W. Weeks and J. B. D. Cogswell. The first president of the Chamber was L. J. Higby. The membership at the outset was not more than 50. In 1863 the members of the organization, then 270 in number, took possession of a new building on the site of the present Chamber of Commerce, which had been erected by Alexander Mitchell and S. M. Ogden, at a cost of $50,000. The opening of the new Chamber of Commerce rooms occurred on the evening of February 3, 1863. Thomas Whitney, who was the orator of the occasion, remarked in the course of his address : " One of the main and most important uses of an institution of this character in this city, I conceive to be the establishment of a just and equitable mercantile tribunal, which shall take cognizance of all matters relating to the mercantile interests of Milwaukee, speaking out and letting its voice be heard in tones of stern reprobation and condemnation of all dishonorable and unmercantile customs and practices in this, as well as in other communities, while at the same time it inspires and encourages to true, pure and lofty purpose, as well as to high-minded, noble, manly action and effort—a tribunal which shall be a beacon in this community, elevated upon high and lofty grounds, warning against perilous and dangerous courses, while at the same time it allures to those of safety and stability; one which shall at all times make a correct public sentiment here upon all questions pertaining to our commercial welfare and prosperity, a sentiment which shall be known and felt all through Milwaukee, and which can neither be withstood nor opposed." To the high principles so earnestly advocated by Mr. Whitney, the Chamber of Commerce has always remained true. No body of men in the United States have earned for themselves a more enviable reputation for integrity, energy, enterprise and liberality than those who compose the Milwaukee Chamber of Commerce. The moral and material support which the Chamber of Commerce gave to the Federal government during the war is more properly part of the political than the industrial history of Milwaukee, and here need be only alluded to in passing. Whenever charitable, patriotic or public objects have wanted financial assistance, the members of the Chamber have always been found open of purse. Many important public measures have gained their first impetus in the Milwaukee Chamber of Commerce. The financial stability of the Chamber is a matter worthy of mention. Even during the panic of September, 1873, when chaos reigned on most of the other boards of trade throughout the country, the members of the Milwaukee institution never lost their heads. From September 22 to October 4 of that year, the price of No. 2 spring wheat was held in Milwaukee at ten to twelve cents above the Chicago market. The members of the Chamber met daily, only to adjourn, and, in accordance with a resolution adopted on the first day of the crash, payments were carried over the entire period of disaster. The magnificent building which the Chamber now occupies is held under a lease from Alexander Mitchell for a period of twenty years, dating from May 1, 1881. It was opened on November 18, 1880, at 3 o'clock in the afternoon, in the presence of an assemblage of visitors comprising a large part of the population of Milwaukee. Previous to the formal exercises, several trades were made by operators in the pit. It is on record that the first transaction in the new Chamber was the purchase by Thomas E. Balding of 1,000 bushels No. 2 spring wheat for January delivery, the seller being Alex. C. Ray. Within ten or fifteen minutes upward of 300,000 bushels had changed hands. President Bodden then called the members to order. After music by a band and the "Chamber of Commerce Choir," under the direction of Will Graham, the formal exercises of dedication were proceeded with. A letter of regret from Alexander Mitchell, who was out of town, was read, and John Johnston, as his representative, tendered the key of the building to President Bodden, making at the same time a brief address, to which the president appropriately replied. A letter from Angus Smith, one of the men who have been prominent in the wheat trade of the city, was then read, and George Godfrey, a pioneer commercial reporter, entertained the assemblage with reminiscences of the Chamber's early days. In the evening the members of the Chamber and a number of invited guests sat down to a magnificent banquet in the dining hall of the old Newhall House. Following is a list of the presidents of the Chamber of Commerce, and a statement of the number of its members at the beginning of each fiscal year since its organization:

Fiscal year.	President.	No. of Members.	Fiscal Year.	President.	No. of Members.
1858-59	L. J. HIGBY	99	1872-73	F. H. WEST	338
1859-60	JOHN BRADFORD	122	1873-74	O. J. HALE	442
1860-61	HORATIO HILL	179	1874-75	O. J. HALE	430
1861-62	DANIEL NEWHALL	239	1875-76	N. VANKIRK	569
1862-63	S. T HOOKER	303	1876-77	N. VANKIRK	575
1863-64	J. J. TALLMADGE	348	1877-78	CHARLES RAY	569
1864-65	J. J. TALLMADGE	353	1878-79	CHARLES RAY	561
1865-66	WM. YOUNG	332	1879-80	M. BODDEN	561
1866-67	WM. YOUNG	389	1880-81	M. BODDEN	561
1867-68	JOHN PLANKINTON	371	1881-82	CHAS. F. FREEMAN	561
1868-69	EDWARD SANDERSON	365	1882-83	CHAS. F. FREEMAN	630
1869-70	ANGUS SMITH	392	1883-84	ROBERT ELIOT	629
1870-71	ANGUS SMITH	341	1884-85	ROBERT ELIOT	628
1871-72	F. H. WEST	338	1885-86	JOHN JOHNSTON	624

The position of secretary of the Chamber of Commerce has been held for nearly twenty years past by W. J. Langson, the present incumbent. Mr. Langson is one of the most accurate and comprehensive commercial statisticians in the Northwest, and to his valuable reports the compiler of this work is indebted for much of the statistical information which these pages contain.

THE WHEAT TRADE.

For a long series of years Milwaukee was beyond dispute the greatest primary wheat market in the world, and though her pre-eminence in this respect seems now to have slipped away from her, on account of the diversification of the agricultural industry of her tributary territory, which was formerly devoted almost exclusively to wheat-raising, her wheat trade is still a conspicuous and important branch of her commerce. John Johnston, in an address on the occasion of the dedication of the new Chamber of Commerce, in 1881, sketched the origin and development of the wheat trade of Milwaukee in the following words: "Wisconsin, little over thirty years ago, raised scarcely enough wheat for its own food, and the means of conveying any local surplus to market were very deficient. There were as yet neither plank-roads nor railroads. The price of grain scarcely justified the hauling of it by wagons over ungraded roads, unbridged streams and undrained sloughs for distances varying from twenty to seventy miles, and many a pioneer farmer can tell how on his return home from a journey to Milwaukee with a load of wheat he found that the expenses of the journey had exhausted the money he received for his grain. A Racine county farmer informed me the other day that at the time when the Cathedral was being built [1847-1852] he hauled wheat to Milwaukee and sold it for 35 cents per bushel. The first load of wheat which ever entered Milwaukee was received in 1839, and brought 50 cents per bushel. The first wheat sent from Milwaukee was shipped on July 8, 1841, on the schooner

'Illinois,' Jonas Pickering, captain, and consisted of a cargo of 4,000 bushels. It took three days to load it. With our present facilities for handling grain, 4,000 bushels can be shipped in about fifteen minutes. The construction of the Red Warehouse, in which a single horse did the elevating, was considered a great advance in the manner of handling grain, and still more of an advance was the Blue Warehouse, for in it two horses were used! Even as late as 1853, when the population of Milwaukee was over 25,000, the shipments of wheat had not reached a million of bushels per annum. The receipts of wheat and flour continued to increase until they attained their highest point on the crop of 1873, being then forty millions of bushels." Thomas Whitney, in his address on the occasion of the old Chamber of Commerce building, in 1863, says of the first load of wheat, referred to above by Mr. Johnston as having been brought to Milwaukee in 1839, that it was brought here from Caldwell's Prairie by a farmer who was not satisfied with the result of the transaction. "This load of wheat," Mr. Whitney continued, "was bought by Messrs. Ludington & Co., and elevated to the upper loft of their warehouse upon the shoulders of Mr. Harry Ludington, who thus acquired to himself the fame of being the first wheat elevator ever established in Milwaukee. This grain was sold to Messrs. Ludington & Co. at 50 cents per bushel, and re-sold by them (whether at the same price or not, I am unable to say) for feed, there being no other use to which the article could at that time be put." At the time when Mr. Whitney's address was delivered, Milwaukee had already acquired supremacy in the wheat trade over all competing cities. One reason for the increase of this branch of the city's business which he gave, is worth noting from a historical point of view, namely, the blockade of the Mississippi during the war.

The total receipts of wheat at Milwaukee in 1884 were 13,193,922 bushels—an increase of about four million bushels over the receipts of the previous year. The through movement for the whole year was 3,026,401 bushels, making the net receipts consigned to and sold in this market 10,167,521 bushels. The amount that went through by rail consisted mainly of wheat in which Milwaukee merchants were interested, billed through to Chicago and other markets at such times as there was any apparent advantage to be gained in doing so. Of the aggregate receipts 8,559,018 bushels were received over the various divisions of the Chicago, Milwaukee & St. Paul railway, 3,442,684 bushels by the Chicago & Northwestern railway, 618,312 bushels by other roads, and 573,908 bushels by lake—the latter chiefly from other Wisconsin ports. The total shipments, including the through movement, were 7,187,838 bushels. Excluding the through movement, the shipments were equally divided between the lake and rail routes. The mills consumed 4,839,613 bushels, leaving 3,963,981 bushels on hand in the elevators, outside warehouses and at mills at the end of the year.

Residence of John Plankinton.

The following table exhibits the total receipts and shipments of wheat at Milwaukee annually for twenty-seven years:

Years.	Receipts.	Shipments.	Years.	Receipts.	Shipments.
1884...............	13,193,922	7,187,838	1870............	18,883,837	16,127,838
1883...............	9,278,922	3,109,439	1869............	17,745,238	14,272,799
1882...............	8,058,422	2,193,539	1868............	12,750,578	9,878,090
1881...............	10,176,098	7,992,665	1867............	12,523,464	9,598,452
1880...............	11,756,463	9,952,629	1866............	12,777,557	11,634,749
1879...............	19,649,352	15,060,222	1865............	12,043,659	10,479,777
1878...............	21,763,312	17,254,453	1864............	9,147,274	8,992,479
1877...............	19,814,949	18,298,485	1863............	13,485,419	12,837,620
1876...............	18,174,817	16,804,394	1862............	15,630,995	14,915,680
1875...............	27,878,727	22,681,020	1861............	15,930,706	13,300,495
1874...............	25,628,143	22,255,380	1860............	9,108,458	7,568,608
1873...............	28,457,937	24,994,266	1859............	5,580,681	4,732,957
1872...............	13,618,959	11,570,575	1858............	4,876,171	3,994,213
1871...............	15,686,611	13,409,467			

The fear has been sometimes expressed, by not very well informed critics, that Milwaukee is apparently too near Chicago for a healthy growth of her trade. The fact of Milwaukee's decreased wheat business, as compared with former years, has been noted in support of this assumption. Not long ago, a New York journal, commenting on the matter, said: "Country customers are going to Chicago, because there is no speculation in Milwaukee, which is over-shadowed and dwarfed by the great city at the foot of the lake."

Much of the purely speculative activity which was observable in the wheat pit of the Milwaukee Chamber of Commerce five or six years ago has disappeared. If the seat of gambling in wheat options has been transferred from Milwaukee to Chicago, the fact need cause no solicitude to the friends of this city. To the thoughtful observer, the weakest point in Chicago's panoply of commercial fame is the feverish proneness to pure speculation which is characteristic of her citizens, and which has led to the concentration upon the floor of her Board of Trade of a species of fictitious business operations that is the bane of modern commerce. Milwaukee is not "too near Chicago for a healthy growth of her trade." Indeed, it may be said, with a close approximation to absolute truth, that the only direction in which her trade is not steadily growing, is a direction in which growth would be incompatible with health.

A study of the statistics of transportation will reveal the fact that an enormous amount of the product of the Northwestern wheat fields now passes through Milwaukee in the form of flour instead of in that of grain. This fact is indeed one of the most striking proofs of the rapid development of the Northwest in recent years. This development, which has comprehended the growth of manufacturing centers like Racine, Janesville, Neenah and Menasha, as well as Minneapolis, among the Northwestern wheat fields, has incalculably increased Milwaukee's possibilities as a commercial metropolis. The merchants of this city have taken advantage of these possibilities, and Milwaukee's trade has been enormously extended of late years.

THE LEADING BARLEY MARKET.

Milwaukee holds supremacy as the leading barley market of the West, Chicago ranking second in this respect. The net receipts of barley at Milwaukee during 1884—that is, the barley actually consigned to the city—amounted to 4,702,766 bushels; while the net receipts at Chicago were only 4,178,638 bushels. Next to wheat, barley is the most important cereal product handled at Milwaukee.

OTHER GRAINS.

In a large part of the territory directly tributary to Milwaukee corn is a less profitable crop than wheat and other grains, and is therefore grown to a comparatively limited extent; yet Milwaukee's corn trade has at times reached important proportions. In each of the years 1872, 1880, 1882 and 1883, the receipts of corn at Milwaukee were over 2,000,000 bushels, the exact figure for the last-named year being 2,256,862 bushels. The shipments of corn for that year were 1,799,936 bushels. In 1884, however, the receipts of corn at Milwaukee were only 841,560, and the shipments 360,833.

The receipts of oats at Milwaukee during 1884 were 2,973,786 bushels, and the shipments 1,870,309 bushels. Secretary Langson, of the Chamber of Commerce, in his report for 1884, says: "The production of oats is constantly increasing in the territory lying tributary to the market of Milwaukee, but being of lower weight and value per bushel than any other grain, oats will not bear the charges per bushel for storage or transferring that might not seem excessive on the heavier and more valuable grains. Hence it is that only a small proportion of the surplus product goes into store at the usual points of accumulation, and the prevailing elevator charges have practically turned the whole transportation of this crop from the waterways to the railroads. Sales in this market and Chicago for Eastern shipment or export are now made almost exclusively on track, and, as has been seen, a constantly increasing proportion of the shipments passes directly through both these markets by rail."

The receipts of rye at Milwaukee during 1883 amounted to 620,873 bushels, and the shipments to 549,020 bushels. The crop of oats in 1884 was exceptionally light, and the receipts for that year were only 340,948 bushels, the shipments being 235,340 bushels.

THE GRAIN TRADE SUMMARIZED.

The aggregate receipts of all kinds of grain and flour at Milwaukee for the year 1884 represented a total equivalent of 41,761,336 bushels, which was an aggregate increase over the total movement of the previous year of 4,800,414

INDUSTRIAL HISTORY OF MILWAUKEE. 53

bushels. Of the total amount received in 1884, the equivalent of 28,922,629 bushels was consigned to Milwaukee, and 12,938,707 bushels were shipped through by rail without transferring at this point.

The storage capacity of the public grain elevators in Milwaukee is 5,630,000 bushels. The Chicago, Milwaukee & St. Paul Railway Company has about three millions available room, and the Chicago & Northwestern Railway about a million and a half. During the winter of 1884–5 all of the elevators were taxed to their full capacity, and, in fact, were obliged to put nearly a million bushels of wheat on board of vessels wintering in the harbor, at a considerable loss of storage. A stock company, with a capital of $100,000, has just been formed, which will put up a new 800,000-bushel elevator at once.

LUMBER AND COAL.

The total volume of the lumber trade of Milwaukee for 1884 did not vary materially from that of the two preceding years. The receipts of lumber proper by lake, mainly from Michigan, showed a decrease of about ten million feet, and those by railroad, all from Northern Wisconsin, an increase of about fifteen million feet. About 59 per cent. of the total supply came from Michigan. In addition to the receipts at Milwaukee, a very large amount of lumber is shipped westward from the pineries of Northern Wisconsin by Milwaukee lumber merchants and manufacturers. In this respect the lumber interest of Milwaukee has increased very largely within the last few years with the extension of her railroads and their connections throughout the northern part of the State. The receipts of lumber in 1884 were 230,162,000 feet, and of lath, 13,386,000 feet. One hundred and eighteen million two hundred and forty-one thousand shingles, and 1,210,444 cedar posts were also received during the year. The shipments were: Lumber, feet, 57,275,000; shingles, number, 45,777,000; lath, feet, 4,090,000.

The increasing receipts of coal at Milwaukee during recent years constitute one of the notably encouraging features of the city's commerce. The record of 1884 showed an increase of 91,577 tons over the receipts of the previous year, reaching the large amount of 703,161 tons, against 177,655 tons in 1874, and 44,503 tons in 1864.

THE JOBBING TRADE.

The general mercantile and manufacturing business of Milwaukee is in a highly prosperous condition. The jobbing trade is more active than that of any other city of equal size in the country. The estimates of commercial agents placed the total sales of merchandise for 1884 at $130,000,000. The estimate is regarded as below the actual amount of business, for the reason that the smaller classes of business, which make up a large aggregate, are invariably overlooked or underrated in all such calculations. The hardware trade was estimated at $4,500,000; drugs, oils and paints at $5,500,000; wholesale grocery trade, $25,000,000; woodenware and woodwork of various kinds, $2,500,000; spices, coffee and baking powder, $3,000,000; dry goods and clothing, $12,000,000; leather tannery and rubber goods, $5,200,000; furs, hats and caps, $2,500,000; tobacco and cigars, $5,500,000; notions, $3,000,000; millinery trade, $1,250,000; china, glassware and crockery, $1,000,000; iron and wood machinery, $5,000,000; stoves and other manufactures of iron not included in hardware estimate, $5,500,000; products of the glass works, $400,000; brick and lime, $2,200,000; carriages, wagons and sleighs, $1,200,000. Other important items which go to round out the aggregate of the city's business to the figure given above are the sums received for the products of the packing houses, the breweries, the boot and shoe manufactories, books and paper, liquors and wines, vinegar, and soap and candles. The figures above reported are not given to the public with the assurance of accuracy, but, as far as they go, are believed to be within reasonable bounds.

No intelligent business man can fail to observe the marked improvement in the jobbing as well as the manufacturing business of Milwaukee within the last two or three years. With scarcely an exception, the wholesale merchants of Milwaukee have completely outgrown the accommodations which served them a few years ago, and have found it necessary to either absorb adjoining buildings or remove to more commodious quarters. In every line of business this evidence of enlargement is apparent. When one contemplates the great field of operations that is now open to the merchants and manufacturers of Milwaukee, without even going beyond the territory occupied by her own railroads, and her wonderful resources and development, it would be difficult to find a location better adapted than Milwaukee for building up an extensive mercantile trade or the successful prosecution of manufacturing enterprises. Intelligence and energy in either direction cannot fail to be rewarded by success.

MILWAUKEE BANKS.

The banking facilities of Milwaukee are first-class in every respect. The stability of the Milwaukee banks is a fair indication of the character of the leading commercial and manufacturing interests of the city, and has justly earned for them the confidence of the public at home and abroad. Their management is, in the fullest sense of the term, liberally conservative, affording all the facilities that their patrons could expect consistent with sound business principles. Their credit is practically unlimited. The deposits received by the banks of Milwaukee during the year 1884 aggregated $553,224,030.

MILWAUKEE AS A MANUFACTURING SITE.

Many of the advantages of Milwaukee as a seat of manufacturing enterprises must strike the most casual observer. She has at her doors a country rich with

THE WISCONSIN MARINE AND FIRE INS. CO'S BANK BUILDING.

many kinds of raw material which come from forests, from mines, and from farms. She has a good water power, and she can buy fuel cheaply. The tract of country naturally tributary to her is large and rapidly filling up, and her transportation facilities, both by land and by water conveyances, are unsurpassed. The economical administration of the city's government, and the consequent low rate of taxation here, is another desirable feature of Milwaukee as a manufacturing site which deserves to be taken into account. The happy fitness of Milwaukee as a dwelling place is an incalculable addition to the other advantages which the city possesses as a manufacturing site. The best class of workingmen are attracted to it so strongly that in many cases their services may be secured here for lower wages than they would be willing to work for in any other town—a circumstance due, of course, partly to the cheapness of living in this city.

The first manufacturing enterprise of note instituted in this section of the country was a saw-mill, erected within what is now the city limits, in the year 1835, by a Mr. Darling, better known in the community at that time by the not very euphonious, though, perhaps, appropriate name of "Old Fixings." This mill was located on the Milwaukee river, a short distance above the present dam, and is reported to have done a very flourishing and successful business for the times. Like the scriptural grain of mustard seed, the germ of Milwaukee industrial enterprise, so favorably planted, has been succeeded by a marvelous growth.

Milwaukee is fast becoming a great manufacturing city. Between 1870 and 1880 her population increased 60 per cent., while the number engaged in manufacturing increased 150 per cent. There are thirteen cities west of Philadelphia whose inhabitants number over 100,000. Of these great cities, Pittsburg and Cincinnati are the only ones which have a larger percentage of the population engaged in manufactures than Milwaukee. Milwaukee not only has a percentage of population engaged in her manufactures greater than any other city west of Philadelphia of 100,000 inhabitants, except Pittsburg and Cincinnati, but the number is absolutely larger than in Buffalo, Louisville or Detroit, and about equal to the number in Cleveland, although the population of Cleveland was 45,000 greater than that of Milwaukee at the date named. A feature of Milwaukee manufactures worthy of mention, is their diversity. In Pittsburg, almost half those engaged in manufactures are connected with iron. In Milwaukee, no one species of industry overshadows the rest so much that any disaster overtaking it would work great harm to the city. In 1880 the manufacture of men's clothing employed the greatest number of hands, being over 4,000. Next come the foundry and machine shop products, which employ some 1,400; then come the breweries, with 1,040; then follow the packers, the tanners and the trunk manufacturers, closely followed by the coopers and the sash, door and blind manufacturers. Bay View is not included with Milwaukee in the census reports, neither are the St. Paul Railway shops, or the showing would be still better.

INDUSTRIAL HISTORY OF MILWAUKEE. 57

STATE CENSUS FIGURES.

In connection with the State census taken in Milwaukee during July, 1885, under the supervision of the city clerk, an effort was made to secure statistics relating to some of the more important industries of the city. Many establishments declined to report, while the proprietors of others, inspired by fear of the assessor, did not give figures commensurate with the actual facts. Despite these drawbacks, however, the following summary of the result of the industrial census will be found interesting and impressive: " During the year the total value of iron products and manufactured articles of iron in the city reached $3,130,500, and the value of leather and manufactured articles of leather was $4,590,400. There were 3,300 wagons, carriages and sleighs manufactured, representing a value of $412,700. There were 969,420 barrels of beer manufactured, valued at $6,054,336; and 400,000 gallons of whisky, at a total value of $500,000. Vinegar seems also to have been in demand as 3,907,000 gallons were made, all being valued at $426,560. The product of woolen fabrics is estimated at $115,000; of earthenware, $33,500, and of drain tile, $38,000. The number of cigars and cigarettes manufactured during the year was 49,318,800, estimated at $1,397,436, while the total amount of all other tobaccos manufactured was 3,637,000 pounds, an aggregate value of $858,000. The flouring mills of Milwaukee show up well, having turned out 1,057,953 barrels of flour during the year, representing a money value of $5,094,-479.39. All other manufactured articles are classed under one head, and the value of their products is estimated at $11,413,359.63. The total value of the real estate and machinery used in the local manufacturing enterprises is $8,395,066.53; of the stock and fixtures, $7,552,851.23, showing a total investment of $15,947,-917.76. The amount of wages paid for labor performed in the enterprises cited above during the year, was $6,210,165.72, while the number of men employed is set down at 15,456. The total value of the products of the local manufacturing interests, according to the reports received by the city clerk, is $34,069,271.02, while the total amount of money invested, including wages paid, during the year, is $22,158,083.48."

THE IRON INDUSTRY.

Foundries and machine shops in 1880 gave employment to 1,467 operatives in Milwaukee. There were thirty establishments of the kind, in which $1,286,445 was invested. The value of the materials annually consumed was set down at $3,795,289, and of the finished product at $4,204,708. As has been heretofore stated, the census returns do not include Bay View or the Chicago, Milwaukee & St. Paul railway shops in the report of Milwaukee industries. Otherwise the iron manufactures of Milwaukee would figure as employing more operatives than any other division of manufacturing business. A small foundry and machine shop, established on the canal in 1842, is probably entitled to the credit of having been the pioneer in its branch of industry. By 1844, mill building was in progress in this city on a large scale. There are now two mammoth establishments in this line in the city, besides a number of smaller ones. There is a demand for Milwaukee-built flouring mills and sawmills from every part of the globe where such machinery is in use. In the manufacture of steam engines, steam boilers, galvanized iron, tools, and architectural iron of every description, Milwaukee has a reputation for good work second to that of no city in the country. There are two large stove foundries here, a bell foundry and a large number of machine shops. There are also two type foundries and five or six brass foundries. Like all the other branches of her trade, Milwaukee's foundry and machine shop business is constantly growing.

The rich mineral deposits in Northern Wisconsin and the northern peninsula of Michigan have attracted the attention of Milwaukee capitalists. A number of iron mining companies, which are developing the mineral riches referred to, are composed entirely of Milwaukee men, several of whom have acquired handsome fortunes in mining.

The works of the North Chicago Rolling Mill Company, at Bay View, one of the environs of Milwaukee, give employment to upward of 1,500 men, one-half of them skilled laborers, who earn from $2.50 to $6.00 per day. Originally these works were constructed for the manufacture of railroad iron. This industry being insufficient to use the product of the two blast furnaces, a merchant iron mill was added. Iron rails having been superseded by steel, the manufacture of the former was abandoned three years ago. The old rail mill was converted into a nail plate mill and a large nail factory added, containing 100 nail machines, having a possible annual capacity of 300,000 kegs of nails. The nail mill has proved a success. During 1884 it turned out 163,000 kegs of nails, all of which were disposed of. The company also manufactured at its Bay View works during 1884, 38,000 tons of angle, bar and plate iron, 10,050 tons of muck bar and 28,000 tons of pig iron. The amount of raw material received at the company's works by lake and railroad during the year was 211,700 tons. The figures will convey some idea of what one successful manufacturing establishment alone contributes to the commerce and prosperity of Milwaukee, for in everything but municipal government, Bay View is practically a part of the city.

THE LEATHER INDUSTRY.

Few persons not directly interested in the business realize the extent of the leather manufactures of Milwaukee. Everybody knows that tanneries have been in operation here for thirty years or more, and that for about the same length of time the center of the tanning industry has been steadily moving west, owing to the exhaustion of the hemlock bark supply in the East. But there the general information stops. Nobody, except persons who have made the subject a special study, is aware of the extent to which Milwaukee's tanning industry has developed. Of late the growth of the business here has been so rapid as to render the showing made in the census of 1880 obsolete. Since 1880 the capacity of the tanneries of this city has been increased 40 per cent. There are fifteen tanneries in the city. Harness leather, upper and grain leather, kipskins, calfskins and sheepskins, in bark and colored, are the principal products of the tanneries of Milwaukee. Three of the tanneries tan sheepskins exclusively. The leather tanned by the other tanneries is two-thirds side leather—cow and steer hides—and the rest small hides—

T. A. CHAPMAN'S PALACE DRY GOODS STORE.

calf and kip skins. Most of the hides used here come from the farming States of the Northwest, the heavy hides from the grazing regions being employed chiefly by the sole leather tanners of the East. The bark used by Milwaukee tanners is hemlock. Three-fifths of it comes from Michigan and the remainder from this State. About 30,000 cords of bark, worth on an average $8 per cord, are consumed here every year. One thousand men are employed in the tanneries and currier shops. The capital invested in the business is about $2,000,000, and the value of the leather tanned and curried in the various establishments aggregates between $4,000,000 and $5,000,000 per annum. Milwaukee tanners enjoy two advantages over their competitors in the neighboring city of Chicago. One is that port charges for unloading bark are lower here. The other is that the wages of labor are also lower, on account of the relative cheapness of rent and board in this city. By reason of these advantages, Milwaukee tanners are enabled to shade prices in competition with the tanners of Chicago. Two-fifths of the leather manufactured in Milwaukee goes East. The rest is consumed in Chicago, Cincinnati, Louisville, Milwaukee and the other boot and shoe and harness manufacturing cities of the West. At times large quantities of Milwaukee leather have been exported to Europe, but little has gone out of the country during the past two or three years.

THE MANUFACTURE OF FLOUR.

Milwaukee was an importer of flour up to 1845. In that year she became an exporter of this article, and has since continued such to a very large extent. In 1840 the entire State of Wisconsin had but four flouring mills, turning out 900 barrels of flour annually, besides twenty-nine wind and water grist mills, yielding altogether an annual income of only a few thousand dollars. Milwaukee to-day has twelve roller flouring mills, with an aggregate daily capacity of 6,500 barrels. The product of these mills during 1884 was 1,070,860 barrels of flour. The total receipts of flour at Milwaukee during the year were 4,076,871 barrels. The shipments during the year amounted to 4,601,267 barrels, leaving a balance of 546,474 barrels, representing the home consumption and the amount on hand December 31, 1884.

BEER AND MALT.

Milwaukee beer has made a reputation which has extended beyond the bounds of the continent. There are nine breweries in the city, with an aggregate capacity of 1,643,000 barrels per annum. During the year 1885 the Milwaukee brewers expended over $575,000 in improvements, and with but one exception, the capacity of every brewery in the city was materially increased. The amount of beer brewed in Milwaukee during 1884 was 1,136,401 barrels, and the sales of beer during that year aggregated 1,112,449 barrels, the gross proceeds of the year's work of the brewers being about $8,900,000. Fifteen hundred men are employed in the breweries of Milwaukee.

A large malt business is done in this city. The receipts of malt during 1884 were 298,073 bushels, and 3,124,837 bushels were manufactured in the city. Of this supply, 1,041,526 bushels were shipped, 2,381,384 bushels being consumed by the breweries in the city.

THE PACKING INDUSTRY.

Milwaukee is not as relatively prominent as a packing point as she has been in former years, but she nevertheless does a very considerable and steadily increas-

INDUSTRIAL HISTORY OF MILWAUKEE. 61

ing business in this line. One of her packing houses, that of John Plankinton & Co., gives employment to 1,000 men when working at full speed, and has a capacity for killing and curing 6,000 hogs per day. The hogs packed here come from Wisconsin, Northern Illinois, Iowa and Dakota. In the great Milwaukee packing houses not a scrap of the "porker" is wasted. The eatable portions are utilized as food, the intestines are cleaned and used as sausage casings, the bristles are made into brushes, the hair is curled and put into mattresses, and the blood and refuse from the tanks are taken by the manufacturer of fertilizing materials, who sells them to the farmer to use in enriching the soil and growing corn, which in turn is converted into hog again. During the summer season which closed October 30, 1885, the hog packing at Milwaukee was 33 per cent. in excess of that for the corresponding season in 1884. The aggregate of the packing was 235,911 head of hogs. The packing in the summer season of 1884 was 136,529 head, and in the winter season of 1884–5, 298,537 head.

THE CLOTHING TRADE.

The two largest Milwaukee establishments for the manufacture of men's clothing were in existence prior to 1850. Started on a small scale and developing gradually, their growth has been commensurate with the growth of the city. One of them now gives employment in the busy season to upward of a thousand hands. The United States census of 1880 shows that there were, at that date, fifty-two clothing manufactories in Milwaukee, employing 4,252 hands, representing an invested capital of close upon two millions of dollars, using $2,243,365 worth of materials in each year, and turning out an annual product valued at $3,763,987. Besides these, the census reported the existence of four manufactories of women's clothing, employing nearly 200 people and having an annual product valued at $147,160. Clothing manufactured in Milwaukee is sold in every State and Territory in the West and South. In the larger establishments machinery driven by steam power is employed, greatly increasing the production and decreasing the cost of the goods. As to quality, style and workmanship, the clothing manufactured in Milwaukee is equal to the best produced elsewhere. The inferior grades of goods in this line are not manufactured here. The showing made by the census falls far short of representing the present condition of the trade. The number of operatives now engaged in it is not short of 6,000, and there has been a corresponding increase in the amount of the annual product as compared with 1880.

OTHER INDUSTRIES.

Milwaukee has five wholesale millinery houses, which give employment to upward of 250 hands, and do a business aggregating upward of $1,000,000 a year. This is exclusive of other establishments devoted to particular branches of ladies' headgear manufacture, the product of which, if included, would swell the aggregate to nearly double the amount named. The trade is assuming constantly increasing proportions.

A fleet of steam and sail vessels and nearly 100 men belonging to Milwaukee are engaged in the lake fisheries. The catch of an average season is about 600,000 pounds of whitefish and trout.

The manufacture of soap in Milwaukee is assuming proportions which entitle it to notice. There are five or six extensive soap manufacturing concerns in the city, and all are obliged to from time to time increase their facilities in a large way.

Within the past few years the knit goods industry has assumed far more important proportions in this city than most persons are aware of. Among the outward and visible signs that the industry is a flourishing one, is the fact that the proprietors of one of the largest of Milwaukee's knitting establishments have lately completed and moved into a commodious new five-story building in the Kinnickinnic valley, which they have erected at a cost of $50,000. There are fifteen or more establishments of this kind in different parts of the city. The fine work is done by hand, but in all the factories where the heavier grades of goods are produced, machinery is employed. The operatives are mostly girls. It is estimated that between 500 and 700 girls find employment in the knit goods manufactories of Milwaukee. Authentic figures bearing on the value of the aggregate annual product are not at present attainable, but that it reaches a large amount is beyond question. The proportions of the industry are the more wonderful in view of the fact that its growth, from a very small beginning, has taken place in less than half a decade.

Five hundred men are employed in the Milwaukee manufactories of trunks and valises. The business has increased materially since 1880 when the annual product was valued at $250,000. One of the trunk manufactories in this city is among the largest in the United States.

About 1,000 men are employed in the manufacture of sash, doors and blinds, and the annual out-put of the Milwaukee factories is valued at a million dollars. The furniture factories employ 800 men and produce nearly $1,000,000 worth of furniture in the course of a year. Recently the demand for parlor frames and other fine furniture manufactured in this city has very largely increased, and these goods are now sold by Milwaukee manufacturers as far east as New York. Carriages and wagons made in Milwaukee are sold as far south as Texas and as far west as California. There are upward of 40 cooperage establishments in the city, and the annual products of the cooperage industry here are worth in excess of three quarters of a million dollars.

The distilleries of Milwaukee produced 21,036 barrels of highwines in 1884, valued at $967,656—nearly a round million. Vinegar distillation has also attained important proportions in this city within the past few years.

Residence of Valentin Blatz.

There are 1,000 cigarmakers in Milwaukee, and 300 men and boys are engaged in the manufacture of chewing and smoking tobacco and snuff. The value of Milwaukee's tobacco products is about $2,000,000 per annum.

A large factory of sewing machines was established in Milwaukee in 1881. It is doing a flourishing business. The manufacture of glass, also recently introduced here, has rapidly attained important proportions. Window glass and bottles are made in large quantities, and preparations for the manufacture of art glass have just been completed.

MILWAUKEE CEMENT.

On the east bank of the Milwaukee river, a short distance north of the city, are the quarry and works of the Milwaukee Cement Company. The works are the largest under one superintendence in the United States, and the cement is of a quality as perfect as first-class machinery and business skill can make it. The natural deposit of rock from which the cement is manufactured was discovered only a few years ago and has been worked since July, 1876. In superficial area the deposit covers between one and two hundred acres, with a depth of indefinite extent. The mill, kilns and other works of the company are modeled after the most approved plans. Spur tracks communicating with three trunk lines of railway run alongside the warehouses. The amount of cement manufactured and sold by the Milwaukee Cement Company during the season of 1884 was about 240,000 barrels. The capacity of the cement works at the present time is half a million barrels. The ordinary production in a day of ten hours is over 1,000 barrels, or about 30,000 barrels per month.

UNITED STATES CENSUS FIGURES.

Despite the fact that the statistics which it contains have been in a large measure outgrown during the five years which have elapsed since its compilation, the following table, taken from the United States census of 1880, will be found interesting and valuable in connection with the subject of the manufactures of Milwaukee:

INDUSTRIAL HISTORY OF MILWAUKEE. 65

MANUFACTURES OF MILWAUKEE.

Mechanical and Manufacturing Industries.	No. of establishments.	Capital.	Average no. of hands employed. Males above 16 years.	Females ab've 15 years.	Children and youths.	Total amount paid in wages during the year.	Materials.	Products.
All industries	844	$18,766,914	16,015	3,922	949	$6,946,105	$28,975,872	$43,473,812
Baskets, rattan and willow ware	4	$ 90,600	108	15	161	$46,660	$38,825	$114,300
Blacksmithing	34	54,850	103			52,264	31,410	122,540
Bookbinding and blank book making	7	21,700	56	47	18	31,505	26,681	78,713
Boots and shoes, including custom work and repairing	59	296,275	462	55	9	162,263	380,074	665,183
Brass castings	6	108,300	140	2	2	51,112	76,436	167,114
Bread and other bakery products	36	61,350	102	16	29	37,254	255,449	358,366
Brick and tile	5	328,500	346		43	89,720	77,276	225,808
Brooms and brushes	4	13,000	50	5		15,240	16,720	47,620
Carpentering	47	149,780	745			311,581	543,315	986,585
Carpets, rag	5	5,100	19	25		4,900	12,550	22,350
Carriages and wagons	11	97,000	148			62,265	76,500	184,000
Clothing, men's	52	1,895,128	1,902	2,350	50	912,657	2,243,365	3,763,987
Clothing, women's	4	64,900	34	163		29,900	109,900	147,160
Coffee and spices, roasted and ground	9	257,621	125	19	15	89,550	693,042	931,640
Confectionery	4	144,054	110	30	20	43,542	378,370	474,922
Cooperage	39	142,250	526		35	234,115	337,880	680,445
Coppersmithing	3	41,500	20			10,692	22,870	44,392
Cordage and twine	3	5,000	9			3,200	10,000	16,600
Dentistry, mechanical	5	8,000	10	1	2	4,500	10,502	30,000
Drugs and chemicals	6	40,872	15	12		9,386	55,179	85,393
Flouring and grist-mill products	11	1,066,000	265			136,266	3,795,289	4,204,708
Foundry and machine shop products	30	1,286,445	1,437		30	673,392	1,173,907	2,252,784
Furnishing goods, men's	3	7,000	9	9	1	1,890	17,000	28,850
Furniture	16	329,800	497	14	15	212,501	223,301	568,268
Furs, dressed	3	61,000	14	38	5	25,000	89,500	136,000
Hairwork		8,500		11		2,800	6,050	13,200
Hand-knit goods	5	26,000	2	538	52	14,500	45,500	83,000
Hardware	5	11,700	19		10	8,600	14,900	32,160
Hats and caps, not including wool hats	3	26,000	8	14		7,500	17,928	34,000
Jewelry	4	15,000	18			8,316	31,000	47,000
Leather, curried	17	800,425	375			160,441	1,874,595	2,219,978
Leather, dressed skins	5	71,500	46			20,900	67,925	104,381
Leather, tanned	17	1,008,525	407			173,861	1,612,400	2,101,195
Lithographing	4	69,125	116	2	73	57,751	79,640	166,860
Liquors, distilled	2	142,000	20			9,180	95,425	145,650
Liquors, malt	13	4,732,909	1,040			525,573	2,259,345	4,034,319
Looking-glass and picture frames	4	12,975	10		11	7,222	19,900	35,470
Lumber, planed	3	70,000	115	4	11	35,000	50,000	117,000
Marble and stone work	11	95,300	167			73,256	106,450	220,396
Masonry, brick and stone	4	8,500	27		2	12,000	14,000	34,750
Mattresses and spring beds	4	3,800	8	5	2	2,550	12,000	17,500
Mineral and soda waters	6	33,200	44	5	5	14,208	31,450	62,950
Painting and paper-hanging	31	53,950	204		2	68,105	95,607	200,546
Plumbing and gas-fitting	8	47,600	95		1	43,600	71,700	138,400
Printing and publishing	24	434,700	518	43	48	268,270	200,486	675,387
Pumps, not including steam pumps	4	4,075	9			3,150	4,622	11,500
Saddlery and harness	29	73,300	107		38	44,451	112,620	199,525
Sash, doors and blinds	7	261,000	512		18	139,100	303,000	557,000
Shipsmithing	8	136,500	227			110,413	133,963	301,700
Shirts	3	2,100	4	17		4,990	5,790	17,655
Slaughtering and meat-packing, not including retail butchering establishments	7	789,000	928		25	187,596	5,529,618	6,009,406
Soap and candles	5	120,000	50	4	11	24,620	204,100	280,090
Stone and earthen-ware	8	69,700	67			17,511	21,755	66,600
Tinware, copperware and sheet-iron ware	29	95,950	152			56,687	106,994	215,444
Tobacco, chewing, smoking and snuff	3	331,000	200	6	20	78,500	786,645	978,281
Tobacco, cigars and cigarettes	56	238,375	733	4	77	301,934	344,939	835,506
Trunks and valises	4	183,000	218		45	76,720	115,800	244,600
Upholstering	6	11,900	46			22,800	97,500	146,500
Vinegar	2	62,000	32			18,415	42,000	149,000
Watch and clock repairing	4	4,100	8		1	3,780	4,800	12,675
Wheelwrighting	13	47,500	67			27,870	29,800	80,950
Wirework	4	4,750	8			3,140	3,185	10,885
Miscellaneous industries (*)	69	2,084,830	2,160	468	125	1,059,440	3,728,001	6,437,945

* The sixty-nine establishments classed as "miscellaneous industries," are grouped in order that the business of individual establishments may not be disclosed to the public. In this group are embraced agricultural implements;

The census returns show that, while the population of Milwaukee increased between 1870 and 1880 a little over 60 per cent., the part of the population engaged in manufacturing increased 150 per cent., and the capital employed in manufacturing increased 125 per cent. The following table shows how much greater proportionately the manufactures of Milwaukee were in 1880 than in 1870:

	Population.	Capital.	Hands Employed.	Value of Products.
1870	71,440	$ 8,200,000	8,433	$18,798,122
1880	115,587	18,766,914	20,886	43,473,812

From the above, it appears that during the decade referred to, the number of hands employed in manufacturing in Milwaukee increased from 8,000 to 20,000. No authentic statistics bearing upon the subject are obtainable, but it is probable that the relative increase of persons engaged in manufacturing has been still greater during the six years which have elapsed since the taking of the last Federal census. It may be interesting to mention, for comparison with the number of artisans given above, that the number of Milwaukeeans engaged in rendering personal and professional services in 1880 was 12,979, while those engaged in trade and transportation numbered 9,322.

---

artificial feathers and flowers; artificial limbs; bags, paper; baking and yeast powders; boot and shoe uppers; boxes, cigar; boxes, fancy and paper; boxes, wooden, packing; bridges; carriages and sleds, children's; carriages and wagon materials; drain and sewer pipe; dyeing and cleaning; electroplating; engraving and die-sinking; engraving, wood; fertilizers; files; food preparations; furniture, chairs; galvanizing; gloves and mittens; ink; iron and steel; lightning-rods; lumber, sawed; mixed textiles; models and patterns; musical instruments, organs, and materials; musical instruments, pianos, and materials; oil, linseed; paints; patent medicines and compounds; pickles, preserves and sauces; refrigerators; roofing and roofing materials; safes, doors and vaults, fire-proof; scales and balances; show-cases; starch; steam fittings and heating apparatus; stencils and brands; stereotyping and electrotyping straw goods; tools; toys and games; type founding; wood preserving; wood, turned and carved, and woolen goods.

A Walk About the City.

SOME OF THE POINTS OF INTEREST TO THE STRANGER.

MILWAUKEE'S fitness for residence purposes is primarily due to Nature herself. Built on a hilly amphitheatre at the edge of an inland sea, and thoroughly drained by three beautiful streams, the city is possessed of a situation at once healthful and picturesque. Its air and its water are as pure as can be found in the world. The natural advantages of the place have not (as in the case of some other cities) been countervailed through the ignorance or indifference of its inhabitants. Its public and private architecture is tasteful and attractive; its streets are handsome and clean. More than one disinterested, traveled visitor has said of it that, with the exceptions of Paris and Washington, it is the most beautiful large city on the globe.

PUBLIC BUILDINGS, ETC.

The Government building, at the northwest corner of Milwaukee and Wisconsin streets, is of marble quarried at Athens, Ill., and cost $161,779, exclusive of the ground on which it stands, and of the expenditure which has been made upon interior alterations. It is 110 feet in length, 60 feet in width and three stories in height, and contains the postoffice, United States Court and other Federal offices. Its erection was begun May 1, 1856, and it was taken possession of January 1, 1859. The business of the Federal officers at Milwaukee has grown so much in recent years that they are now cramped for room, and a new Federal building, of greater dimensions than the present one, has become an imperative necessity.

The Milwaukee County Court House, which contains the county and circuit court rooms, the city council chamber, the county offices and most of the city offices, is situated at the north end of the handsome public square on the East Side which is known as Court House Park. The square is bounded by Biddle, Jackson, Oneida and Jefferson streets, and was given to the city by Solomon Juneau, the founder of Milwaukee. The architect of the court house was the late L. A. Schmidtner. The building was completed in the spring of 1873, at a cost of $650,000. It is constructed of Milwaukee brick, veneered with Bass Island sandstone. The colossal Corinthian columns, which form a striking and handsome feature of its exterior, are of iron. The greatest length of the building, from east to west, is 210 feet; the greatest width, from north to south, 130 feet. The distance from the ground to the main cornice is 80 feet, and from the ground to the topmost point of the gilded figure, which surmounts the dome, 208 feet 6 inches. The park in front of the court house is set out with elm trees, grass plats and ornamental walks. A large and handsome fountain enhances the beauty of the square.

The Central Police Station, situated at the northeast corner of Broadway and Oneida street, is a model edifice of its class. It was erected in 1884 and taken possession of in the spring of 1885. The numerous fire-engine houses in different parts of the city are well adapted to the purposes for which they were constructed. The water works pumping-houses, of which there are two, are among the points of interest to visitors. No city in the country has finer public school buildings than Milwaukee. There are fourteen district school buildings and several branch schools. One of the State Normal Schools is also located in Milwaukee, and the building which it occupies is large, handsome and well arranged. The new County Jail, in process of erection, on Broadway, near the new police station, will be as handsome as is compatible with the use for which it is designed, and will embody the modern improvements in jail architecture.

Among the important institutions of Milwaukee is the Milwaukee Insane Asylum, organized and governed under the State law. It is situated in the town of Wauwatosa, a short distance west of the city. The large and handsome buildings of the asylum are surrounded by ample grounds, and are set in the midst of beautiful rural scenery. The most modern and approved methods of treatment are in vogue at this institution, which is both an asylum and a hospital, and it is regarded as a model establishment of its kind. It is the only public institution in the State where the care and treatment of the insane and inebriates at private cost is provided for by law. The cost of the maintenance of the inmates maintained at public charge is borne partly by the county of Milwaukee and partly by the State of Wisconsin. The affairs of the asylum are under the immediate control of a board of trustees.

One of the embellishments of this work is a fine illustration of the magnificent new depot which the Chicago, Milwaukee & St. Paul Railway Company is erecting in Milwaukee. The new depot will face north on Everett street, with the Fourth Ward Park in the foreground, and will occupy the width of the block between Third and Fourth streets. The main building is to be 320 feet long by 62 feet wide. Outwardly the style of the building will be a modern treatment of the Gothic. The foundations are of limestone, with a granite facing above the grade. The building is to be built of red pressed brick, trimmed with red sandstone and red terra cotta. It will be surmounted by a slate roof, on a fire-proof foundation of tile, supported by iron beams. Over the main entrance a clock tower will rise, its height to the top of the finial being 173 feet. The building is to be warmed by steam and thoroughly ventilated. The inside finish of the principal rooms on the first floor will be hardwood, with cut glass windows and stained glass transoms. The corridors will be finished in enameled brick and marble. South of and joined to the main building will be a train building, wide enough for five trains. This building is to be of iron and open on three sides. The cost of the depot will be about $300,000.

Milwaukee's leading hotel, the Plankinton House, is owned by John Plankinton, who was moved to build it more by public spirit than by money-making considerations, although the establishment is now and has for several years past been a source of considerable profit. The architecture of the hotel is French Renaissance in style. The interior is commodious and elegantly finished, and furnished, the large dining-hall, wainscoted with colored marbles and richly decorated, being one of the most magnificent apartments of the kind in this country, and standing well in comparison with the celebrated hotel dining-halls of Europe. The hotel has, at present, accommodations for 600 guests, and an addition is now under way by the construction of which its capacity will be nearly doubled.

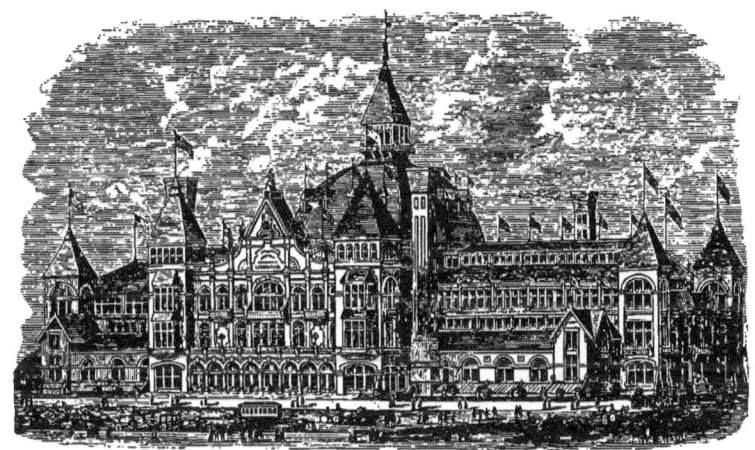

EXPOSITION BUILDING.

The Milwaukee Exposition building occupies the entire square bounded by Fifth, State, Sixth and Cedar streets. The main entrance is on Fifth street. The building is in modified Queen Anne style, and is surmounted by a huge polygonal dome 175 feet in height. The material of the structure is Milwaukee brick, trimmed with light sandstone. The building is pronounced one of the handsomest of its class in the country. It was finished in July, 1881, and cost $200,000. John Plankinton, who made to the Exposition Association a loan of $70,000, which enabled the erection of the building to be proceeded with without delay, was elected the first president of the Association, and has held the position ever since. He is the largest stockholder in the Association.

It is a matter of just local pride that since its inception Milwaukee's Exposition has been successful in an artistic and educational as well as a financial sense. Its art gallery has from year to year contained what is universally admitted to have been the finest series of picture collections ever shown in the West. Its machinery department has been large and well-ordered, containing much of interest and valuable suggestiveness. Its display of the natural products of the Northwest has been such as to each year newly impress the beholder with the variety and vastness of the resources of this rapidly-developing section. In short, the Milwaukee Exposition is not, as enterprises bearing that name sometimes are, a sham, and the visitors who annually come to Milwaukee to see it go away delighted and come again the next year.

At the northeast corner of Mason and Jefferson streets work has been begun upon an art gallery, which will cost about $100,000. The structure is being erected, at his own expense, by Mr. Frederick Layton, whose intention is, when it is completed, to present it and the ground upon which it stands to the city. The building will occupy a plat of ground 120 feet square. It will be constructed of Milwaukee pressed brick, Ohio gray sandstone and terra cotta. Its ground dimensions will be about 80x100 feet, and it will be a single lofty story in height. The style of its architecture will be what is known as Thompsonian Greek—a style in which Egyptian solidity is happily tempered with Greek grace. Besides retiring rooms for visitors, a curator's room, unpacking rooms and other offices, the building will contain a sculpture gallery, 25x38, in the center; small picture galleries, each 25x40, to the right and left of this, respectively, and the main picture gallery, 30x80 feet, in the eastern end of the museum. The floors of the sculpture gallery and the entrance way will be of marble. The offices in the front of the building will be lighted by windows in the walls. All the galleries will be lighted from the roof. The building will be heated by steam. The architects are W. and G. Audsley, of London, and E. T. Mix & Co., of this city.

The corner-stone of the new Light House Squadron Armory was laid with imposing ceremonies on the 14th of August, 1885. The site upon which the building stands was purchased by the Squadron with money the chief part of which was contributed by public-spirited citizens. The money with which the building was erected was loaned to the Squadron by the State. The armory stands on the east side of Broadway, between Oneida and Biddle streets, and adjoins the new police station. It covers a ground space of 120x120 feet. The front portion of the building, comprising 40x120 feet, is three stories in height. The remainder, about 24 feet in height, constitutes one story, on the rear of the lot, and is used for a mounted drill and exercise room. Several other military organizations have leased apartments in the front part of the building. The armory is severely plain and solid in construction, in keeping with its purposes. It is built of brick, faced with Waukesha limestone. Its cost has been in the neighborhood of $30,000.

The house of the Milwaukee Club, a social organization comprising most of the more prominent business and professional men of the city, is a sightly building standing upon the northeast corner of Jefferson and Wisconsin streets. The architecture of the building is modern English, and the material is pressed red brick. The cost of the building and furniture was about $100,000. The club took possession of the handsome establishment in the spring of 1884. Several other cities have club houses that are larger, but none has a club house that is better appointed or more elegant.

The Mitchell building and the Chamber of Commerce are perhaps the finest business buildings in the city. Both were erected by Alexander Mitchell. The former is occupied by the offices of the Chicago, Milwaukee & St. Paul Railway Company, the Northwestern National Fire Insurance Company and the Wisconsin Marine and Fire Insurance Company's Bank. The Chamber of Commerce is partially held under a long lease from Mr. Mitchell by the commercial body whose name it bears, the remainder of the building being rented for business offices. Both buildings are magnificent structures. The two together have a frontage of an entire block, on the south side of Michigan street, between East Water street and Broadway. As Charles L. Colby once remarked, they "stand side by side, like Chang and Eng, united by a ligament through which the stream of life is constantly flowing." They are built of granite and light gray sandstone. Illustrations of both buildings appear in this work.

The Colby and Abbot block, at the northwest corner of Mason and Milwaukee streets; the new office building of the Northwestern Mutual Life Insurance Company, at the northwest corner of Broadway and Milwaukee street, and John Plankinton's Library block, on Grand avenue, between Fourth and Fifth streets, are all large, substantial and elegant business buildings, which would do credit to any city in the country.

T. A. Chapman's dry goods store, at the southeast corner of Milwaukee and Wisconsin streets, is one of the sights of Milwaukee. It is spacious, elegant, artistic and in many respects unique. The store occupies the site of the one destroyed by fire on the 23d of October 1884, and its erection was begun almost before the smoke of the conflagration had cleared away. The depth of the store from the Wisconsin street front is 210 feet, and from the Milwaukee street front 120 feet. The height is five stories. The main entrance is on Wisconsin street and the carriage entrance on Milwaukee street; both are very handsome. At the latter is a handsome Greek portico of white granite, with columns and shafts of polished Scotch granite. The style of the building is modified classic. The foundation is of rock-faced red sandstone, and the superstructure of brick with trimmings of red sandstone and terra cotta. The exterior is richly and elaborately decorated in colors. The pediment of the Wisconsin street front is appropriately surmounted by a large phœnix in terra cotta. Of the interior arrangements and decorations of the store it would be impossible to speak in detail in this brief sketch. It is sufficient to say, that the lighting, heating, ventilation and all the provisions for comfort are as nearly perfect as they can be made. The triangle-shaped chimney, with three fire-places, with its triple mantel of carved English oak, is one of the first things that attracts the notice of the visitor. Another notable adornment is the series of large decorative paintings of "The Seasons," by Tojetti, a well-known Italian artist, living in New York. An illustration of the exterior of the Chapman store appears on page 59.

Architecturally, the most notable ecclesiastical edifice in the city is St. Paul's Church (Episcopal), at the northeast corner of Marshall and Knapp streets. The building was begun in 1882 and, although its main tower is not quite finished, has been occupied for upward of a year. The church and chapel occupy the entire length of the lot, 180 feet on Marshall street, while the front of the church and rectory, that is to be, will fill nearly the depth of 127 feet on Knapp street. The church is cruciform, the front flanked on either side by towers, between which runs an ample vestibule. A high-arched cloister joins the west transept with the chapel and is a beautiful feature of the exterior design. The style of architecture is Norman, the round-topped windows adding in effect to the massiveness of the material, a rich-brown sandstone brought from Bass Island, Lake Superior. The high clerestory carries up the roof to a height of 67 feet, giving to the exterior a grand and imposing effect, which is relieved from heaviness by the graceful lines of the great windows, with their mullions of yellow sandstone. The deep recesses of the doorways, with their clustered columns of red granite, the rich carving abundantly bestowed, the solidity and reality of everything, make the building one which has been seldom equaled in this country, and one which will be, for many years to come, without a rival among the churches of the West. The interior is solidly and richly finished. A notable feature of the church is its decorative windows of stained glass, many of which are unsurpassed in the United States. Each of the large transept windows cost $3,500. The cost of the church, when completed, will be $250,000.

Immanuel Presbyterian Church, on Astor street, between Martin street and Juneau avenue, is one of the conspicuously handsome church edifices of the city. It was dedicated January 3, 1875. The building, site and furniture cost $200,000. The church is built of gray, rock-faced limestone from Wauwatosa, with trimmings of red Potsdam stone. The main entrance is flanked by two square towers, the larger of which rises to a height of 147 feet. The smaller tower is 100 feet high. The peak of the main roof is ninety feet above the sidewalk. The main audience-room of the church seats 1,400 people. The architects of Immanuel Church were E. T. Mix and P. B. Wright.

An illustration on page 37 shows the property of All Saints' Cathedral (Episcopalian). The property embraces six lots—60x120 feet each—and comprises one-half block on the north side of Juneau avenue, bounded on the east by Marshall street, and on the west by Cass street. The Cathedral occupies the Marshall street corner, and is shown on the extreme right of the cut. It is a handsome and substantial structure of Milwaukee pressed brick. Next to it stands Cathedral Hall, a building used for Sunday-school, meetings of charitable societies, diocesan councils, etc. Adjoining this is All Saints' Chapel, in the wings of which the church-school is held. On the Cass street corner of the block stands the clergy-house. Back of the latter, and fronting on Cass street, is St. John's Home, an asylum for aged ladies. The Home is built of brick. The other buildings, except the Cathedral, are frame structures.

Calvary Presbyterian Church, at the southeast corner of Grand avenue and Tenth street, was erected in 1870, at a cost of $60,000. It is a large and handsome Gothic structure, of Milwaukee brick, ornamented by two graceful spires of unequal height.

The Methodist denomination has several large and handsome church edifices in different sections of the city. Summerfield M. E. Church, at the northwest corner of Van Buren and Biddle streets, is shown in an engraving on page 38. It was dedicated in 1858. The interior was remodeled in 1879-80. The Grand Avenue M. E. Church is a commodious and sightly edifice of Gothic design, which was completed and dedicated in 1871.

Trinity Evangelical Lutheran Church, a Gothic edifice, at the southeast corner of Prairie and Ninth streets, attracts much attention from strangers for the beauty of its exterior design, as well as the richness and tastefulness of its interior finish. It is built of Milwaukee brick and trimmed with Illinois sandstone. The tower is supplied with a clock and a chime of bells. The building was dedicated in 1880. The architect was F. Velguth. Another handsome Lutheran church is that which the St. Peter's congregation have just erected at the southeast corner of Scott street and Third avenue, at a cost of $30,000. It is of Gothic architecture, with massive buttresses and a high and tapering spire.

Among the more notable of the numerous Roman Catholic churches in the city are St. John's Cathedral, on Jackson street; St. Mary's Church, on Broadway; St. Gall's, on Sycamore street; and the Church of the Capuchin Friars, on Fourth street, near the reservoir. The last named is in the Norman style of architecture, and has one of the finest interiors in the city. Several others among the eighty churches, which the city contains, are worthy of the sight-seer's attention, but space does not permit descriptions of them here.

The Milwaukee Young Men's Christian Association, which was organized in

1876, will soon be in possession of a handsome building, plans for which have already been prepared. The structure, with its furniture, and the site upon which it is to stand (on Fourth street, near Grand avenue), will represent a value of upward of $75,000. The money was raised by subscription, and cheerfully contributed by citizens of all denominations. The building is intended to be a center of recreation and culture for young men. It will contain a lecture room, a reading room, a gymnasium, a natatorium, and class rooms. All its privileges will be free. The Y. M. C. A. maintains a department for work among railroad men, which has headquarters at 294 South Water street, and also a German department, with headquarters at 340 Third street.

The residence of Alexander Mitchell, a beautiful engraving of which adorns this work, is pronounced by competent critics to be one of the finest city residences in the United States. It is situated on Grand Avenue, opposite Grand Avenue Park. A few blocks west, on the same thoroughfare, is the palatial residence of John Plankinton, an illustration of which also appears in this work. One of the handsome residences which have recently been erected on the East Side is that of Valentin Blatz, situated at the southwest corner of Van Buren street and Juneau avenue. The residence of John L. Mitchell, on the South Side, is a magnificent structure, and is finished in princely style. Numerous other wealthy Milwaukeeans have dwellings on which the architect and the decorator seem to have lavished all the cunning of their respective arts.

The eastern end of Grand Avenue Park is adorned with a monument of granite and bronze, surmounted by a heroic statue of George Washington, which is said to be the only public statue of Washington west of New York. The monument was designed by R. H. Park, of Florence, Italy, and presented to the city by Miss Elizabeth Ann Plankinton, being unveiled with imposing ceremony November 7, 1885. It cost $20,000. The monument stands on a foundation of solid masonry. The base is light gray granite from Mount Desert, Me. It is thirteen and a half feet square on the ground and thirteen feet high. The heroic bronze statue of Washington surmounting it is ten and a half feet in height. Two supplementary figures, also of bronze, which stand upon the two uppermost of the steps leading to the pedestal, are about life-size.

Miss Plankinton's liberality and taste have stimulated like qualities in other wealthy citizens, and Milwaukee is promised a soldiers' monument, a monument to Solomon Juneau, and statues of Daniel Webster, Henry Clay and Matt H. Carpenter, one or more of which will probably be placed in position during the coming year.

The Western Branch of the National Asylum for Disabled Volunteer Soldiers is located one mile west of the city limits, in the town of Wauwatosa. The grounds belonging to the Home comprise 410 acres, beautifully laid out, and partly under cultivation. The portion not devoted to agriculture—about one-third of the whole tract—constitutes one of the most beautiful parks in the country.

The new buildings erected in Milwaukee during the season just closed aggregated in value $4,500,000. The real estate sales recorded during the year ended September 1st, 1885, aggregated $4,654,158.

The architectural beauty of Milwaukee is an element of the city's attractiveness which cultured visitors never fail to note. To E. Townsend Mix, more than to any other man, the Cream City is indebted for the sightliness of the great edifices which adorn her principal business streets. The Mitchell building, the Chamber of Commerce, the Plankinton House, the Library Block, the Exposition building, the new Chicago, Milwaukee & St. Paul depot, the *Evening Wisconsin* building, the Chapman store, the Milwaukee Club House, St. Paul's Church, and a number of other important edifices, combining in their construction the essential elements of good architecture—fitness, stability and beauty—are creations of the genius of Mr. Mix. Besides contributing so much to the fair appearance of Milwaukee, the firm of E. T. Mix & Co., of which Mr. Mix is the senior member, has at different times furnished designs for and superintended the construction of large and handsome buildings in most of the important cities of the Northwest.

MILWAUKEE NEWSPAPERS.

No city of equal size in the country has a more creditable newspaper press than Milwaukee. The oldest newspaper in the city, by succession, is the *Evening Wisconsin*, which is the direct descendant of the *Milwaukee Advertiser*. The latter was the first paper in Milwaukee and the third in the State. Its first issue made its appearance on Thursday, July 14, 1836. D. H. Richards was the first manager of the paper, and Hans Crocker acted for a time as its editor. In March, 1841, Mr. Richards sold the *Advertiser* to J. A. Noonan, who changed its name to the *Courier*. John A. Brown became editor of the paper in 1843, and in 1845 William H. Sullivan became the publisher. The *Courier* was a weekly publication until March 19, 1846, when it began to be issued as a morning daily. On the 9th of July of the same year the daily publication of the paper was suspended, the weekly edition being continued. On June 2, 1847, the paper passed into the hands of William E. Cramer and Joseph Curtis, who continued its publication under the name of the *Wisconsin*. Mr. Curtis sold out his interest in September, 1850, but Mr. Cramer has ever since remained senior proprietor and editor. A. J. Aikens became a partner of Mr. Cramer in 1857, and John F. Cramer entered the firm in 1864. The style of the firm, "Cramer, Aikens & Cramer," has remained unchanged since that year. In 1879 the establishment was moved into its present quarters, in a spacious and handsome building, at the northeast corner of Michigan and Milwaukee streets, erected by the proprietors with a view of making a model printing office. Such it certainly is. No printing office in the country is better arranged for the comfort of its employés and facility of work. The *Wisconsin* has no superior among the afternoon dailies of the country. In politics it is independently Republican.

The *Sentinel*, the principal morning newspaper of the city, is another journal which reflects credit upon Milwaukee and upon the State at large. It was founded as a weekly in 1837, by John O'Rourke, the capital with which the office outfit was purchased being furnished principally by Solomon Juneau. The first issue of the daily edition appeared December 9, 1844. A history of the vicissitudes of ownership which the *Sentinel* has undergone, would occupy far more space than can be devoted to the subject here. A long line of brilliant writers has been associated with the paper. The name that is most closely identified with its earlier history is that of Gen. Rufus King, who occupied its editorial chair almost uninterruptedly from 1846 to 1861, when he received the appointment of United States Minister to Rome. The *Sentinel* is now owned by the Sentinel Company, of which Charles Ray is president. Horace Rublee is the editor-in-chief. The literary tone of the *Sentinel's* editorials is very high, and it has a finely organized news service. The paper has been an exponent of Republican principles ever since the Republican party was formed.

The *Daily Journal*, a comparatively recent addition to the English press of the city, is a bright two-cent afternoon newspaper, of Democratic predilections, and has a large constituency of readers. It is owned by the *Journal* Company. L. W. Nieman is the editor, and Michael Kraus the publisher.

Milwaukee has three dailies printed in the German language—the *Herold*, the *See-Bote* and the *Freie Presse*. The *Herold* is published every morning by the *Herold* Company, of which W. W. Coleman is president and chief stockholder. When he entered upon the management of the paper it was a puny, ill-supported sheet. Now it is one of the largest and most influential German newspapers in the United States, and a source of wealth to its proprietors. In politics the *Herold* is an independent supporter of the Republican party. The *See-Bote*, which was started in 1851 by a stock company, is owned by P. V. Deuster & Co. Mr. Deuster has been its principal proprietor since 1856. It was an afternoon paper until February 25, 1886, when it began to be issued in the morning. The *See-Bote* is a handsome, well-edited journal, devoted to the cause of Democracy. The *Freie Presse* is an independent Republican newspaper, and is published every afternoon except Sundays. It is owned by the *Freie Presse* Publishing Company, and ably edited by Hermann Sigel.

THE MILWAUKEE COLLEGE.

(FOR LADIES.)

This institution was established in 1850 while the city was young, has been frequently enlarged and improved to keep up with the growing demands, and is now one of the best organized and most fully equipped schools either west or east. It has adequate facilities for every grade, primary, preparatory and collegiate; regular courses leading to graduation, and for special courses; and for both day and boarding students.

MILWAUKEE COLLEGE. (For Ladies.)

Few cities can be found so well adapted for the location of a ladies' college as Milwaukee; its beauty of situation, variety of relief, broad streets lined with shade trees, and especially the vigilant care of its sanitary conditions, provoke enthusiastic praise from all visitors as well as from its own people, now numbering 150,000. The facilities for all educational interests are constantly growing and multiplying: the Public Library, the Public Museum of Natural History, the prospective Layton Art Gallery, the Industrial Exposition and the music concerts of societies, all indicate the spirit of the place, and are more or less available to all students and studious people in the city.

The College Home, contiguous to the College, has excellent accommodations, for the President's family, the ten resident teachers, and fifty boarding students. These students are divided into six groups of families, each under the special care of a teacher in charge, acting under the general direction of the president. The family government thus distributed, and the basis of the government being *personal worthiness* rather than a set of rules for universal application, has proved here eminently successful. All apartments in both the College and the Home are heated with steam, lighted with gas and well ventilated; all floors are provided with bath-rooms and hot and cold water; the class-rooms and study hall have also open fire-places for ventilation.

The several departments of study are equipped with all useful aids and instruments; as that of Astronomy, with a complete observatory, a five-inch refracting telescope by Clarke & Sons, a transit instrument by Browning of London, solar and siderial chronometers by Tobias, of London; that of Natural History, with cabinets of mineralogy, geology and zoology, by Ward, of New York; articulated and inarticulated human skeletons from Paris, manikins and models from Berlin, etc.; that of Physics with Ritchie's large rotary air-pump, Duboscq's heliostat and solar microscope with a power of 1500 diameters, a Toepler-Holz electric machine, a fine thermo-electric pile, and astatic needle, etc.; that of Chemistry with a laboratory well arranged and furnished for real practice as well as for illustration; also with cabinets of materials for examination by the pupils; that of Painting and Drawing with sky-light studios and full-size casts of the most important antique statues and busts.

The libraries have 3000 volumes, mainly books of reference, the balance being selected not so much for general reading as for collateral use in connection with the various lines of study.

The methods of instruction are eminently practical, employing the senses to the utmost, where it can be done at all, so that the concrete may come before the abstract, things before words, and phenomena before scientific statements or discussion.

The frequent lectures by the President in the several departments are generally illustrated with Steward's large optical lanterns from London and selections from the stock of more than 5000 transparencies; these lectures, together with class visits at the various commercial and manufacturing establishments in the city, are highly valued in the work of education. The department of Vocal and Instrumental Music, under the direction of Prof. Dwight F. Stillman, has won a high reputation by thorough instruction and careful training, embracing critical attendance upon concerts and operas in the city.

President of the Board of Trustees: WM. P. McLAREN, Esq.
President of the College: CHAS. S. FARRAR, A. M.

THE CATHOLIC NORMAL SCHOOL OF THE HOLY FAMILY AND PIO NONO COLLEGE.

St. Francis, Wis.

PIO NONO COLLEGE.

This institution was founded by the Rev. Dr. Salzmann in the year 1870, and opened on the 2d of January in the following year. In appreciation of such a praiseworthy and beneficial project, the generous Louis I., King of Bavaria, before all others, donated the sum of $1,704 towards the erection and completion of this institution, the first and only Catholic Normal School in America.

Beautifully located two miles south of the city limits of Milwaukee, near Lake Michigan, on the Chicago & Northwestern Railroad, the building presents an aspect at once grand and inviting. Elegant in its proportions, it is constructed and arranged with the utmost care and regard for the comfort and convenience of pupils. The house is thoroughly supplied with water from an artesian well, lighted by gas, heated by steam, and amply provided with all modern improvements. As special care is taken to promote the health and vigor of mind and body, the spacious grounds around the institution are intersected by pleasant, shady walks, and in bad weather a large hall is provided for healthful exercises and youthful recreation.

The entire building comprises two departments, viz.: The Catholic Normal School and the Pio Nono College. In the former, Catholic young men are educated, trained and prepared for the profession of teaching. In the latter department, Catholic youth are grounded in the principles of Christian faith and educated for the various branches of literary and commercial life.

The united effort for the restoration of Cecilian music to its pristine purity and grandeur had its origin in this institution, under Dr. Salzmann, in the year 1873, when a society known as "the Cecilian Society" was established under the presidency of Sir John Singenberger, graduate of the Musical School at Regensburg, Bavaria, and Professor of Music at the Normal School.

The members of this society, extending as it does, over the whole United States, now number almost five thousand (5,000), amongst whom are many priests, bishops and archbishops. Sir John Singenberger, who is yet president of the society, edits "The Cecilia," a beautiful literary organ of church music, published at the Normal School.

The faculty of the Institution are: Rev. Chas. Fessler, Rector and Professor of Exegesis, Pedagogy and German; Rev. Aug. B. Salick, Master of Discipline, Professor of Christian Doctrine and German; Rev. J. F. McMullen, Professor of Christian Doctrine and English; Chevalier J. Singenberger, Professor of Vocal and Instrumental Music; Mr. J. T. Kelly, Professor of English, Geography, History and Penmanship; Mr. Dominic Schuler, B. S., Professor of Natural Science, Mathematics and Book-keeping.

The course of studies in the Normal School comprises four years. The programme of studies embraces Christian Doctrine, Exegesis, Liturgy, Church History, Pedagogy, Music (vocal and instrumental), English, German, Latin, Arithmetic, Algebra, Geometry, Natural Science, Geography (political and physical), U. S. History and Government, Penmanship and Drawing.

In the College department, the course of studies comprises Religious Instruction, English, Arithmetic, Algebra, Geometry, Geography, Commercial Law, Book-keeping, U. S. History and Government, Penmanship, Drawing and the optional studies, viz.: German, Latin, Music and Natural Science.

Connected with this institution is the St. John's Deaf-Mute Asylum, under the direction of Rev. Chas. Fessler. It was founded in the year 1875 by the Rev. Theo. Bruener, now Rector of St. Boniface Church, Quincy, Ill.

Every care and attention is paid towards promoting the knowledge and advancement of these pupils. The boys are instructed by Mr. Louis Mihm, and the girls are taught by the good Sisters of St. Francis.

A BUSINESS COMPENDIUM

OF

Representative Mercantile and Manufacturing Establishments

OF

MILWAUKEE.

T. A. CHAPMAN.

ON the following page, is a portrait of one of the best known merchants of the Northwest, Timothy Appleton Chapman. Mr. Chapman is a typical American. A farmer's son, he went forth before he had attained the age of manhood, to seek his fortune in the world of business, and, by the exercise of his native capacity, energy, enterprise and honesty, has achieved in his chosen pursuit a measure of success as full as it has ever fallen to any man to enjoy. Mr. Chapman was born in Gilead, Me., on the 23d of May, 1824. During his boyhood he assisted his father on the farm. His education was obtained in the district school of his native town and the academies of Bethel and Yarmouth. For a time, in the intervals of attending school, he was occupied as a teacher. At the age of 20, with less than $10 in his purse, he went to Boston, where he remained thirteen years—the first six years as a clerk in a dry goods store and the remainder of the time in business on his own account, in company with his brother, under the firm name of T. A. & H. G. Chapman. Becoming convinced that the West would be a better field for his operations, Mr. Chapman came to Milwaukee in 1857. He established himself in business on East Water street, under the firm name of Hassett & Chapman. Mr. Hassett retired at the end of five years, and was succeeded by Charles Endicott, who remained three years. Since the retirement of Mr. Endicott, Mr. Chapman has been alone. His business has steadily expanded. In 1872, the necessity for increased room having become imperative, he erected at the southeast corner of Milwaukee and Wisconsin streets one of the largest and most handsomely appointed store-buildings in the West at that time, and removed from his old quarters. In 1883, his new store was outgrown, and he built an addition nearly doubling its size. Not content with building for utility only, he called decorative art to the aid of architecture, structure, with its entire contents, was destroyed by fire. Milwaukeeans looked upon the fire as a public calamity rather than a merely private loss. Business men asked the question, "Will Mr. Chapman rebuild?" with much concern, for they

and created an establishment that fitly came to be spoken of as "the Palace Store," and was the wonder and the pride of the whole Northwest. On the night of October 23, 1884, this magnificent appreciated that the beautiful store and the large and elegant stock which Mr. Chapman always carried had brought a great many people and a great deal of trade to the city which would go elsewhere if the store were not replaced. Most men of Mr. Chapman's years would have been inclined under similar circumstances to avoid the responsibilities and risks of beginning anew. His insurance money and his other property would have enabled him to "crown a life of labor with an age of ease." But after carefully summing up the situation he decided upon the opposite course, and before the ashes of the old store were cold he had completed plans for rebuilding upon even a grander scale than before. An engraving and a description of Mr. Chapman's new store appear in another part of this work. The store is conceded to have no superior in the world, for the purposes for which it is designed, and in many of its excellent features it is entirely unique. One of these is light. The store is so arranged that there is not a dark corner nor a deep shadow in the whole building. The ventilation is as perfect as science can make it. Three large open fireplaces, which contribute to the purification of the air, give a cheerful and homelike effect to the store. Ample provision is made for the comfort of the employés as well as the patrons of the establishment. It is not alone his high standing as a business man that gives Mr. Chapman his place in the esteem of his fellow citizens. He is more than a successful man of business. Broad-minded, cultured, and public-spirited, a patron of art and education, he is looked up to as one of the representative men of the time.

The portrait which is presented herewith will be recognized as a very good likeness of Mr. Chapman.

GOODRICH & WAGNER,

Successors to Ball & Goodrich, Wholesale Grocers.

301 and 303 East Water Street.

AMONG the large wholesale firms in the city of Milwaukee whose names have attained a prominence in the history of the Cream City, we particularly mention the house of Goodrich & Wagner. The business was established in 1845 by P. W. Badgley, whose name was for many years connected with the solid commercial interests of the city of Milwaukee. A few years after the business was organized, J. A. Dutcher was admitted into the firm, then taking the name of P. W. Badgley & Co. In 1853 Mr. Badgley died, and the firm became Dutcher & Sexton. Mr. Goodrich became connected with the firm in 1853 as book-keeper, and a member of the firm in 1856, the name being changed at that time to Dutcher, Sexton & Co. In 1859 Sexton retired, and in 1862 Mr. Ball became interested in the firm, then being known as Dutcher, Ball & Goodrich. Mr. Dutcher retired from the firm in the year 1868, the business being continued under the name of Ball & Goodrich. In 1878 Mr. Ball died, the firm, however, continuing under the same name until March 1st, 1885, when Mr. Wagner purchased the interest formerly owned by Mr. Ball, when a final change was made and the present name assumed. The business has been carried on in the same location since its organization, having added, however, another store to their first quarters, and now have four floors 52x150 feet in dimensions.

They employ twenty-four persons in the establishment, and eleven traveling salesmen. Their goods are sold throughout the West, and among their customers are numbered some of the largest dealers in the Western country. Mr. John R. Goodrich was born in New York, and came to this city in 1850. He has for sixteen years been a member of the Board of Trustees of Beloit College, is Vice President of the Exposition Association, and director in the Merchants' Association, and has filled other offices with credit to himself and honor to the societies which he represented. Mr. A. H. Wagner was born in Germany, coming direct to Milwaukee in 1860. He was for twenty-two years and up to the time of his connection with this firm, connected with the Englemann Transportation Company, and also the Northwestern Transportation Company, as secretary and treasurer. Both gentlemen occupy prominent places in the commercial world, and the firm receives the cordial support of its many patrons, and is rapidly extending its trade relations throughout the Northwest.

MILWAUKEE CEMENT CO.,

Manufacturers of Hydraulic Cement.

Office, 184 West Water Street.

OF all the industries of the city none has so large a shipment, with the exception of the breweries, as the Milwaukee Cement Co. It is an enterprise of which Milwaukee can be proud, and has extended its name and fame to all parts of the Union. The works of this company are situated on the Milwaukee river, within a few miles of the city. In superficial area, the territory of this company contains about 300 acres, with a depth of cement rock of an indefinite extent, of the best quality, and fully adequate to meet the requirements of this extensive industry. This territory lies on both sides of the Milwaukee river, and is in close connection with three principal trunk lines of railway. This company was incorporated in 1876 with a capital of $350,000. The first kiln was completed during the same summer, and from that time to this the mills have been in almost constant operation. The full capacity of manufacture is about 1,000 barrels per day, or nearly 350,000 barrels per annum. The amount manufactured at the present time is at the rate of 250,000 barrels per season. The business has been extended to about twenty States, and the sales are much larger than from any other mill in the West, and perhaps larger than from any one mill in the country. The purchasers of this cement in large quantities are the government of the United States, and all the principal railroads of the West, including the C. M. & St. P., C. & N. W., C. B. & Q., A. T. & S. F., B. & M., and Canadian, Northern, Central and Southern Pacific Railways. Nearly all the large government buildings, as well as the principal railroad bridges crossing the Mississippi and Missouri rivers, erected during the past five years, have been built with the aid of this material. The superiority of this cement over all others, as regards the average tensile, breaking and crushing

Works of the Milwaukee Cement Company.

strength, and greater adhesion to brick, has been unquestionably established by upwards of 3,000 most careful and severe tests, as well as by the most complete analysis. These have been made under the direction of Mr. D. J. Whittemore, for many years Chief Engineer of the Chicago, Milwaukee & St. Paul railroad, and other gentlemen of practical character and scientific attainments. Ten kilns, 22 feet square and nearly 50 feet high, are in operation. The pulverizing mill, three or four heavily timbered warehouses for the storage of cement, and numerous large dwelling and boarding houses for accommodation of employés, are especially noticeable on the premises, and built in the most substantial manner. The machinery is new, and of the most complete patterns, equal, and in many cases superior, to any of the best concerns in this country. They have in successful operation nine run of burrs of the most perfect mechanism for the purpose to which they are applied. The motive power for driving the ponderous machinery is supplied by four boilers and two large steam engines, having an aggregate of 160 horse-power. Nearly 100 men are employed in the works. The shipments are two large train-loads of cement every day. The peculiar quality of the soil where the mills are located, was first known to Prof. I. A. Lapham, one of the most skillful geologists of the country. The following gentlemen constitute the present officers: H. Berthelet, President; Geo. H. Paul, Secretary; John Johnston, Treasurer; Goe. S. Bartlett, Superintendent of Sales; J. R. Berthelet, Jr., Superintendent of Works. It is by the able management of this corps of officers that the company has achieved a success so highly creditable to themselves, and of so much importance to the city of Milwaukee. The various departments of this company are connected by telephone with their city office, 154 West Water street, owned and operated by themselves, so as to insure prompt shipments and attention which the trade demands. The company have published in pamphlet form a handbook for engineers, architects, masons, contractors and builders, giving the most practical information regarding hydraulic cement, which will be sent by mail on application.

R. P. ELMORE & CO.,
Dealers in Coal and Pig Iron.
Office, 400 East Water Street.

FROM the earliest period in the world's history until a comparatively recent date, wood was the universal article of fuel.

The subsequent discovery of coal was providential, as the demand increased with the development of higher civilization and the necessities of the arts and manufactures. Coal mining is now one of the great industries of the United States, and coal is rapidly supplanting wood as fuel, even where the latter is to be found in abundance, owing to its cheapness and ease of handling, as well as its superior quality as fuel.

R. P. Elmore is the pioneer coal-dealer in Milwaukee. The firm began in 1851 as S. L. & R. P. Elmore. Later it became Elmore Bros., but for twenty years past has been R. P. Elmore & Co. The following clipping from the *Milwaukee News* of Jan. 23d, 1867, will give an idea of the beginning of the coal business here:

"Prior to 1851 there was no coal kept in this city. Those who were compelled to use it in manufactories or preferred it for domestic consumption, supplied themselves as they best could from vessel owners and warehousemen who generally had a little on hand. It was then sold by the bushel. During this season Messrs. S. L. & R. P. Elmore concluded to engage in the business, and opened a small yard on East Water street, a short distance east of 'Walker's Point' bridge. As their capital was small they could not afford to make a trip East to buy of miners, or their agents in person, so they made a contract to take a small quantity of Ohio bituminous coal 'unsight, unseen,' as the saying is. The price was paid in advance, and in due time the coal arrived. As they had never seen any bituminous coal, and knew almost nothing of its quality or the best methods of using it, they were naturally anxious to inspect their new purchase, and when it came they were dismally disappointed by its appearance. They stood looking at it mutely for some minutes, then both turned away and walked down the street together for several blocks, neither saying a word. They both felt the venture was a failure, and strove to draw forth from his own heart the consolation he failed to find in the countenance of the other. A further investigation of the subject, however, and a better acquaintance with the wants of the market and the merits of bituminous coal, enabled them to dispose of the lot without loss, and thus lay the foundation of the present trade of R. P. Elmore & Co.

Their first winter's supply was about 600 tons, which proved ample for all demands, and was so far as they knew, the total amount of coal of any kind sold in the State.

The Elmores put up the first coal scales in the city, and from that day to this they have kept pace with the growth of the city and country. Some years ago Mr. Elmore found it necessary to add to their permanent facilities for storing and delivering coal and wood, and made a purchase of dock property on River street, and adding to it from time to time they now have an immense retail yard, affording ample room for all seasons of the year. From the difficult sale of 600 tons in 1851, they have advanced to a business over eight States, amounting to nearly one million dollars annually.

Besides the yard mentioned, they have two shipping yards on the different railroads, and have a dock front of 1,400 feet.

They do an extensive wholesale business, handling all the various kinds of anthracite and bituminous coals, imported and domestic pig iron, foundry supplies land plaster, cements, etc.

R. P. Elmore, the founder of this enterprise, was born in Connecticut in 1815, and came to this city in 1851. He has an enviable reputation as a business man and is accorded a prominent place among the esteemed citizens of Milwaukee. His long connection with the business interests of the city has earned him a name that will always be identified with the leading men in the State.

He has the finest coal office in the city, in the Iron Block, corner East Water and Wisconsin streets.

MEINECKE & CO.,

Importers and Jobbers of Toys, Fancy Goods and Notions, Children's Carriages, etc.

348 and 350 East Water Street.

AMONG those houses in Milwaukee entitled to special notice, is that of Meinecke & Co., importers and jobbers of toys, fancy goods and notions, at Nos. 348, 350 and 352 East Water street. They are principally engaged in the wholesale trade, which extends throughout the entire Northwest. They occupy the whole building, which comprises four floors and the basement, 60x120 feet in area, and carry the most extensive stock in their line in the West. The great proportion of their goods come from Europe, although some are of home manufacture. They also have a large stock of willow-ware, children's carriages, etc., which are manufactured at the factory of A. Meinecke & Son, at the corner of Mason and Front streets, and elsewhere mentioned in this volume. Besides stock already mentioned, they also carry a complete stock of Bohemian glass and china ware, druggists' sundries, bird cages, fishing tackle, etc. They employ a force of thirty-five hands in the store, and do an immense annual business. The members of the present firm are A. Meinecke, Sr., A. Meinecke, Jr., C. Penshorn and F. Goetz.

MENDEL, SMITH & CO.,

Importers and Wholesale Grocers.

East Water and Huron Streets.

IN presenting a review of the mercantile houses of Milwaukee, the above house is representative. They are centrally located on East Water street, and occupy the whole of their large store, consisting of five floors and basement. Twenty-five employés are on their pay-roll, besides seven commercial travelers, who represent their firm throughout the West. Their strict integrity and the superior quality of their goods has gained them a standard reputation with the trade, and the popularity of their house is constantly increasing. A great many articles are prepared especially for them to order, and are marked with the famous "Cabinet Brand." They make a specialty of teas and tobaccos, importing the former from Japan, where it is put up expressly for them and known as the "Badger Brand," and has been highly satisfactory to their large number of customers. Their trade lies exclusively in Wisconsin, and they endeavor to meet the wants of the home merchant in every case, and their large and growing trade warrants the assumption that they have been successful, as their annual sales do not reach less than one million dollars. This satisfactory result has been achieved by the exercise of a straightforward system of dealing, and the house of Mendel, Smith & Co. has attained a prominence accorded only to those whose operations have been characterized by the strictest principles of mercantile honor. Henry M. Mendel, the head of the firm, was born in Germany in 1839, and came from there directly to Milwaukee in 1854. He occupies a high position in business circles. He is a director and vice-president of the Exposition Association, president of the National North American Sängerbund, president of the Milwaukee Musical Society, which is one of the oldest organizations of the kind in the country, and is also a trustee of the Academy of Music. Mr. Ira B. Smith was born at Fox Lake, Wisconsin, in 1850, but has resided in Milwaukee the greater part of his life. He is well known throughout the city and State, and is the oldest son of Ex-Governor Wm. E. Smith, who was one of the founders of this business and senior partner until his sudden death two years ago.

THE HOFFMAN & BILLINGS MFG. CO.,
[LIMITED],

Manufacturers of Steam, Gas, Plumbers' and Brewers' Supplies.

Office and Salesroom, 141 to 147 West Water Street.

A WORTHY example of business thrift, illustrating what energy and enterprise can accomplish, is the house of the Hoffman & Billings Manufacturing Company. For thirty years they have been connected with the business interests of this city, and have always been the recognized leaders among the manufacturing industries of this community. Beginning with but one lathe, operated by foot power, this establishment has advanced step by step, increasing their trade and resources, until they have grown to be one of the largest houses of the kind in the Northwest. The business was established in 1855 by Mr. J. C. Hoffman on State street, between Sixth and Seventh, on a very small scale and limited capital. He received Mr. Chas. F. Billings into partnership in 1870, under the style of Hoffman & Billings. In this relation their business steadily advanced, and they were very successful in every branch of their trade. In the spring of 1882 the present firm was incorporated under the laws of the State of Wisconsin, with a large capital, which was necessary for the extension of their growing trade. This firm manufactures, on a large scale, a full line of brass and iron goods for steam, gas and water service, supplying dealers and fitters all over the North and West, and even ship to Eastern markets, where their goods are in great demand. They have many important inventions of their own. The most important of the many articles manufactured by this house is cast-iron pipe, heating apparatus, radiators, tools, steam pumps, cocks, gauges, whistles, couplings, valves, expansion joints, fittings, boiler tubes, flanges, branch T's, steam and gas fitters' tools, and engineers', brewers' and plumbers' supplies in general. They also carry a full stock of rubber hose, belting, packing and leather belting, besides being agents for various kinds of pumps, the principal of which are the Knowles steam pumps and Rumsey iron well pumps. Their extensive catalogue is replete with a list of every article manufactured and handled by them, and no dealer should be without it.

It can be procured free of charge by addressing the firm. The value of their large stock reaches to upwards of $150,000. The large salesrooms are situated at Nos. 141, 143, 145 and 147 West Water street, the dimensions of which are 75x150 feet. The main works are located between Sixth and Seventh streets, on Cedar, occupying one-half of the block, and include three large buildings, fully equipped and used for a machine shop, brass foundry and iron foundry, respectively. This part of their works has had the misfortune of being burned out several times, but they have always repaired the damage, and continued, if anything, on a larger scale. They are also establishing a plant on Becher street, in the southern limits of the city. It consists of an area of three acres, on which are being erected mammoth buildings for shops, foundries, etc., where all the latest improved machinery will be introduced, among which we mention the Colliau patent furnace for melting iron, the 40,000-pound boring mill, the ten-ton traveling crane, and the large engines used to drive this vast machinery, which aggregate 100 horse-power. Upwards of 200 skilled mechanics are employed in the various departments. The sales, which extend to every part of the Union, amount to nearly one-half million dollars annually, showing the importance of this large industry to the city of Milwaukee. The officers of this company are: J. C. Hoffman, president; B. Hoffman, vice president, and J. B. Kalvelage, treasurer and secretary—all efficient business men, and fully conversant with every detail of their vast business. The firm court the patronage of dealers in all sections of the country, and are prepared to do any kind of work in their line promptly and at living prices. All large contracts receive their special attention, and parties desiring bids will find it to their interest to open correspondence with this house.

BUNDE & UPMEYER,

Manufacturing Jewelers.

121 and 123 Wisconsin Street.

THIS popular firm, although of recent origin, has become as well known as many of those of earlier date. It was established in 1880 as a wholesale, retail, and manufacturing concern, and has met with deserved success. It is one of the representative houses in the city, and is a great point of attraction for shoppers of superior jewelry. Their rooms are nicely fitted up with show cases, and they are just preparing to make other large and important additions to their facilities in this line. The firm started on rather a small basis, but a system of upright and honorable dealing, combined with energy and perseverance, have placed them at the head of all other concerns of the kind in the city. They employ thirteen skilled and experienced artisans in their shops, and are continually turning out jewelry of all kinds, most exquisite in design and finish. They make a specialty of watches and diamond settings, their stock of diamonds being especially complete and valuable. Both gentlemen are natives of Milwaukee, Mr. Louis W. Bunde having been born here in 1859, and Mr. Upmeyer two years earlier. The former has had eleven and the latter thirteen years' experience in the business, so that both are especially fitted for conducting the large establishment of which they are proprietors. They have lately added increased facilities in the way of new machinery, adapted to all their wants, making them better prepared than ever to do first-class work.

W. H. LITTLE & CO.,
Milwaukee Beef and Pork Packing Company.

114 to 120 Sycamore Street.

THE packing industry of our city is among the first in importance. One of the four leading houses of this kind in the city is that of W. H. Little & Co., formerly established by Mr. D. C. Abbey. It is situated at Nos. 114, 116, 118 and 120 Sycamore street, and consists of a large two-story brick building, 100 by 120, with basement. The various departments of this establishment are ample in every respect for the large and growing trade. The plans for the construction of this building, which was erected in 1872, were elaborate and perfect, and taking into account its central location, it is the most accessible of all the packing houses in the city. The building is fitted up with all modern appliances for handling and preparing beef and pork. Everything for the packing and curing of beef and pork is carried on in this building, with the exception of slaughtering, which is done at the city abattoir. It contains facilities for all departments associated with a business of this kind—cutting, drying, salting, barreling, etc. The various apparatus for steam and kettle lard rendering, and rooms for smoking and curing hams and bacon, are among the largest in the city. The capacity of the large refrigerator room is 1,600 tons of ice, and will contain 100 hogs, or 25 head of slaughtered cattle. The excellency and reliability of the various products of this firm have long been established, and Little's lard has an unrivaled reputation throughout the United States for purity and cleanliness. The boiler used for the generation of steam is of forty horsepower. Upwards of fifty hands are employed for conducting this large business. The shipments extend all over the United States. The aggregate sales per annum are upwards of half a million dollars. Mr. Little is a native of New York city and came to Milwaukee in 1868, and was interested with his brother in the dry goods business, until he entered the present establishment with Mr. D. C. Abbey in 1872.

GOLL & FRANK CO.,
Importers and Dealers in Dry Goods, Notions and Gents' Furnishing Goods.

Corner East Water and Buffalo Streets.

IT IS with pleasure that mention is made of the mammoth institution of Goll & Frank, at the corner of East Water and Buffalo streets. It is the largest business of the kind in the city, and one of the largest in the West. It dates its birth back to 1850, when it was established in a limited way on East Water street, by

Mr. Julius Goll. Two years thereafter Mr. August Frank was admitted into the firm, and it has since continued under their name. On January 1, 1885, the firm was incorporated, with the following officers: President, August Frank; Treasurer, Julius Goll; Secretary, O. Loeffler. The capital stock is $250,000. From the start the success of the firm was assured, under the efficient management of the two partners, and its business soon assumed such magnitude that their quarters were not sufficient to allow them the room necessary, so they decided to build, and erected the handsome and imposing structure which they now occupy, and took formal possession in 1862. It is five stories in height, with high and well-lighted floors, and presents a front on East Water street of one hundred feet and on Buffalo of one hundred and thirty feet. Its interior is systematically and tastefully arranged, the office appointments being elegant and well adapted to their purpose. The basement is large and well lighted, and contains the domestic goods. On the first floor are the offices, and dress goods in large variety. On the second floor can be found a large and varied stock of embroideries, laces, gloves, hosiery and notions, covering everything in this line. The third floor is devoted to the woolen goods, and the fourth is given up to jeans, flannels, blankets and manufactured goods. Fifty employés are on the pay roll in connection with the establishment, and besides these the company employ outside parties in the manufacture of furnishing goods, this force consisting of several hundred. Eight commercial travelers represent the house throughout the Western States to the larger retail firms. During the thirty-five years of this firm's existence they have built up a reputation for honest dealing and good goods second to none in the West, and this city is deeply indebted to the energy and perseverance of these gentlemen, which has resulted in the building up one of the finest institutions in the West, and of which its owners may justly feel proud.

CONWAY, CLEMENT & WILLIAMS,

Manufacturers and Dealers in Furniture.

137 and 139 Wisconsin Street.

AT the above location we find the elegant establishment of Conway, Clement & Williams, occupying a fine large structure five stories in height, including the basement, with a frontage of forty-five feet and a depth of one hundred and sixty-five feet. Within we find a most magnificent and complete stock of everything in the way of furniture, some the most elegant in design and finish. Fine chamber suits with marble-topped stands and French plate glass mirrors are here found in every style at all prices, with all the splendid appointments in demand by the public. This institution was established here the present year, and started with a stock of $35,000, which has recently been increased to about $75,000, in order to meet the increased demands of trade. Notwithstanding its recent origin, it now takes its place among the first of the furniture houses, and enjoys a large patronage, and counts some of our most wealthy and influential citizens among its customers. Mr. Conway was born in Danbury, Conn., in 1851, and came to the city the present year. He served for two and one-half years in the late war in the 2d Connecticut as a private, and was an active participant in several hard-fought battles. Mr Clement is a native of Neenah, this State, was born in 1861, and had been engaged in business at that point for three years before entering the present firm. Mr. Williams was born in Columbia county, Wisconsin, Dec. 14, 1848. He has been for the last fourteen years employed as salesman by the large furniture firm of Matthew Bros. in this city, and thoroughly understands the wants of the trade. The business is under the supervision of three very energetic business men, who deal in a systematic and honorable manner with their customers, and it will doubtless be numbered with our substantial institutions. A cabinet department is run in connection with the store, and a specialty is made of manufacturing upholstery to order.

J. P. THOMPSON & CO.,

Dealers in Dye Woods, Chemicals, Acids, Oils, etc.

No. 105 West Water Street.

THE Northwestern Woolen Manufacturers' Supply House is situated at 105 West Water street, where are found all kinds of dye woods, chemicals, acids, oils, woolen machinery, supplies, burlaps, wool sacks, twine, needles and hop sacking. This enterprise was started by the present firm, J. P. Thompson & Co., in 1868, at 124 West Water, where they remained for six years, after which they removed to their present central and commodious quarters. The building they occupy is ample in every respect for the storage of their large stock of supplies. The structure is two stories in height, with a commodious basement, and has a frontage of 25 feet, with a depth of 120 feet, the location being enhanced by the fact that they have the corner store, using all that side on Clybourn street, which during the busy season presents a lively scene. The specialty of this firm is Woolen Mill Supplies, which they handle in large quantities to supply their growing trade. Their dye woods are received through the large importing agencies of the East, while their acids are all obtained here in Milwaukee. Besides enjoying a fair city trade, they also have a large patronage throughout Wisconsin, Minnesota and Iowa, which aggregates upwards of $75,000 per annum, the stock carried being valued at $20,000. This firm are Northwestern agents for Beach & Co., Hartford, Conn., who are United States agents for Brooke, Simpson & Spiller, of London, the great manufacturers of aniline colors. Mr. Thompson, the sole proprietor, is a native of Connecticut, and came to Milwaukee in 1863, and soon after established his present business, which, by his personal attention and practical business methods, has grown to take such an important position among the commercial features of this city.

KIECKHEFER BROS. & CO.,
Manufacturers of Stamped, Japanned and Pieced Tinware, etc.
113 to 128 Clybourn Street.

AN establishment of most rapid growth, the result of continuous earnest toil and ability, well directed, is that of the above named firm. From an individual business of comparative insignificance the three members of this firm united themselves but a few years ago into a company for the manufacture of all forms of tinware, with a capital of $15,000. They have been able in the short period of their existence to increase their business to that extent that it has reached colossal proportions, excelling anything of its kind in the Northwest, and carrying a stock of over $100,000. The firm was incorporated in 1880, and leased the three upper floors of the Reis Block, southeast corner West Water and Sycamore streets. They manufacture all forms of tinware and sheet iron goods, but in the short space of two years their business grew to such magnitude that they erected a large commodious building of their own on Clybourn street. It is 80 feet front with a depth of 120 feet, and has four floors. The establishment of this industry effected an entire revolution in pieced tinware and sheet iron goods throughout the city and country. Their large factory is furnished with dies, presses and all ingenious devices and contrivances by which the separate pieces, or the entire article, are at once struck into the required shape, reducing the work of the tinman to the mere act of soldering the different parts. By this means the firm has been able to manufacture these wares at so great a reduction in price that retail dealers, who heretofore manufactured these articles, can purchase them from this establishment cheaper than they can make them. Incredible as it may seem, this firm has lately again enlarged their premises by the erection of a large brick block adjoining their old one. It has just been completed and is five stories high and 50 by 140 feet in size. They have among their innumerable machinery undoubtedly the largest and heaviest presses used by any similar establishment in the Union, with a weight of from 3,000 to 40,000 lbs. All this vast machinery is propelled by a superior Corliss engine of over fifty horse-power. In all the departments of their business they require the aid of about 200 operatives, many of whom are skilled artisans. This important home enterprise turns out every description of pieced and stamped tinware, dripping pans and elbows, besides dealing extensively in stamped, japanned and granite wares. The shipments of this firm are to almost every State in the Union, reaching from New York to San Francisco, and have an annual trade of upwards of $300,000. The tin plate is procured direct from England, while the sheet iron comes from Pittsburg. The members of this firm are F. Kieckhefer, W. Kieckhefer and S. Walter, all native Milwaukeeans, and are among the most enterprising business men in the city. The trade is largely indebted to this energetic firm for many important improvements—inventions of their own —in this direction, which have been adopted by other large tinware factories.

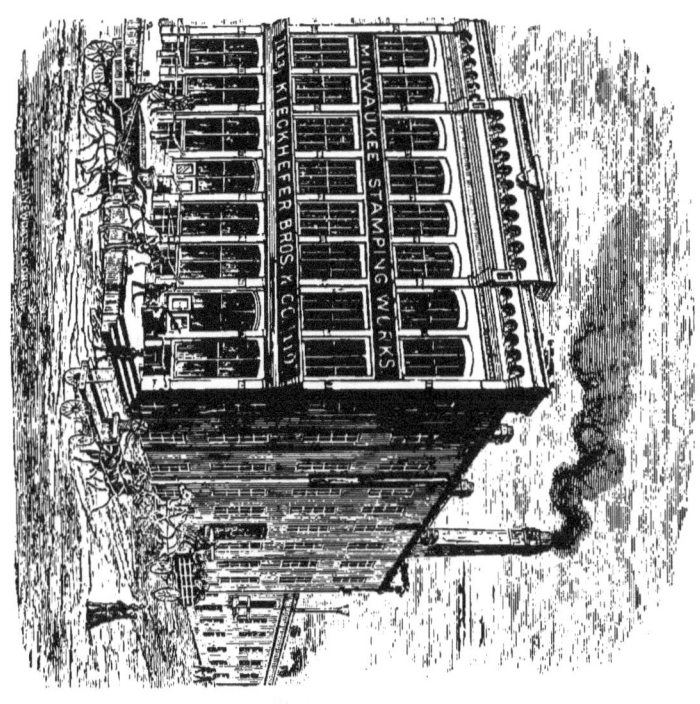

FACTORY.

OFFICE AND SALESROOMS.

KIECKHEFER BROS. & CO.

ALBERT TROSTEL,

(OF THE LATE FIRM OF TROSTEL & GALLUN.)

Tanner and Dealer in Leather, Findings, Tools, Oil, Etc.

104 West Water Street.

ONE of the most successful houses of the leather industry in our city, is that of Albert Trostel, the senior partner of the late firm of Trostel & Gallun. Mr. Trostel began with a small tannery twenty-seven years ago on the Milwaukee river, adjacent to the present site of the State street bridge. Without a store, and doing only job work for his customers, he steadily advanced in business, and about nine months subsequently, took August F. Gallun into partnership. Their progress was rapid, and at the outbreak of the rebellion they were among the fortunate ones to hold large stocks, and reap the benefit of a heavy increase in value. Their first tannery of importance was the "Star" tannery, well known for its production of the celebrated "Blue Star" harness leather. About eight years since they built the Empire tannery, and subsequently purchased the Phœnix tannery on the canal. A dissolution of the firm was effected May 1st, 1885, Mr. Trostel retaining the Star tannery, 891 to 903 North Water street, and also the Phœnix tannery on the canal, the main buildings of which are respectively 60x150 and 60x300, besides the necessary buildings, land and dockage to accommodate his supplies, and his immense stock of bark, the majority of which he receives by vessel from Michigan while the lake is open to navigation. A forty horse-power engine is used in each tannery, with four large boilers to drive the various machinery, and every modern device and appliance of actual benefit in the manufacture of leather. From 150 to 200 men are constantly engaged by this firm, who turn out annually upwards of 65,000 sides, kips, and calf skins, all of the best green, and green salted western slaughter stock, which calls for the use of 8,000 cords of bark. The specialties made by Mr. Trostel from these hides and skins are russet and black harness, saddle, collar and line leather, boot and shoe grains, wax upper, kip and calf skins. The old store at 202 and 204 West Water street having been retained by August F. Gallun for the purpose of carrying on a similar business with his son (*though not as the "successors" of the late firm of Trostel & Gallun*), it became necessary that Mr. Trostel should find a store for the sale of his products and for his extensive retail trade in findings, tanners' and curriers' tools and supplies, oils, etc. He was most fortunate in securing and purchasing the fine four-story and basement brick building conveniently located at 104 West Water street, near Huron street bridge, in the fitting up of which he displayed commendable taste and good judgment. Extensive as the sales are, they are still increasing, and embrace a territory bounded only by the oceans, gulf and British provinces. The stock carried by this firm varies from $200,000 to $300,000, while the sales aggregate $500,000 per annum. Mr. Trostel is a native of Wurtemburg, in Germany and came to this country in 1852. Being a thorough practical tanner, he is acquainted with every feature of the business. This, together with his sterling integrity and straightforward business principles, has enabled him to reach the high position accorded him in commercial and manufacturing circles. He has two sons undergoing instruction in the "art," "trade" and "mystery" of the tanning business, who, when graduated, will take their places as members of the firm, and will undoubtedly prove valued acquisitions to the business of their esteemed parent.

BRADLEY & METCALF,

Manufacturers of and Wholesale Dealers in Boots, Shoes, etc.

389, 391 and 393 East Water St.

IN reviewing the business interests of Milwaukee, it is our desire to briefly mention those houses who have attained a reputation as representatives in their particular lines of trade. There is no establishment that has done more for the benefit of Milwaukee, or more widely advertised it as a desirable manufacturing point, than the firm of Bradley & Metcalf, manufacturers and dealers in boots and shoes. This is one of the oldest establishments of the kind in Milwaukee, having first been instituted in 1843, and has since been under the supervision of its originators. Their building is at Nos. 387, 389, 391 and 393 East Water street, and consists of twenty-four floors, 20x120 feet in dimensions, besides three basements of the same size. The four lower floors are devoted respectively to the retail and wholesale departments, and warehouse. The manufactory is divided up into the various departments, both for heavy and light work. First we come to the cutting-rooms, of which there are two, where the uppers are cut for boots and shoes. The next are the stitching-rooms. One hundred and eighty-five girls are employed in this department, besides a large number of machines. In the next department, we find several machines being operated in cutting soles, turning them out very rapidly and perfectly. In this department we see the Fisher Channel Turning " machine," which does the work formerly, and until lately, done by hand, and which is a very great saving of time and labor. In the next department, called the "bottoming department," we find several objects of interest. First is the " Standard " screw machine, which is a comparatively recent invention, and one which is destined to take the place of all other modes of fastening the uppers and soles together. The screws come in a continuous roll weighing about seven pounds, and this machine cuts them off and screws them into the soles at the rate of ninety a minute, placing them half an inch apart. Three years since, Messrs. Bradley & Metcalf put in one machine at a cost of $400, but felt it was taking a large risk. The machine was such an unqualified success that they soon added another, and still another, and now have four. Here we also find the National Heeling machine, which, with the assistance of a man and boy, heels 800 pair a day. They have four of these machines, costing $500 each. Here we also find the McKay sewing machines, for sewing on soles. This right was bought of the inventor some twenty years since for a small sum, and the purchaser has realized from this one machine $10,000,000 in royalties. In the shoe department we find the Reese Button-hole working machine, cutting and stitching much better than can be done by hand, and finishes three thousand holes per day. This is a new invention, and is a very valuable machine. We then come to the last department, where the bottoms are finished, sand-papered and burnished, and stamped with their trade-mark. The fine work is then put in boxes bearing the trake-mark, kind, size, width of sole, and number. This firm is also the owner of the patent on a machine for making a patent corded seam, which was invented by Mr. Shaw, who for thirty years was foreman of this establishment. It makes a good seam, less prominent and objectionable than is generally used, and is cheaper to make. They have equipped and fitted a new stitching-room, which they occupied lately, and which is the finest in America. It is on the top floor, and finely lighted by ten large sky-lights. They have in the last two years increased their capacity from 300 to 2,000 pairs of shoes a day, and are now making preparations to increase this large number one-half, which will necessitate the employment of 150 more hands. This large concern is under the supervision of Mr. John A. Walden, who was educated in the business from his boyhood in Worcester, Mass., and has been superintendent of various factories since nineteen years of age. Five ten-horse gas engines are employed for driving the machinery. The working force is upwards of 425 persons, and the weekly pay-roll amounts to $4,000. The stock kept on hand is estimated at half a million dollars, and the yearly sales reach an immense sum. They employ from eighteen to twenty commercial travelers, and their goods are in demand over the entire country. Mr. Bradley was born in Massachusetts in 1818, and came to Milwaukee in 1843, with a valuable business experience obtained in New York City. Mr. Metcalf is a native of New York, was born in 1822, and came to Milwaukee with Mr. Bradley. They commenced business the same year together, on a small scale, which has gradually increased until it is second to none in the Union, thus showing what a spirit of energy and perseverance will do. Milwaukee is justly proud of this vast enterprise, and it is with pleasure we give it a place in these pages.

HARRY S. SUTTER,

Photographer.

No. 128 Wisconsin Street, and Corner Oneida Street Bridge.

MR. SUTTER'S establishment at No. 128 Wisconsin street, is well known throughout the entire Northwest. He has by far the most complete and elegant gallery in the city, and occupies two floors, 20x120. On the upper floor are two sky-lights, laboratory and dark rooms, especially designed by Mr. Sutter for the purpose of producing nothing but strictly artistic work in all the various branches of photography.

Mr. Sutter opened in 1873, and has established a trade that is vast in its proportions. His business amounts to over

$25,000 per annum. His register of negatives shows the enormous number of 78,000. The duplicate orders from these plates are a source of a large revenue, which is especially gratifying, inasmuch as it shows that his untiring study and work are well received and appreciated by his friends and patrons. The studio on Wisconsin street, spacious and well appointed as it is, falls short of room, and consequently obliged Mr. Sutter to procure the Grand Central Gallery, corner Oneida street bridge, one of the handsomest buildings in the city, and especially built for the purpose of doing platinum and chemical prints—pictures ranging from 8x10 to 54x100 inches. This studio contains besides photographic portraiture, rooms for artists doing water coloring, India ink, crayon, etc., in all sizes. The most important part is the printing to any size by electric light. Mr. Sutter has devoted many days and nights in his efforts, and after years of persistent study and labor, finally accomplished the desired result. He owns not only the first electric plant in this city, but is the first one who purchased such a costly outfit for this purpose in this country. This plant contains a seven horse-power engine, and a dynamo which produces 10,000 candle power, furnishing light at all times to work eight solar cameras. Mr. Sutter is more than a mere "taker of pictures;" he is an artist in the best sense of the word, and also an inventor, an originator of new ideas and new methods. He has taken out patents for several useful, in fact indispensable, articles of studio furniture, among them a composing chair, and an automatic grader of tints for making life-size vignettes. A large and paying part of his business is photographing samples for factories and wholesale houses—such things as crockery, glassware, furniture, etc., etc. He has a light specially provided for this class of work, and is thus enabled to do it quickly and in first-class style. Mr. Sutter uses American-made materials altogether, finding that they are far superior to the best imported goods in the market.

Harry Sutter looks like Dan. Manning, the present secretary of the treasury, and is one of the really live, energetic and intelligent business men of the city. He was born in Zürich, Switzerland, in 1855, and came to America and to Milwaukee two years after. He is a charter member of the light-horse cavalry of Milwaukee, and has served on the staff of the 4th battalion, 1st regiment Wisconsin militia.

EXCELSIOR BUSINESS AND SHORTHAND COLLEGE,

H. M. Wilmot & Co., Proprietors.

S. W. Cor. East Water and Wisconsin Streets.

THE great benefit derived from the schools and colleges of our land is quite apparent, and the importance they hold in a community is unquestioned. But of all institutions of learning, a well ordered and conducted business college to a large city is of inestimable value. They impart an education which, while especially important to all aspirants in purely business or mercantile pursuits, is also of great value and use in every other human vocation. In fact, there is no branch of education that can be mastered in the same length of time, which is so useful, practical, beneficial and productive of good results as a "business education."

In this line we wish to direct our many readers to the claims presented by the "Excelsior Business and Shorthand College," which is situated in the "Mack Block," southwest corner East Water and Wisconsin streets. The building is one of the newest and finest in Milwaukee, easy of access by street cars from all parts of the city. That part occupied by the college has been finished especially with separate study-rooms and wardrobes for ladies and gentlemen; also, a fine reception-room, office and recitation-rooms. Prof. H. Mitchell Wilmot is principal, and with five efficient assistants constitutes the faculty of the institution. Its course in book-keeping is superior, as it comprises the work of at least a half dozen authors in addition to about fifteen years' actual experience of the principal as an accountant and teacher. The systems of shorthand taught are the standard and are employed by fully 80% of all reporters in the United States. Thorough and practical instruction is also given in pen-

INDUSTRIAL HISTORY OF MILWAUKEE. 101

manship, correspondence, arithmetic, business law, business forms, business practice, typewriting, etc. Students of both sexes are admitted to day or evening sessions at any time, and allowed to pursue any one or more studies or courses, according to means or inclination.

Those who cannot conveniently attend the college, on account of business or otherwise, can take a course in shorthand by their improved and perfected method of postal instruction by mail. School teachers, lawyers, ministers, merchants, clerks and others, will find this a grand opportunity to improve their spare time, and acquire a thorough and practical knowledge of this most fascinating and useful art.

Rates of tuition are very reasonable and compare favorably with the rates of Eastern colleges, and the reduction of price in commodities generally. This college was founded in the "Iron Block" by the present proprietor in 1881, but on the completion of the "Mack Block" in 1883, moved to its presents quarters. During the four years of its existence there has been an enrollment of 500 scholars. All departments are fully represented, and the method of instruction in all branches is superior to many of the larger colleges of our country. Prof. Wilmot is a native of New York, spent his boyhood in the West, but returned East to finish his education in the schools of New York city. He is also a graduate of the Northwestern College, Madison, Wis., where he, prior to his removal to this city in 1880, successfully conducted a similar institution.

O. L. PACKARD,

Machinery and Tools for Iron and Wood Workers.

Nos. 85 and 87 West Water St.

THE trade in machinery and tools has now an important part in the commercial history of this city, a representative and leading house in this branch of trade being that of O. L. Packard, founded Jan. 1st, 1866, on a small scale, at 138 West Water street. Gradually increasing, and always maintaining that high grade of excellence among its specialties for which it is so well noted, this house long ago reached the front ranks of the commercial industries of this city. The first great question for the accommodation of its trade, was the means for greater facilities and more commodious quarters, which finally were found at 85 and 87 West Water street, the present location. The firm occupy six floors, two large basements, 25x100 feet each, with two sheds, 20x50 feet in the rear, used for storage. The building is fully fitted with every facility and all modern appliances for this branch of trade. All the manufacturing done by this firm is confined to articles for the salesrooms and repairing of machinery. A duplex engine, lathes and drilling machines of the latest pattern are found in the workshop. This house deals in all kinds of machinery and tools for iron and wood workers, Sturtevant's blowers and exhausters, shafting, pulleys and hangers, engines, boilers, mill, foundry and machinists' supplies, steam and centrifugal pumps, inspirators and governors. The stock of this firm is drawn from various localities from New England to Missouri, and is the largest and best general assortment of any house of this kind in the West. The sales have aggregated upwards of a quarter million of dollars annually, extending from Lake Superior to Florida, but mainly through this and adjoining states. About a dozen persons are employed, three of whom are skilled and experienced mechanics of long standing. In the firm's opinion, manufactories in wood, iron, wool and glass, would materially advance the commercial interests of our city, and reward the sensible, diligent and wide-awake manufacturer. The native place of Mr. Packard is Lonsdale, R. I., where he was born in 1836, coming to Milwaukee in April, 1865, and the following year commenced his present business. Mr. Packard is a gentleman possessed of large practical experience in all the branches of his business, and gives close personal attention to the successful workings of every department. He has been secretary of various Masonic, Co-operative, Loan and Building, and Religious associations, also secretary, general agent, treasurer and manager of several iron manufacturing establishments.

H. BERTHELET & CO.,

Manufacturers of Hydraulic Cement, Sewer and Culvert Pipes.

Office, 152 West Water Street.

AN important branch of industry, and one requiring special mention in a brief review of the leading business interests of this city, is the large manufactory of cement stone sewer-pipe of H. Berthelet & Co. This is entirely a home industry which was begun in a moderate way by the present firm about twenty years ago in the lower part of the Third Ward. The rapid growth of the city brought in demand this article of manufacture, and the firm receiving the patronage of the city, as well as from the public in general, looked around for more extended quarters where they could have ample room for their increasing trade. In the year 1870 they moved their manufacturing establishment to what was then the extreme southern limits of the city, at the junction of Kinnickinnic Ave. and Clinton streets, with the office at No. 650 Clinton street. The city office is now at No. 152 West Water street, which is in direct telephonic communication with their factory, and it is here where Mr. Berthelet, the head of the firm, is always found superintending the city trade. The factory proper consists of a large building 98 by 116, while the grounds occupy nearly three acres. The history of the manufacture of this article would be full of interest, but time and space will not permit. They have a large, latest improved, 10-horse-power engine, which besides running the various machinery operates the large Blake Crusher, used to prepare the stone for mixture with the cement and sand. They also manufacture chimney tops of all forms and styles, drainage, connection and well pipe of all descriptions. Their specialty, sewer pipe, which has acquired such an extensive use and reputation, is made of the best hydraulic cement and *crushed gravel*. They are perfect in their interior finish, and in point of economy, durability and perfection are superior to any other pipe manufactured for sewerage and drains, as acids or alkaline matter will not affect them and grease will not adhere to them, besides the egg shape of the large pipe aids this latter, besides giving the pipe great strength. The annual products are over 25 miles of pipe. The shipping facilities are perfect the N. W. R. R. having a switch located in their yard. Mr. Berthelet was born in Detroit, Mich., and came to Milwaukee in 1860, since which time he has built up this large industry and gained the enviable position he now occupies among the standard concerns of the Cream City.

VAL. BLATZ,
Brewer and Maltster.

TO form some idea of the greatness of Milwaukee's popular industry, all that is necessary would be to visit the institution of Valentin Blatz, which has gradually risen from a primitive beginning to its present proud position as one of the leading breweries in the United States.

In the year 1851 Valentin Blatz became the proprietor of the brewery, which was then located on the corner of Broadway and Division streets, occupying only half of a city lot. Its sales at that time were 150 barrels annually and its storing capacity 80 barrels of lager beer. Year after year its sales increased, owing to the superior quality of its product and the enterprise of its owner, rendering additional facilities and storing capacity necessary, so that now the brewery proper, with its connecting buildings, occupies two blocks of the most valuable property right in the heart of the city of Milwaukee. Mr. Blatz furthermore owns forty lots bordering on both shores of the Milwaukee river, below Racine street bridge, about a half a mile from the brewery, which are occupied by coal sheds—where coal is delivered by the cargo—and by a number of spare ice-houses.

To illustrate the popularity of Blatz beer and to show how it has ingratiated itself with the trade and the public in general, the following figures will demonstrate:

		Barrels.
Sales for	1868	15,366
"	" 1873	44,639
"	" 1878	48,671
"	" 1879	77,493
"	" 1880	94,935
"	" 1881	107,065
"	" 1882	117,976
"	" 1883	125,273
"	" 1884	136,143

After the close of 1885 the sales are anticipated to foot up at least 150,000 barrels.

In 1872 the malt and ice houses on the corner of Johnson street and Broadway, together with their entire contents, were destroyed by fire. Their re-erection was immediately begun and in the incredible short space of three months the buildings loomed up, enlarged and provided with all modern improvements. Beginning in a very small way, the establishment has attained its present high rank through the energy and indefatigable industry of its owner, whose sole propaganda was and still is his superior brew. Using nothing but the choicest of materials attainable, both in this country and abroad, which he procures regardless of cost, he has been enabled to manufacture beer which has received the highest encomiums wherever introduced.

At the Philadelphia exposition the Val. Blatz beer was awarded a gold medal, the highest premium, for its excellent qualities and because it excelled in point of body, flavor and purity.

The fact remains that the beer has won an international reputation for its unsurpassed quality, and in order to satisfy the demands of the trade, agencies have been established in all of the leading cities in the United States and elsewhere. Special depots under the management of efficient agents are now located as follows: At Chicago, corner Union and Erie streets and corner 16th and Canal streets; at Kansas City, Mo., foot of Walnut street; at Minneapolis Minn., 245 Second Ave. South; at St. Paul, Minn., 282 Jackson street; also Iron Mountain, Mich.; Marinette, Florence, Berlin, Wis.; and various other places.

The capacity of the brewery at the present time is 200,000 barrels and its storing capacity 60,000 barrels. The number of employés is about 200. 50 wagons and over 100 horses are in constant use. The machinery and accommodations in use at this brewery are of the latest designs and best inventions known to science.

Making a tour of inspection through the different departments, where the most delicate cleanliness is observable, there are found two enormous brewing kettles, holding 500 and 350 barrels respectively, several large mash tubs with a capacity

BLATZ'S BREWERY.

of 900 and 700 bushels each, a powerful Corliss engine of 150 horse-power, to which is attached a fly-wheel 14 feet in diameter, weighing twelve tons. Mention is made of these utensils to show how the establishment has enlarged. Its proprietor is still adding to its buildings and machinery, making improvements every year. At present a large grain elevator is being built to hold 300,000 bushels of barley, and an additional malt kiln is under construction. The brewery turns out the very best of domestic beer, and the original " Wiener " beer, which is the pride of its manufacturer.

Mr. Blatz has the credit of establishing the first bottling department in Milwaukee, which now occupies capacious quarters on the corner of Knapp and Broadway streets, one block from the brewery. Messrs Torchiani and Kremer have the management of this branch of the business, which is carried on by them in an enterprising way and with the most signal success. They are the sole bottlers of Val. Blatz's Premium Wiener Export Beer, which they ship to all inland and foreign points at the rate of 2,000 bottles per day.

During the recent exhibition held at New Orleans, a wonderfully unique and well adapted exhibit was displayed, representing Mr. Blatz's manufacture, which has been described at length in the daily papers owing to its grandeur, and which no visitor passed by unnoticed.

Mr. Blatz was born at Miltenberg on the Main, Bavaria, in 1825. Being a practical brewer, he took an active part in business and by hard labor and business foresight has successfully brought it to its present foremost rank.

He was elected an alderman in 1872, ably representing his constituents in the city council. Mr. Blatz is connected with the Second Ward Savings Bank of Milwaukee, being its president since Jan. 2, 1866.

GEORGE S. LYON,

Practical Plumber, Gas Fixtures and Plumbing Material.

410 Grand Ave., Library Block.

THERE is no branch of industry that adds more to the general welfare of a city than the plumbing business. Classed with the prominent and practical plumbers of Milwaukee is the above named house of George S. Lyon, formerly Spence & Lyon. His establishment is located at 410 Grand Avenue, in the Library Block, and consists of two floors, 20x130 feet in dimensions. His office and salesrooms are as fine as can be found in the city. Mr. Lyon makes, at the annual industrial exposition, a fine display of goods in his line which attracts much notice and favorable comment from all. His exhibition of gas fixtures, chandeliers, lamps, shades, etc., for variety and beauty cannot be surpassed by any other firm of the kind in the city. He is agent for the Siemen's

patent regenerative gas-lamps, which are so popular with the public. For economy and illuminating power it is acknowledged to be the best lamp of the kind patented. Mr. Lyon is thoroughly acquainted with every branch of the plumbing, steam and gas fitting business, and by carefully selecting competent workmen, and personally superintending their work, has built up a sound reputation for promptness and reliable work in this important line. He has under employ from 30 to 50 hands, according to the season. He opened up his present business in 1883, after having dissolved partnership with Mr. George A. Spence, with whom he had been in the business for several years.

Mr. Lyon's fine stock of goods is procured in the East and represents a value of $10,000, while the sales will aggregate fully $50,000 per annum. Mr. Lyon has been closely connected with this industry for years, and has always been an advocate of the idea of appointing an inspector in this branch of business, which has lately been accomplished.

R. W. PATTERSON,

Undertaker and Embalmer, and Dealer in Metallic Cases, Caskets, etc., etc.

No. 461 Milwaukee Street, between Mason and Oneida.

TWO floors at 461 Milwaukee street are occupied by Mr. R. W. Patterson, one of the oldest and most successful undertakers in the city. The business was established in 1869 and has been characterized by gradual and substantial growth from the start, until to-day the establishment ranks among the leading houses of the kind in the West. Mr. Patterson is a man well adapted for the work, having the accomplishment for the embalming part of the business of a thorough knowledge of anatomy, being a graduate of Victoria School of Anatomy at Coburg, Ontario. Several assistants are employed. Fine caskets from the leading manufactories of the country are used, while there is always a full line of goods for people of limited means and in moderate circumstances. Mr. Patterson, with that refinement and delicacy of feeling which characterizes the man, has recently remodeled his premises in such a way that everything in any manner relating to the business is kept out of the public view, and so people who pass his store are not shocked by seeing in the show windows a display of caskets, coffins, and other things of a like cheerful and enlivening character. This is a reform in the right direction, and it ought to be followed by every coffin dealer and undertaker in the land. Mr. Patterson carries a stock worth from $6,000 to $10,000, and does a yearly business amounting to about $30,000. Born in Canada, July 4th, 1831, Mr. Patterson came to Milwaukee in 1855, and after engaging in photography several years, established the business which, under his careful personal management, has grown and developed with the growth and development of the city.

Speaking of some of Milwaukee's present needs, Mr. Patterson remarked that more factories of all kinds ought to be put up without delay, there being no city that has a more favorable location than this one for the successful running of factories.

IRA M. DAVIS & CO.,

General Commission Merchants.

165 and 167 West Water Street.

IN a detailed account of the leading houses in the commission business in this city, prominent mention is made of the firm of Ira M. Davis & Co., whose transactions in this important branch of commerce are among the most extensive in the city. The business was begun by Mr. Ira M. Davis, the senior member of the firm, in 1861, at 157 West Water street. Now they are permanently located in the large and handsome block at 165 and 167 West Water street. They took up their position here about nine years ago, and in that time have won the reputation of not only being the oldest, but also most successful commission house in the city, and have the largest produce trade of any firm on the street. The building they occupy is three stories high with a large basement. It has a frontage of 40 feet and a depth of 100 feet, affording ample facilities for the storage of all consignments made them, which are received from all sections of the country. The specialties of this firm are butter, eggs, cheese, apples, oranges, lemons, seeds, etc. From thirteen to fifteen hands are constantly employed and two beautiful large wagons are run in connection with their city trade. Their country trade is very great, and includes all the Northwest. Liberal cash advances are made on all consignments, and prompt and satisfactory returns are rendered. Mr. Davis is a native of New Hampshire and came West in 1861, locating and entering the present business in Milwaukee the same year.

EDWARD KEOGH,

Printer.

437 East Water Street, Corner Mason.

THE business of the job printer has attained such a degree of perfection, that some of the finest lithographic designs will scarcely excel in beauty, excellence and finish, the work of a practical job printer. In variety, style and price they have a great advantage, while it takes less time to turn out work, and allows the customer to choose his own styles. In the first rank of Milwaukee firms we find the name of Mr. Edward Keogh. In 1867 he established a small business, with a few cases of type and one press. The superior quality of the work turned out soon established a reputation second to none, and the large increase of orders compelled him to add to the facilities of his house from time to time, until he now

occupies two floors with his printing and ruling departments, has three modern printing presses and a four-horse-power Otto gas-engine, and a fine stock of the latest styles in type. He employs ten workmen, and has an extended trade throughout the State. He makes a specialty of job and book work, and has also a book-bindery in connection. Mr. Keogh was born in Ireland, Jan. 21st, 1835, and came to this country in 1841, first settling in New York. In 1842 he came to the Cream City, working at his trade until 1867, when he established his present business. What he has accomplished has been gained by untiring energy and devotion to business, united to an inherent capacity for business management. That he is deservedly popular among his acquaintances is shown by the fact that he has represented the 3d district in the assembly for nine years, having first been elected in 1860, and thereafter consecutively in 1861, 1875, 1876, 1877, 1878, 1879, 1880 and 1881. In 1862 and 1863 he served as state senator, having been elected by a good round majority. He is now the city printer.

HADFIELD & CO.,

Dealers in Coal, Wood, Lime, Cement, Salt, etc.

Office, 119 West Water Street.

THE enormous proportions to which the wood and coal trade has attained in this city, brings before the notice of the public the firm of Hadfield & Co. They also deal in lime, cement, stucco, salt, land plaster, plaster hair, fire brick and fire clay. The city office is conveniently situated at 119 West Water street. They have three large yards, capable of holding a sufficient amount of coal for their extensive city and country trade. The yards are located at First Avenue and Canal street, SouthWater near National Av., also at Canal and Muskego Ave. They own large stone-quarries at Waukesha, which are unexcelled by any in the State. This firm has been engaged in their present business for years, and are well known throughout the commercial circles of this city as enterprising and practical men in this branch of trade.

The firm consists of J. Hadfield, G. A. Hadfield and A. H. Hadfield. Through their efficient management the trade has grown to large proportions, represented in the States of Wisconsin, Michigan, Iowa, Illinois and Dakota. They ship upwards of 50,000 tons of coal per season. The shipments from their stone quarries are forty to fifty cars daily, besides manufacturing 1,000 bbls. of lime daily. This firm employs over 150 men to assist them in the various departments of their business. Having advantage of railroad and water transportation, with all the facilities for extending and increasing their already large business, this firm holds an important relation with the commercial features of this city.

WM. FRANKFURTH HARDWARE COMPANY.

(LIMITED.)

Wholesale Hardware.

116 and 118 Clybourn Street.

IN an historical review of the old established and prominent mercantile houses of Milwaukee, it is a pleasure to give space for a sketch of the widely known and universally respected establishment of the Wm. Frankfurth Hardware Co. It traces its origin as far back as 1862, when it was established by Mr. Wm. Frankfurth, who, in 1874, took as partner Mr. Lorenz Maschauer. During these twenty years this house has maintained a prominent position among the representative business establishments of this kind in the city, and has come to be well known throughout the Northwest. From a comparatively small beginning the business has grown to its present magnitude, and is still rapidly extending its business relations. On April 15, 1885, the interests of Wm. Frankfurth & Co. were merged into and absorbed by the Wm. Frankfurth Hardware Company (Limited), with a capital stock of $200,000, at which time they took possession of the splendid new structure which was then just completed and ready for occupancy, where, in quoting their own language at the time, "they aim to retain the confidence which the old firm enjoyed, and to serve old and new customers promptly and satisfactorily." The dimensions of their new building at 116 and 118 Clybourn street, is 50x200 feet, being four stories high and built of brick with terra cotta trimmings. This building is fitted up in the most complete manner and arranged expressly for the large business controlled by this house. The shelving is especially complete and convenient, being constructed on a plan which does away with the step ladder for reaching the higher shelves. It will repay any dealer in hardware, whether in the city for business or pleasure, to visit this house and note the complete facilities for transacting business on a

large scale in this, the model hardware house in the Northwest. A walk through the house will give any one new ideas as to how completely a business of this magnitude can be systematized. These large premises are filled with a full line of foreign and domestic hardware, including every kind of mechanics' tools, builders' hardware, shelf goods, heavy hardware, locks, latches and house-furnishing goods of every description pertaining to this branch of trade. In connection with their general trade, they manufacture all forms of tinware, wire screens and stove polish. Among a few of the numerous articles which are inventions of this firm, are the copper-rimmed tinware, "Daisy" ash sifters and patent fuel savers. Their sales are very extensive, and shipments have been made as far distant as South America. The annual sales will reach no doubt to one-half million dollars. Mr. William Frankfurth is a native of Germany and came to Milwaukee in 1850, since which time his name has become familiar to the whole country in connection with the hardware trade, the standard of which he has so materially aided in elevating.

The original firm of Wm. Frankfurth & Co., a retail establishment, is located at 367 Third street, but has no business connection with the Wm. Frankfurth Hardware Co., as now existing.

GEO. A. SPENCE & CO.,
Fine Gas Fixtures and Plumbing.
132 Grand Avenue.

A BUSINESS that adds much to the comfort and health of the inhabitants of a city, is the gas-fitting and plumbing industry. One of the principal firms engaged in this business in Milwaukee, is that of Geo. A. Spence & Co., at 132 Grand Avenue. This establishment was founded in 1867 by J. P. Rundle, on Milwaukee street. It was then changed to Wisconsin street, and in 1869 moved to the present quarters. Mr. Thomas Spence entered the business in 1870. In 1881 the establishment was sold to Mr. Geo. A. Spence and Geo. S. Lyon, and was conducted under the firm name of Spence & Lyon, the business soon thereafter passing into the hands of the present firm. The commodious quarters of this firm consist of two floors, 25x110 feet in dimensions, and a large basement. The first floor is divided into salesroom and office, and their exhibition of the most costly and latest designs of gas fixtures, shades, lamps, chandeliers, polished brass and bronze goods, constitutes as fine a display as can be found in the city in this branch of trade. They employ upwards of fifty men to meet the demands of their large and growing trade. Their fine stock of goods and most of their material is purchased in the East, and is valued at $20,000. The business of this firm extends all over the city and various portions of the Northwest, and aggregates an amount of $125,000 per annum. They are exclusive agents for the Mitchell, Vance & Co.'s gas fixtures, and the Detroit Combination Gas Machine, and also the Jas. L. Sharp "Dome," "Ætna" and "Active" gas stoves, which are meeting with such great success. The members of this firm are both Milwaukeeans, and are proficient in their business, and are in every way worthy the support and patronage accorded them.

ADOLPH MEINECKE & SON,
Manufacturers of Baskets, Willow Ware, Children's Carriages, etc.
Corner Mason and Front Streets.

FIRST and foremost among the manufacturing firms of Milwaukee, we find that of A. Meinecke & Son, by reason of their large trade extending over the length and breadth of the United States, and on account of the business ability of the two gentlemen conducting the establishment. Adolph Meinecke, Sr., was born in 1830, near Bremen, Germany. His father was a country physician, and allowing him a good education, he passed the mercantile school at Osnabrück, and served an apprenticeship in a business house at Bremerhaven, and came to America in 1848. After being employed some years by an importing house in New York, an occasional trip west drew his mind to the idea of establishing himself at Milwaukee. This he finally did in 1855, and a fancy goods and toy store was the starting point that grew into a wholesale and importing establishment. The great demand for finer willow ware and ladies' baskets, gave rise to the manufacture of these goods on the place. In 1864 work was begun with a German foreman and a few hands. Innumerable obstacles presented themselves, which, with competing low prices of imported goods, were soon overcome

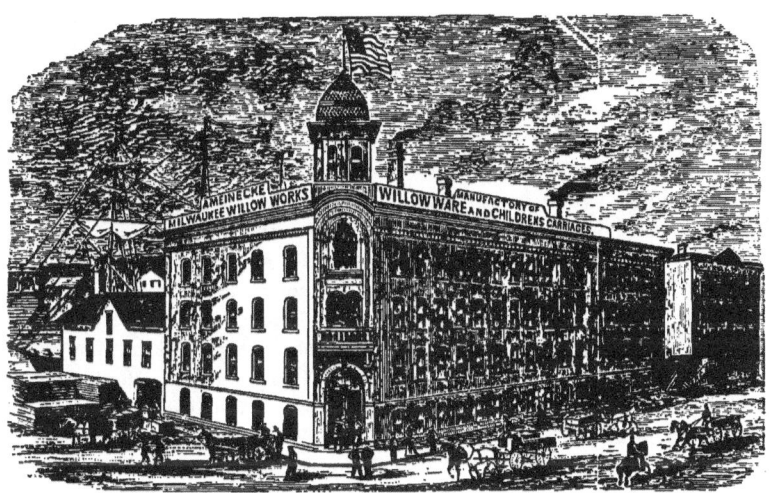

by a well regulated working plan, making goods more adapted to the requirements of this country, and by raising the willow used in manufacture on their own plantations. Under this system the demand for Milwaukee baskets grew largely, until now many of the most extensive dry goods and notion houses from every part of the United States receive their supply from the Milwaukee Willow Works, as the factory was named.

The extensive works which were put up at the foot of Mason street, occupying nearly the entire block, were erected in 1870, and employ over three hundred hands, and has many outside shops connected therewith. Besides baskets, the works make a specialty of children's carriages, of which over fourteen thousand were made last year. There are also made hobby-horses, boys' wagons, croquet games, toy furniture, rattan and willow ware, and various other articles too numerous to mention. Another of their specialties is the manufacture of wooden shoes, these being extensively used by the Germans in warm weather. This work was formerly done by hand, but they have invented a machine which does the work better, and in a much less time. They have induced the farmers in this neighborhood to grow willow on the banks of brooks, and this has turned out to be a good investment. Their business has constantly been on the increase, and the sales last year amounted to the sum of $250,000. Ferdinand Meinecke, the son, was born in 1856, in this city, and was admitted to the firm in 1878, since which time the business has been conducted under the name of A. Meinecke & Son. They have engines and boilers of one hundred horse power in their factory, and other labor-saving machines and inventions. Their name is known far and wide, and bears a high reputation in the commercial world for the honorable and business-like manner in which their affairs are conducted, and their straightforward manner of dealing with all.

STRONACH LUMBER CO.

Manufacturers of Salt, Piece Lumber and Timber.

Office 149 West Water Street.

ONE of the important factors of commercial advancement in this city is that of the lumber and salt trade. A well known and exceedingly popular establishment of this branch of industry is the Stronach Lumber Co., with extensive mills and timber lands in and near Manistee, Mich. Their main office is in this city, 149 West Water street, where all the business of the firm is transacted. The capacity of the mills of this company is 18,000,000 feet of lumber and 100,000 barrels of salt annually, and they employ upwards of 200 men. This company was incorporated some 15 years ago with mills and office as above stated.

They manufacture piece lumber and timber for all kinds of construction and manufacture salt in connection. The trade of this company is very extensive, large sales being made to firms of this city, Chicago and the Northwest, but principally in Milwaukee, reaching to over $200,000 annually. The officers of the company consist of John Thorsen, President; W. R. Thorsen, Secretary, and W. B. Remington, Treasurer. Mr. John Thorsen has charge of the business at this place and Chicago, Mr. W. R. Thorsen giving his attention to the mills at Manistee, while Mr. Remington looks after the interests of the company's large tracts of pine lands. A new and important feature of this company's business is the manufacture and sale of salt,

INDUSTRIAL HISTORY OF MILWAUKEE.

which has been found in large quantities near their mills. They have just begun working this new branch, and in the start were very unsuccessful with their well, losing a large number of tools, besides so much valuable time. Being men of mettle and determination, however, they still pushed forward with that energy which is indicative of success, and now manufacture 400 barrels per day, which finds a ready sale in this market. The superiority of these wells may be assumed when it is stated that the brine contains 97 % of pure salt.

SIELAFF, LOEBER & CO.,
Wholesale Paper and Twine Dealers.
103 West Water Street.

AT No. 103 West Water street is situated the wholesale store of Messrs. Sielaff, Loeber & Co., dealers in all assortments of paper and wooden wares, twines and ropes. Their large building, two stories high, with a basement, is fully stocked with a complete line of wares for their large trade, which extends to all parts of the Northwest. For the past four years, since the incorporation of this firm, they have succeeded in establishing a large and growing trade. A specialty of this firm is becoming popular all over the country, and is known as "the Yak-Tail Duster," for which they are sole agents in the United States east of the Rocky Mountains. The superiority of this duster over all others is so great that it does not admit of comparison. It is matchless for beauty, symmetry, durability, usefulness and cheapness. After the tail of the yak has been prepared for artificial use, it is about twenty inches long, fine and flexible as human hair. It is jet black, and can be used on the finest and most delicate surface, without marring it in the least. Its merits are readily attested, from the fact that it is in use by all the large railroads, hotels, banks and public buildings of note in the country. This firm are also large dealers in, and always have on hand, a full assortment of wrapping and building papers, and are manufacturers' agents for woodenware, brooms, brushes, manilla and sisal rope, manilla and sisal clothes-lines, and are also agents for Bentley & Gerwig's twines. Their telephone, No. 171, puts them in communication with all parts of the city. All in all, this is a standard house.

THE WISCONSIN MARINE AND FIRE INS. CO. BANK.

THE Wisconsin Marine and Fire Insurance Co. Bank is the pioneer bank of the whole Northwest. It was established as early as 1839, and for forty-five years it has had the same president and the same cashier. Between 1840 and 1850 it furnished currency for the whole country between Detroit and St. Louis and, although this circulation had no security but the personal honesty of the officers of the bank, every dollar presented at its counter has been redeemed in gold. It still does the largest business of any bank in Wisconsin, and maintains its high character for honesty and conservative management. Its bank building, of which we give a cut on page 55, is a fine specimen of architecture, and is a credit to the city.

PHILLIP BEST BREWING CO.,
Manufacturers of Beer.
Milwaukee, Wis., U. S. A.

THE manufacture of beer has contributed more to make this city famous than all the other interests combined. It is noted all over the civilized world for the superiority of its products in this line, and some idea of the importance of this industry may be formed when it is stated that over $8,000,000 are invested, and the sales amount to upwards of 1,500,000 barrels annually. One of the oldest and most important establishments of this kind, not only in Milwaukee, but in the world, is that of the Phillip Best Brewing Co. This company has over three and one-half million dollars invested, and the product of their breweries is the standard for excellence and purity wherever it is known. The business was founded in 1842, on a small scale, by Jacob Best and his four sons, Phillip, Jacob, Jr., Charles and Lorenz. The amount produced was only about 300 barrels a year. After a number of changes, the entire business was taken charge of by Philip Best, in 1860, who laid the foundation for the immense business now controlled by this company. In 1864, Capt. Frederick Pabst, his son-in-law, was admitted to partnership. The next year Phillip Best withdrew from the business, and Mr. Emil Schandein, also a son-in-law, was received into partnership. The firm was then called Phillip Best & Co. So extensively had the business grown, the demand surpassing the supply, that in 1873 a stock company was formed, and the name of the business changed to the "Phillip Best Brewing Co.," and was incorporated under the laws of the commonwealth of Wisconsin. The following officers, who are still serving, were elected: Capt. Frederick Pabst, president; Emil Schandein, vice-president; Chas. Best, Jr., secretary.

MAIN BREWERY.

For the benefit of visitors to our city, and information to the readers of this work, we give an account of the location

SOUTH SIDE BREWERY.

and description of the mammoth buildings of this company. Their plant, or main buildings and beautiful general offices, are situated on both sides of Chestnut street from 9th to 11th. They are located on six different blocks, and the life and action in these quarters is equal to that of a small city, yet everything is done with a precision and dispatch that is truly wonderful. The monster structure of this establishment is the Empire Brewery, consisting of six large buildings, from the top of any one of which can be obtained a commanding view of the entire city, the surrounding country and Lake Michigan. These buildings are well fitted with all modern improvements and machinery of the latest patterns. The capacity of these buildings alone is over 400,000 barrels per year. The yards, fire-engine house and "pitching department," with their full force of well-disciplined firemen, constitutes one of the interesting features. One of the largest buildings in the world, of this kind, is the extensive malt house. It is ten stories high, and has the best and most perfect arrangements for malting in the world. Just east of this large malt house is the company's elevator "A," which has a storage capacity of 300,000 bushels. The general offices are next to elevator "A." They are beautifully decorated and fitted up in the most perfect manner. The business is all transacted here by a great number of clerks, book-keepers, etc. The elegant private offices of President Pabst and of Secretary Best are also situated in this building. The extensive stables are situated on the corner of Chestnut and 11th streets. Other interesting features are the engine-room, ice machine and plant of electric lights, and elegant residence of Capt. Fred. Pabst, with its fine grounds, adjoining.

Then, there is the South Side Brewery, with a capacity of 100,000 barrels per year, and the bottling department, where over 200 hands bottle nearly 15,000,000 bottles of beer per annum, where the railroad and lake facilities for shipping are not equaled by any other establishment in America. Near here is also situated the large malt house, elevator "D," and Vice-President Schandein's beautiful residence and grounds, on the bluff near the brewery. His private offices are also connected with this brewery. There are also two large and commodious shipping depots, one connected with the Chicago & Northwestern, and the other with the Chicago, Milwaukee & St. Paul Railway. The business of this company, from a small beginning, has reached the enormous sales of nearly 500,000 barrels annually. The company manufacture different varieties of beer, to satisfy the various tastes of their patrons. Each variety is marked by a peculiar characteristic, and made of the purest materials and by the best processes known to science. These varieties are known as the "Export," "Select," "Bohemian," "Bavarian" and "Standard." They ship in bulk to all parts of the United States and Mexico, and in bottles all over the civilized world.

This company secured the gold medal at both the Centennial Exposition at Philadelphia, in 1876, and at the great World's Fair at Paris, in 1878. This company's exhibit also took the first prize at the famous Southern Exposition at Atlanta, and at the World's Cotton Centennial Exposition in 1885. The monster strides of this company's business can readily be seen from the simple statement that the production increased from 3,677 barrels in 1863, to 385,049 in 1884. The capital invested is $3,387,825; number of employés, 643; wages paid per year, $385,523.22; number of horses, 207; taxes paid in 1883, $30,246.18; revenue taxes, after deducting 7½ per cent. rebate, $348,150.50; beside other expenses on the same large scale, making their total expenses for the year 1883, $3,042,551.28. The company has branch offices and wholesale houses in nearly every important city in the Union.

CENTRAL WAREHOUSE.

E. J. Tapping, Agent.

Office, 136 West Water Street.

A NEW feature of commercial industry was added to Milwaukee with the opening of the Central Warehouse, about two years ago. It is every way just what its name indicates, central to the business part of Milwaukee, and commodious for the storage of any kind of goods, including furniture, household goods, pianos, organs, flour, wool, vinegar, sirups, etc. It is in the Reese Block, which is four stories high, with large basements. The dimensions are 100x200 feet, and the facilities are enhanced by its location on the river. It includes nine large stores, and every department is fitted up with elevators and all conveniences necessary for a great storehouse. The management of this enterprise is under the direction of Mr. E. J. Tapping, an efficient and experienced business man, who conducts it after the plan of the large New York warehouses. It is mainly through Mr. Tapping's personal energy and attention that this warehouse has met with such great success. Not only is the patronage of the city received, but parties all over the United States consign their wares direct to this warehouse, to be managed and sold by them. All forms of merchandise are received for storage on moderate terms. Storage rooms are also rented to firms in the city, or large establishments who ship in large quantities to this place, and desire to have a central distributing point for their goods. Insurance can be placed on all goods desired, so as to render them safe from loss. Goods can be forwarded to any destination from this warehouse; also sold on commission, if desired. Goods can be packed, unpacked, re-packed, also repaired and polished, when desired. As the merchants of our city and country understand the convenience of this warehouse, the more they patronize it, until now it plays no small part in the city's trade.

JABEZ M. SMITH,

Confectionery, Fruits and Cigars.

441 Jefferson Street.

GOOD candy has become one of the necessaries of life with many worthy people in this progressive age, and it is, therefore, a sweet satisfaction to know that good candy is sold in our otherwise bitter world, and that Jabez M. Smith, at 441 Jefferson street, keeps always a full stock of the best and purest candies in the market. He keeps also fruits and fancy confectionery generally, as well as an alluring variety of things to please and charm the young people. Mr. Smith was in the grocery business a great many years, at 419 Milwaukee street, having a large trade and being among the leading men in that line at that time. He established himself where he is now in 1875, beginning in a small room with a small stock, and enlarging and increasing year by year, until the present respectable proportions were attained. As an old settler, Mr. Smith is full of interesting information about early times in the city of cream-brick houses. Born in Trowbridge, England, in 1839, he came to this country when only three years old, and lived with his people in various parts of York State until 1852, when he came to Milwaukee, which was then a town of less than 20,000 inhabitants. Mrs. Smith's father, as is well known, was the Rev. Chas. S. Macreading, who, for forty years, was a most zealous worker in the field of ministerial Methodism. In an early day he had charge of a church which stood opposite where the Plankinton House now stands. Mrs. Macreading was an active and faithful worker in the missionary cause.

The "Eureka" Mineral Spring was discovered by Mr. Smith some years ago, while boring a well on his premises in this city, and advertised by him extensively, by means of circulars and certificates, throughout the country, but the time was hardly ripe for mineral water, and the enterprise proved to Mr. Smith a failure. If the well could be re-opened, and its wonderful waters put on the market now, a fortune could be realized thereby, as the water is said to be superior to that obtained at Waukesha and at Sparta.

SCHLITZ'S PARK.

Accommodations for 20,000 Persons.

Milwaukee, Wis.

SCHLITZ'S Park is one of the largest and most beautiful pleasure resorts of the Cream City. It covers an area of about eight acres, and is situated at the north end of Eighth street, near Walnut. It is accessible by three of the principal street railways of the city. It has all the hotel accommodations and attractions connected with a first-class pleasure resort of this kind. This beautiful place was formerly known as "Quentin's Park," and was arranged and occupied by him as a family residence until his death, in 1862, when the grounds were fitted for public use and managed by his heirs, and subsequently by lessees. They kept charge of it until July, 1879, when it was purchased by the brewing company whose name it bears. They invested over $150,000 in improving and refitting it. In the centre of the park is "Lookout Hill," on which is erected a lofty pagoda, from the summit of which can be obtained the finest view of all parts of the city, Bay View, west and northern suburbs, and a large portion of Lake Michigan. The next point of interest is the Park Theatre, which is fitted in the most attractive and comfortable manner. It is used for concerts, theatricals and balls, and has a seating capacity of 5,000. The stage scenery is as perfect as any theatre in the city. The Schlitz Park Hotel is a large establishment, 80x150 feet in dimension, near the main entrance, and is run in connection with the park and under the same management. It is two stories in height, and is furnished in the most beautiful manner. It contains restaurant and dining-rooms, parlors and four bowling alleys, the largest and best arranged in the State. To the right of the main gate is located the park menagerie, containing various domestic and wild animals, which are a source of great attraction to visitors. The main entrance grounds to the park are fitted up with two large, beautiful fountains, 250 colored gas globes formed into an arch, terraces and rustic scenes, besides flowers and plants, all of which add greatly to the attractions of this popular resort. The entire park, hotel, opera house and grounds are emblazoned with thirty-two electric lights, which present a most beautiful sight, and remind one of the Oriental gardens of old.

F. W. HARTMANN & CO.,

Distillers and Jobbers in Fine Whiskies, and Importers of Wines and Liquors.

206 and 208 West Water Street.

THE headquarters for pure unadulterated wines and liquors is at F. W. Hartmann & Co.'s, which is one of the best known and the largest wholesale liquor firms in the city. It was established in 1864 under the firm name of Her-

Schlitz's Park.

mann & Hartmann, at 258 Third street. In 1868 the firm was dissolved, and Mr. Hartmann retained charge of the business for the next seven years, locating at 278 West Water street, at which place he remained until 1875, when he removed to 206 and 208 West Water street. In 1877, Mr. Henry Schoenfeld, who had heretofore been engaged in the distilling business, entered into co-partnership with Mr. Hartmann, and has continued in the same up to the present date. In 1883 the present quarters were enlarged, extended and improved, so that to-day they have the most commodious, conveniently located and best arranged establishment in the city. The building is three stories in height, with a large basement, all of which have an area of 40x110 feet. They carry one of the largest and most extensive stocks in the Northwest, consisting of the choicest wines and liquors of their own importation from the most celebrated and reputable houses in the old country. They also have on hand a large supply of Kentucky bourbon and rye whisky, in bond and free, besides domestic brandies, gins, cordials, etc., of their own manufacture. This firm are also noted distillers of alcohol, cologne spirits, bourbon and rye whiskies. Their entire stock is valued at upwards of $200,000. Both Messrs. Hartmann and Schoenfeld are well known among not only the business circles of this city, but also the large houses of the old world. Twelve men are under the employ of this firm to assist with their large trade, and the fame of this firm as distillers and jobbers is extended all over America, especially in the Northwest, where the greater portion of their sales are distributed. The business of this house amounts to about $350,000 a year. Mr. F. W. Hartmann was born in Prussia in 1835, and came direct to Milwaukee in 1855. Mr. H. Schoenfeld is a native of Syracuse, N. Y., and settled in this city in 1866. Both gentlemen have been prominently connected with the business interests of the Cream City, and have built up a profitable business, which represents their ability and sound business policy.

J. M. FOX,

Dealer in Staple and Fancy Groceries.

117 Wisconsin Street.

THIS house dates its inception from 1869, having passed through several hands before Mr. Fox become the sole proprietor. It is one of the oldest and best equipped stores of the kind in this city and enjoys a large patronage among all classes of people. A large stock of staple groceries is always kept on hand, while they have as fine and complete a stock of foreign and domestic groceries and table luxuries as can be procured in this or other countries, and of a quality that will meet the wants of the best trade. His line of canned goods embraces everything that can be obtained, soups, meats, fish of all kinds, fruits and vegetables. Also keeps relishes, preserves, dried fruits, nuts, teas and coffees, crackers, spices, fine flavoring extracts, baking powders, etc. His coffees and teas are especially superior, being the best in the market, and strictly pure and unadulterated. Mr.

J. M. Fox together with his brother purchased the business in 1882, and conducted it under the name of Fox Bros. His brother retired in 1885, and he is now the sole proprietor. Mr. Fox was born in Madison, Wisconsin, in 1851, and was long engaged in business in that city. He is a pushing business man, and has succeeded in establishing his enterprise on a firm foundation.

H. C. KOCH & CO.,

Architects and Superintendents.

Corner Wisconsin Street and Broadway.

ONE of the standard firms of this city, who are architects and superintendents, is that of H. C. Koch & Co., who have conducted business here for a number of years, and have achieved a reputation or sound and artistic workmanship. The business was begun by the senior partner in 1866, who entered into co-partnership with Mr. G. W. Mygatt, then one of the leading architects of Milwaukee. Ten years prior to this time Mr. Koch entered this office as an apprentice, just after completing his academic course. In 1862 he enlisted as a private in the 24th Wisconsin Volunteers, but his profession soon brought him into prominence, and he was placed on Gen. Phil. Sheridan's staff as topographical engineer, where he served until nearly a year after the war. He has in his possession some valuable letters of recommendation from Gen. Sheridan, attesting to his ability and the great service rendered his country. In 1870 he severed his connection with Mr. Mygatt, and the present firm was organized. The special feature of the work of this firm is that of designing public and assembly buildings, in which they rank foremost among the architects of the United States. Over a dozen court houses in the West have been built after their plans. In 1880 they took the third premium out of a list of ten, offered by the sanitary engineer of New York to the architects of the United States for the best designs and plans for school buildings, 184 plans being submitted in all. Mr. H. P. Schnetzky, a brother-in-law of Mr. Koch, is the company of the firm, and is eminently qualified for such association. He is the inventor of the patent Malt House Ventilator, which is by far the best in use. By the introduction of this system more equal and richer malt can be obtained, while the process is much cheaper. This firm occupies commodious quarters in the Pfister block, corner Wisconsin and Broadway. From eight to ten persons are employed in the various branches of this business. One of the features of this firm is plans for malt houses, ice houses, elevators, kilns and breweries. Prominent among their work we mention the Hospital and Memorial Hall at the National Soldiers' Home of this city; the Milwaukee County Insane Asylum; the State Insane Asylum at Oshkosh; Science Hall, State University, Madison; court houses at Madison, Racine, Appleton, and Jefferson, this State, Oskaloosa, Ia., and in various parts of Illinois, Iowa and Minnesota. Specimens of their work in this city consist of the Opera House, Calvary Presbyterian Church, numerous prominent residences, and most all the public school buildings erected during the past ten years. They well merit the prominent position they have gained as architects and superintendents, and all those desiring work of this kind will find able exponents in this firm.

CITY CARRIAGE WORKS.

R. Sherin & Co., Manufacturers of Fine Carriages and Sleighs.

448 Milwaukee Street.

THE City Carriage Works of Milwaukee were established on a small scale in 1869, but business began to increase at once, and it was not long until the present roomy quarters at 448 Milwaukee street were occupied. The room here is ample, there being two floors, each 40x 120, and so arranged that the utmost economy of space is secured. From fifteen to twenty skilled workmen of the first class are constantly employed. Four departments are maintained, and every vehicle turned out is completely finished in the establishment. The woodwork, the blacksmithing, the painting and the trimming are all done, and well done, in the company's works at 448 Milwaukee street. Fine carriages and sleighs of all kinds are manufactured. The best of material is used, and the best of work is, of course, the result. Much of the work is made to order, and some of the best private carriages, buggies and coupés in the city bear the well-known trade-mark of the City Carriage Works. The sleighs manufactured are sold largely in Minnesota, where the sleighing, as a rule, is more reliable than in Wisconsin. From three to five thousand dollars worth of stock—manufactured vehicles—is usually kept on hand.

Mr. R. Sherin, the genial and gentlemanly head of the firm, is a native of Ontario, Canada, where he was born, in 1827. He has resided in Milwaukee 21 years. While a citizen of Canada, Mr. Sherin held several municipal and other offices, but since coming to this city he has held aloof from politics and given all his time and thought to his business. He also did military duty in the Dominion, and knows something about "the pomp of glorious war."

F. R. BUELL & CO.,

Shippers of Anthracite and Bituminous Coal.

Office, 357 Broadway.

COAL is rapidly becoming the chief article of fuel, and the number engaged in the trade in this city is large. Among these, deserving of especial mention, we name the firm of F. R. Buell & Co., of No. 357 Broadway, in the Chamber of Commerce building. This concern was first started in 1882 as Guthrie & Buell, and so continued until June 1st, 1885, when Mr. Guthrie withdrew, the firm being now conducted alone by F. R. Buell, the "company" being nominal. He is engaged solely in the wholesale trade, doing business mainly in Wisconsin, Minnesota, Illinois, Iowa and Nebraska, and his sales aggregate a quarter million and upwards per year. He receives all of the best grades of anthracite and bituminous coal from large

Eastern mines, and handles the famous "Enterprise" coal of Wilkesbarre, and also from the mines of the Grassy Island Coal Co. and Edgerton Colliery, of Scranton. His yards are on the North Menomonee canal, and his shed is 175x250 feet in dimensions. Trade has more than doubled each successive year since its inception, and the future outlook is gratifying in the extreme.

Mr. Buell was born in New York in 1854, and studied for a civil engineer, and graduated from the State University. He followed this profession for a number of years, coming to this city in 1882. The business has grown rapidly under his able and efficient management.

A. W. RICH & CO.,

Dry Goods.

413, 415 and 417 Broadway.

MILWAUKEE is particularly fortunate in the possession of staunch business houses, and especially those engaged in the sale of dry goods. One of the foremost among these enterprises, by reason of the magnitude of trade, is the firm of A. W. Rich & Co. This name has long been identified with the history of our city, and is one of the early landmarks in the field of trade. In 1867, Mr. Rich first started in business at No. 103 Wisconsin street, with the enormous capital of *four hundred and thirty dollars*. He was naturally a business man, and this he soon proved by the unexampled success which met him at every step. He handled only good goods, put them down to a living price, and—*advertised*. The wisdom of this course was soon apparent. A few years later his quarters were found to be entirely too small, and he determined to increase his stock, and so secured more room, at Nos. 101, 105 and 107 Wisconsin street, besides the original store, No. 103 Wisconsin street. He handled the business alone for seven years, then, in 1874, associated with him Mr. Silber, and for ten years the business was conducted under this firm. Last year Mr. Silber retired, and the name was changed to A. W. Rich & Co. Mr. Rich, however, is the sole proprietor of this large business. In 1882, the business was moved to its present eligible location, Nos. 413, 415 and 417 Broadway. The premises occupied consist of a spacious four-story building, 60x115 feet in area, admirably arranged and equipped for the prosecution of the business, employment being furnished to about two hundred persons. The store is fitted up with the cash-railway system, elevators and everything of the latest invention to expedite business. The first and second floors are stocked for retail trade. The third floor contains their wholesale stock, and also the various offices. The fourth floor is given up to the manufacturing of ladies' and children's cloaks and suits, hoop-skirts, etc., and this branch of the business has increased to something enormous. The estimated value of the stock is $250,000, and is constantly being replenished. Mr. Rich was born in Somos, Hungary, July 27th, 1843, and came to this country in 1854, and to Milwaukee ten years later. By indomitable pluck and perseverance, he has arisen from a small position to the proprietor of one of the handsomest stores in Wisconsin. Personally, Mr. Rich is esteemed highly in business circles for his integrity and upright character. He is a benevolent gentleman, and never fails to remember the unfortunate, even amid the cares and worry which are attendant on the management of his business.

out annually from this establishment. Mr. Ogden is a native of Milwaukee and a veteran in this business, and during the past years has made many improvements which have not only established his reputation, but added much to the general character of Milwaukee for its famous manufacturers. Mr. Ogden makes a specialty of fine work in his line of business.

G. W. OGDEN & CO.,
Carriages.
218 and 220 Grand Avenue.

THE G. W. Ogden & Co. carriage manufactory has acquired a merited popularity throughout the city and environs for the superior quality of vehicles turned out and their uniform reliability. John Ogden, father of the present proprietor, commenced business in 1849 on West Water street, and four years after moved to the present large and commodious quarters, 218 and 220 Grand Ave., so that the present extensive enterprise is the outgrowth of scores of years, sedulously devoted to his business. This manufactory covers an area of 33x200 feet, containing three floors of equal dimensions. Everything is arranged with perfect system for effective operations and prompt attention to all orders. Only the very best material is used and finest goods manufactured. A force of twenty-five hands is constantly employed to meet the demands of the large trade which extends all over the Northwest. The stock consists of the finest assortment in the city and the best quality of goods. From 300 to 500 carriages, buggies and sleighs are turned

JOS. SCHLITZ BREWING CO.,
Manufacturers of Beer.
Milwaukee, Wis.

THE renown of Milwaukee lager beer extends all over the civilized world. The value of beer manufactured here is upwards of $10,000,000 annually, and the greater portion of this vast sum is realized from the jobbing sales made outside of the city, thus bringing this immense sum here, in cash, to be expended for the general advantage of the city. One of the great establishments of this kind in Milwaukee is that of the Jos. Schlitz Brewing Co., whose main plant and offices are located on the three blocks from Third street east to the railroad track, and south from Walnut street to Cherry. The business of this company was begun by August Krug, in 1849, who erected a small brewery on Chestnut street, between 4th and 5th. The next year the first beer vaults were built on the present site of the company. The capacity was then only about 250 barrels, and the annual business, up to 1855, only amounted to $1,500. Mr. Krug died in 1856, and Jos. Schlitz, his book-keeper, took charge of the business. In 1874 a stock company was organized, and called the Jos. Schlitz Brewing Co., with the following officers: Jos. Schlitz, president; August Uihlein, secretary, and Henry Uihlein, superintendent. In 1875, Mr. Schlitz was lost on the steamship "Schiller," while on his way to visit his native country. The officers of the company have been since then: Henry Uihlein, president; August Uihlein, secretary, and Alfred Uihlein, superintendent, while Edward Uihlein has the management of the Chi-

JOSEPH SCHLITZ'S BREWERY.

cago branch. The large plant of this company consists of about seven acres. The main brewery and general offices occupy the entire block, bounded by Second and Third and Walnut and Galena streets. The buildings are six stories in height, and contain all the latest facilities and machinery for the manufacture of beer. Their mammoth steam engine is of 150 horse-power. They also have two other engines of 20 and 25 horse-power respectively, used in other departments. On the block bounded by the railroad and First and Walnut and Galena streets, is situated the bottling department, cooper shops, repair shops, ice houses and railroad tracks of the company, while fronting on Second street is located the extensive malt house, 150 x 300 feet, one of the largest in the city; also mammoth grain sheds and wagon yards.

An interesting feature is the large ice machine, run by an engine of 150 horse-power. It is of the Linde patent and the first imported machine of its kind received in America. It was purchased last year in Switzerland. The refrigeration produced by this machine is perfect. One of the vast refrigerators, or beer storage houses, covers an area of 100x140 feet, is five stories in height and constructed entirely of stone, iron and brick, and has a capacity of nearly 50,000 barrels of beer. They are now erecting a new elevator, with a capacity of 400,000 bushels. A feature of interest is their great cellars or vaults, which are twenty-five feet under ground, and contain vats of astonishing size, and so numerous that one would think all the beer in the country could be stored in them. This company own twenty acres north of the city limits, along the Milwaukee river, where are situated their large ice houses, twelve in number. They harvest each season over 100,000 tons, nearly one-half of which is used in their shipment of beer by rail, nearly 10,000 carloads of which are sent out from their brewery every year, and over 6,000 pounds of ice are put into every car, which is capable of preserving the necessary temperature during the longest shipment.

The Schlitz beer is shipped all over the United States, as well as to Mexico, Central America, Winnipeg and Brazil, in barrels as well as bottles. To get at the general extent and increase of this business, we append the following interesting figures of beer sold: In 1850, 250 bbls.; 1865, 4,400 bbls.; 1871, 12,381 bbls.; 1873, 49,623 bbls.; 1876, 71,017 bbls.; 1877, 79,538 bbls.; 1878, 102,538 bbls.; 1879, 139,154 bbls.; 1880, 195,119 bbls.; 1881, 253,371 bbls.; 1882, 277,307 bbls.; 1883, 330,597 bbls.; 1884, 345,554 bbls., which is more than any one brewery in the United States has sold within the same period. The capacity at the present time is over 500,000 barrels annually. Of all the beer manufactured by this firm only about one-sixteenth of it is sold at home. A stock of 120,000 barrels of beer is constantly kept on hand, also 400,000 bushels of malt and barley. Nearly 800,000 bushels of barley are used every year; two-thirds of this amount is received from Wisconsin and Minnesota, while the balance is purchased from California and Canada. About 1,000,000 pounds of hops are received annually from New York State and the Pacific coast. The magnitude of this business would necessarily call for the employment of a large number of men, which at present is nearly 500, while over fifty double-team wagons and trucks and 125 horses are in use. About $3,500,000 is invested in this business, which is increasing so rapidly that greater improvements are contemplated for the near future.

BENJAMIN MOCK'S

Riverside Livery and Boarding Stables.

Foot of Mason Street.

OCCUPYING a standpoint gained by an honorable policy and hard labor, the livery stable of Benjamin Mock enjoys the enviable reputation of being the largest and best equipped stable in the State, which reputation it certainly deserves. The business was founded thirty-seven years ago on a small scale, and during that time has developed into an institution of great magnitude, and become a permanent factor in the commercial prosperity of Milwaukee. The premises occupied are very spacious and commodious and compise a three story building, excellently located at the foot of Mason street, and well equipped for carrying on his business. Mr. Mock employs eighteen men and eighty horses in connection with the stable, and has a large number of carriages, buggies, tea carts, coupés, coupelets, landeaus, omnibuses, etc. Mr. Mock is a native of Baden, Germany, where he was born in 1829, and came to this country about 1852 direct to Milwaukee. He has long been identified with the business interests of the city, and is highly esteemed by the community as an honorable business man, and an upright private citizen.

NEUMAN'S

English Chop House.

No. 120 Grand Avenue.

FOR the benefit of our readers abroad, and those of our citizens who take meals down town, we refer them to the newly established firm of Neuman & Manasse, proprietors of the English Chop House at 120 Grand Avenue. This site has been used for a restaurant about six years. Mr. Thurson first had charge of the business and kept it for two years, then Mr. Chester had a successful run up to a short time ago, when he disposed of it to the present proprietors. Messrs. Neuman & Manasse have entered upon this business with a determination of making the establishment a place equal to anything of the kind in the city. The elegant dining hall has dimensions of 20x80 feet, and everything presents a model of neatness and attraction. Here are arranged a series of inviting tables furnished in the most tasty manner, with polite waiters in attendance to promptly serve the guests. The meals are all served on the "European Plan," and persons may rest assured that they will be served with the best of everything which the market can supply at very liberal prices, and served in the most satisfactory manner. Mr. Neuman is a first class cook of long experience and gives his close personal attention to this branch of the business, feeling confident of not only gaining the favor of Milwaukeeans but also the transient trade. They have a capacity of serving from 200 to 300 for dinner, and are always open at the close of the opera, park, theater and other amusements. Two private dining parlors are being arranged on the second floor, and will be luxuriously fitted up, and adorned with paintings, mirrors and flowers, while the choicest viands of the season will be served. When all their plans are perfected, they will have a force of from 12 to 15 persons. The promptness and efficiency with which the business is conducted, insures the popularity and success of the English Chop House.

GEO. BURROUGHS,

Manufacturer of Trunks and Traveling Bags.

424 and 426 East Water Street.

MR. Burroughs has the satisfaction of having started an industry that has been a credit to himself and the city of Milwaukee. In 1867 he first commenced operations, and speedily discovered that the field of labor was a wide one, and deserving of attention. He occupies the whole of his large three story double building, and has it fully stocked with goods. He employs 20 to 25 workmen, and is continually turning out every variety of articles usually found in a general tourists' outfitting depot, such as trunks, valises, traveling bags, etc. He makes a specialty of sample trunks and cases, also heavy trunks for the theatrical profession, and has testimonials from many of the bright lights in that profession. He also took the first premium for excellent, tasty and thorough workmanship at the Wisconsin State Fair. His reputation is world wide, as he has made trunks, cases, etc., for use in all parts of the globe. His work is all of the best quality, and will bear the test of wear and time, and his large trade is ample evidence that his work is of an extra class. The greatest share of his trade is in the West, although he sends many fine cases to the East. Mr. Burroughs was formerly a resident of Aurora, Ill., having come to that place from England in 1857, of which country he is a native and where he was born in 1842. His business in the Cream City was started in 1867, and now ranks among the leading industries of Milwaukee.

JOHN LUICK,

Confectioner and Caterer.

433 Milwaukee Street.

AMONG the varied industries that contribute to the wealth and prosperity of this city, is the confectionery business, one of the most noted and reliable firms of this class being that of John Luick, successor to James Curry, deceased. His handsome store is located at No. 433 Milwaukee street, and is fitted up in the best style, everything being attractively and comfortably arranged. His specialty is in taking charge of wedding and picnic parties and socials in this line of business, and being a skillful caterer and confectioner, he is the right man to employ. He has a great reputation for his cakes and creams, and to know that they came from Luick's is sufficient guarantee of their quality. His small cakes and confections are in great demand by the public, while his ice cream parlors in the summer season have a large patronage. The business conducted by Mr. Luick was established twenty-five or thirty years ago by Mr. Curry, but sold to the present proprietor twelve years ago. A force of experienced hands are constantly employed to keep up with the demands of the trade, while to facilitate the prompt delivery of orders a horse and wagon is kept on hand. The latest devices and most modern improvements are used by this house, consisting of all sizes of freezers, a small gas engine of three horsepower being used to run the machinery for freezing the cream. The fancy articles of this house are procured in

New York and Philadelphia. The patronage is very large and extends throughout the city and surrounding country, aggregating over $15,000 per annum. Mr. Luick was born at Niagara Falls, N. Y., and came to Milwaukee in 1851, and has long been connected with the business interests of this city.

THE WHITEHILL SEWING MACHINE COMPANY.

PROMINENT among the manufacturing interests of Milwaukee is the Whitehill Manufacturing Co., which has developed the fact that American skill and inventive genius are quite as successful in this branch as in any other. The establishment was founded in this city about four years ago. The premises occupied are very spacious and commodious, comprising a splendid four-story building for the main department, while in the rear is their large and well arranged foundry. These machines are regular home-comforts, and meet the requirements of the public so well that they are styled "Everybody's Favorite." One engine of 150 horse-power and a battery of boilers are required to move the machinery, much of it complex, and all of it invented or adapted especially for the performance of special work. The location of these works is Nos. 179 to 195 Becher street in Kinnickinnic Valley, which gives them all the advantages of lake transportation as well as railroad facilities. The city offices and salesrooms are situated at No. 234 West Water st. The centennial commission recognized the merits of this machine in their awards for "the most rapidly running sewing machine." The inventor and manufacturers of the new Whitehill Sewing Machine have been guided in their new enterprise by a practical knowledge of the wants of the public and the requirements of a perfect sewing machine. With this aim in view they have selected the best tools and machinery, and the moulding, cleaning, inspecting and annealing departments are models in their arrangements. The Whitehill Machines are now manufactured in the best equipped factory in the country, where every detail of each machine receives a thorough inspection and a careful re-adjustment which insures perfection. The

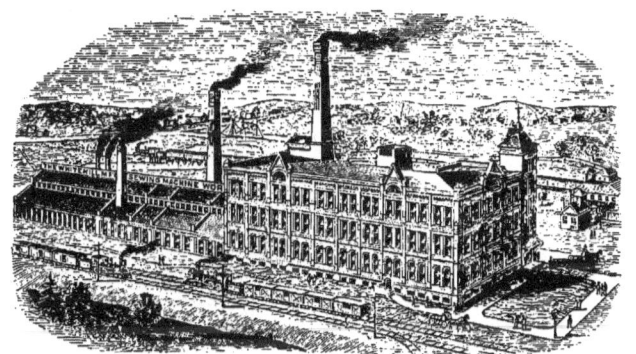

WORKS OF THE WHITEHILL SEWING MACHINE CO.

main department, while in the rear is their large and well arranged foundry. These machines are regular home-comforts, and meet the requirements of the public so well that they are styled "Everybody's Favorite." One engine of 150 horse-power and a battery of boilers are required to move the machinery, much of it complex, and all of it invented or adapted especially for the performance of special work. The location of these main requirements of a good machine are simplicity, durability, ease, quietness and rapidity of motion, a perfect stitch and a large arm. These are the points which the public has a right to expect, and these are the main features of the Whitehill. To these are added beauty of design and finish with harmony of outline, and a perfect set of attachments for every variety of work. The Whitehill is the first and only shuttle machine constructed with a purely crank motion, forming a loop, entirely superseding the noisy and irregular cam motion, enabling it to run at a much higher rate of speed than ever before attained, and transmitting such an evenness of motion to the take-up, that every stitch is drawn in with perfect precision. The tensions applied both to the upper and lower threads are so evenly proportioned that the machine will stitch perfectly under a range of thread from No. 200 down to No. 60 without a change of tensions having to be made, so that the range of family sewing can be performed without the necessity of regulating tensions. This is a feature which families will especially appreciate as overcoming the greatest annoyance in a family sewing machine—the regulating of tensions.

The shuttle is large and of the cylinder type; it is perfect in construction, and will sew evenly with coarse as well as with fine thread. The feed motion is positive in its action and of the simplest construction, all of which is derived from a single eccentric. The machine has a loose band-wheel of a very simple and novel construction, which is connected and disconnected by simply turning a locking-nut half way around. The woodwork is handsome in proportion and artistic in design, combining strength with durability, and fine finish with utility. It is built up in sections to prevent warping and splitting.

The officers of the company are: Henry Fink, president; John Bentley, vice-president; G. C. Trumpff, secretary; Robert Whitehill, superintendent. The company have an extensive nickle-plating department—the most complete in the Northwest—where they do a general nickle-plating business for the trade, and invite the patronage of manufacturers in this department.

F. M. SEYMOUR,
Wholesale Millinery.
382 and 384 Broadway.

ONE of the oldest wholesale millinery and fancy goods houses in the city is the establishment at Nos. 382 and 384 Broadway, of which Mr. F. M. Seymour is the proprietor. Its inception dates back to 1857, over a quarter of a century, when it was first established by H. N. Dunn, who continued the business alone until 1865, when Mr. Seymour was admitted as a partner in the firm, under the title of H. N. Dunn & Co. In 1867 Mr. Dunn died, and his interest in the concern passed into the hands of W. S. Hand, the firm continuing as Hand & Seymour until 1876, when the former retired, since which time it has been conducted by its present proprietor. It was established as a retail house, but gradually expanded its facilities until it was merged entirely into the wholesale trade, and now has an extensive patronage through the several adjacent Western States, the annual business reaching $100,000. The premises occupied are two floors, 36x112 feet in area, well lighted and finely fitted up for the efficient prosecution of trade. The stock carried is most complete in the several branches. The millinery kept in stock consists of all the newest and latest styles, direct from the fashion centers of the world, and selected especially for the Western trade by those comprehending the desires of trade in this direction. Ribbons, laces, etc., in endless variety are also found here; hat decorations, beautiful in quality and design, and in fact, everything designed to delight the heart of the most fastidious.

The proprietor, Mr. Seymour, was born in Hartford, Conn., in 1841, and resided there until the breaking out of the civil war. He enlisted as private and served one year, and was promoted to the rank of sergeant-major, taking part in several well-known engagements. He came to this city in 1863 and entered his brother's store on Broadway, where he remained two years, and until the time of embarking in the present trade. His patronage has undergone a steady and healthy increase since the start, and he now does a lively and growing business, this gratifying result being the outcome of his own unaided efforts, combined with energetic and systematic methods of conducting his affairs.

HANSEN'S EMPIRE FUR FACTORY.

J. D. INBUSCH,

Wholesale Grocer and Jobber of Teas.

333 and 335 East Water Street.

AMONG the leading houses in this line we mention particularly the name of J. D. Inbusch, who has been identified with the business history of Milwaukee for the past thirty-four years. The present enterprise was established in 1850 by Jacob Morawetz, who conducted it until the present year, when he disposed of it to the above named gentleman. Mr. Inbusch had, prior to this time, been a member of the firm of Inbusch Bros., at 238 and 240 East Water street, where they had conducted business as wholesale grocers since 1849. His present location at 333 and 335 East Water street has a front of forty feet, with a depth of one hundred and twenty feet, five stories in height. He conducts a general wholesale grocery business, and the quality of his goods and his methods of transacting business are steadily gaining him trade through the vast field in which his house is known. He has four commercial travelers on the road continually, and employs a large number of assistants in his large store.

Mr. Inbusch is a native of Germany, and was born in 1820. In 1837 he came to New York, and in 1849 settled in Milwaukee, since which time he has been identified with the interests of our city.

A. L. BOYNTON,

Livery, Boarding and Sale Stable.

449 to 463 Milwaukee Street.

THAT large building with the attractive front, on the west side of Milwaukee street, between Oneida and Wisconsin, is the largest livery stable in the city, and as a matter of course, the largest in the State. It is known as the "Palace Stable," and was built by the energetic proprietor, Mr. A. L. Boynton, three years ago. The building is 60x120, three stories high above basement, and has a neatly designed sandstone front. There is room for nearly one hundred horses, and more fine vehicles of all kinds than one would care to count. The stable, contents, etc., represent an investment of over $100,000, and the amount of business done yearly is $30,000 and upward. Sixteen men are constantly employed. Mr. Boynton has been in the livery business thirty-five years, and understands the work thoroughly in all its details. He was born in Monroe County, New York, in 1828, and came to Wisconsin in September, 1840. He began his career here with no means to speak of, but by strict attention to business and by downright hard work has accumulated business and other property worth considerably over a hundred thousand dollars. The "Palace Stable" is a great favorite with everybody, and its capacity is taxed to the utmost daily, to supply the demand for carriages, buggies, phaetons, saddle horses, etc. The finest carriages and barouches of the latest styles and the richest finish are kept in stock, and are always seen in important civil processions and on other important occasions. Boynton's stable is a credit to Milwaukee, is in fact an establishment which would show to good advantage in San Francisco or in Chicago.

C. E. ANDREWS & CO.,

Manufacturers of Andrews' Pearl Baking Powder, Ground Coffees, Spices, etc.

287, 289 and 291 East Water Street.

THIS establishment dates its birth back to 1873, when it was started in a small structure 50x60 feet in dimensions, and on rather a limited scale. Each year the business increased, compelling them to add new facilities, until it has grown into a business of large proportions. They now occupy a three story building at Nos. 287 to 291 East Water street, sixty feet front with a depth of one hundred and eighty feet. They manufacture coffee, spices, baking powder, etc., and employ forty persons in their mills, which are fitted up with all of the latest improved machinery, and driven by a forty horse-power engine. Their specialty is, as we have before mentioned, Andrews' Pearl Baking Powder, which has achieved great popularity on account of its purity and freedom from all injurious or unhealthy substances. It has stood the test for years, and still stands a favorite with the intelligent public. Their goods are largely in demand throughout the West, where the majority of their business is transacted. Mr. C. E. Andrews is a native of Massachusetts, but has long been a resident of this city. Mr. W. B. Johnson, the new member of the firm, was born in Jewett City, Conn., and has been an active business man in the West for ten years—his main business being in Chicago with a branch in Milwaukee. Mr. Andrews is Secretary of the Milwaukee Merchants' Association, and is prominent in business circles. The business is established on a firm foundation and its uniform success is due to the efforts of its members, and they deserve great credit for building up an institution which has brought great credit on both the city and themselves.

DUTCHER, COLLINS & SMITH,

Importers and Jobbers of Teas.

95 Huron Street, Cor. Broadway.

AMONG those who are engaged in the wholesale tea trade in this city, we make particular mention of the firm of Dutcher, Collins & Smith, who for the last fourteen years have been identified with that branch of trade. Their house was first established at the corner of East Water and Huron streets, and moved to their present commodious location in 1880. The structure now occupied is a three story brick building besides the basement, thirty feet in width by one hundred and twenty-seven in depth. They deal exclusively in tea, tobacco and cigars, and have a large trade throughout the West, amounting to at least two hundred and fifty thousand dollars per year. Established in 1871, they have enjoyed a career of unbroken success, which is attributable to the honorable method of conducting business they adopted from the first, to which they have strictly adhered in all their transactions. Mr. Dutcher is a native of Connecticut, and came to this city in 1849. He has long been identified with the business interests of Milwaukee, and is well known in business circles. Mr. Collins was born in 1843 in New York State, and came to Milwaukee in 1857. He is a patriotic citizen, and this he proved by enlisting in the Union army during the war of the rebellion, in which he served three years, being mustered out with the rank of major. Mr. Smith was born in Massachusetts in 1845, but has long been a resident of this city. He served in the 42d Wisconsin during the late war as a private. All three members of the firm are sound business men and have established their house on a sound basis.

THE SINGER MANUF'G CO.,

F. W. Noyes, Agent.

236 West Water Street.

THE conspicuous advantages enjoyed by Milwaukee, from a geographical position with reference to a great system of navigation, as well as superior railroad facilities, makes it a central point of transshipment, so to speak. As a result of this position and these advantages, certain industries and manufactories have sprung into successful operation during the past decade, that have lent an impetus to the growth of this community at once healthful and vigorous. Among such industries that have assumed an importance which demands detailed recognition is that of the "Singer Manufacturing Co." This Company, years ago, took advantage of all these inducements presented by Milwaukee and established an agency in 1859 in the Newhall House block. This was in a small way, and compared with the handsome and extensive quarters of to-day, was very insignificant. These machines are too well known to the public to require an extended description. The commodious quarters of this Company occupy a conspicuous and central site at No. 236 West Water street, southeast corner of Wells. The building contains three floors and basement, which are fitted up and equipped in a style commensurate with the character and transactions of the large business. All the departments are arranged in the most systematic manner for the orderly prosecution of the trade, and the exhibition and handling of the immense stock carried. Over 50 persons are required in this city alone to look after the interests of the Company; while 400 are employed throughout the entire territory, which embraces all of the Northwest. There are 250 wagons and horses all under the control of 40 branch offices, each of which does its business through the Milwaukee office. All machine parts and attachments come from the factories at Elizabethport, N. J., and South Bend, Ind., and are fitted and put together in complete shape at this office, and then distributed throughout the territory. In 1875 Mr. F. W. Noyes took the management of the business as general agent, having been connected with this agency since 1864, first as bookkeeper and clerk and as purchasing agent. Since his connection with the Company the sales have increased from 500 machines a year to over 1,000 a month. Mr. Noyes was born in Pulaski, N. Y., in 1834, and came to Milwaukee in 1861. He was two years in the Quartermaster's Department during the war. After leaving the army he was Deputy Internal Revenue Collector of this district for nearly two years.

E. D. BANGS,

Photographer.

86 Wisconsin Street.

AMONG the prominent artists of Milwaukee is E. D. Bangs, who is one of the pioneers in the business in this city. He is known for his excellent work all over the States, and has achieved a reputation second to none in this section of the country. He is full of business enterprise and enjoys a very lucrative trade. His photographs are admitted to be unexcelled in quality and style of work. He was born in New York in 1840, and came to Milwaukee Sept. 17th, 1849. In 1869 he opened his first gallery, and now occupies the same stand. He showed his patriotism in the late war by enlisting in the First Minnesota for three months. After the expiration of that time he re-enlisted in the First Wisconsin cavalry for three years. He was appointed master blacksmith for his regiment, and held the rank of Brevet Lieutenant. He was wounded twice, once at Kingston, Mo., receiving a severe wound in the side, and again at Chalk's Bluffs in Kentucky. He occupies a prominent place in the business circles of Milwaukee.

WILLIAMS & BRENCKLE,

Manufacturers of and Dealers in Cigars.

408 Grand Avenue.

ONE of the large manufacturing interests of our city is that of tobacco, and in this line Milwaukee is far in advance of any other city in the Northwest except Chicago, which, in the value of annual production, it closely approaches. Ranking with the first establishments of this kind is the above firm of Williams & Brenckle, at No. 408 Grand avenue, in the Library Block. They opened business in 1872 at 117 Cedar street, where they remained two years, but this business demanding greater facilities, they moved to the southeast corner of Grand avenue and Sixth street in 1874, coming to their present location in 1880. They are manufacturers of and dealers in all grades of cigars, tobaccos, etc. In the cigar line their special brands are the "Grand Avenue" and "Margarita," which have become so popular with smokers. They also keep on hand a full stock of smoking and chewing tobacco, snuff, cigarettes and pipes. They import in large quantities the best of Cuban tobacco for their fine cigars. Their stock is valued at $20,000. The trade of this firm extends all over the Northwest, and aggregates $100,000 per annum. A force of twenty-five skilled workmen is employed to supply the demands of the trade. Mr. Williams is a native Milwaukeean, while Mr. Brenckle was born in Buffalo, but came to this city when only 15 years old.

R. S. BAIRD & CO.,
Art Printers.
149 West Water Street.

MR. R. S. Baird, the head of this firm, embarked in the printing business about six years ago, establishing himself then at 149 West Water street. His trade is mostly confined to the city, and he makes a specialty in art printing, and the work executed in this line is of a high order of merit. Being a practical printer, and in every way familiar with his trade, Mr. Baird bids fair to surpass many older firms of the city. Having all the facilities at his command, he is able to turn out promptly and neatly all orders for letter heads, folders, bill heads, cards, and all kinds of office printing.

J. H. NICHOLS & CO.,
Jobbers in Foreign and Domestic Fruits, Cigars, etc.
175 West Water Street.

THE commission trade is fast becoming one of the most important in this city. Among all the firms of this class none have made more advancement, or increased their business more rapidly than J. H. Nichols & Co., at 175 West Water street. They deal in foreign and domestic fruits, besides carrying a large and well-assorted stock of grocers' specialties and various first-class brands of cigars. This business has risen in the space of eight years from small proportions to its present magnitude. The business was carried on at various locations, until Mr. Nichols succeeded in obtaining possession of his present commodious quarters, which bid fair to become too small for his growing trade within the next few years. He employs ten men to assist him in the business and to manage the large patronage he receives. He has two men constantly traveling in the North and Northwest, who procure the best the market affords, giving his customers advantage of fresh goods at moderate prices. Mr. Nichols was born in Watertown, this State, and came to this city over twelve years ago, since which time he has steadily advanced to the front rank in the commission trade.

SAVILLE, BUTLER & CO.,
Jobbers and Wholesale Dealers in Wooden Ware, Grocers' Sundries, Willow Ware, etc.
287 Broadway.

CONSPICUOUS among the public-spirited and enterprising firms of Milwaukee, whose efforts to secure and retain trade from abroad, may be mentioned that of Saville, Butler & Co. They are jobbers and wholesale dealers in wooden ware, grocers' sundries, household and dairy furnishings, willow ware, cigars, tobacco, etc. This house was established Jan. 1st, 1884, and already has a large trade in the adjacent States of Michigan, Minnesota and Iowa, besides the large home patronage they enjoy. They occupy for their office and salesroom a four-story building besides the basement, 40x120 feet in dimensions, and filled from top to bottom with a miscellaneous stock of goods in their line, well chosen and systematically arranged. The basement contains the stock of house-furnishing goods; on the first floor are the offices and shipping room ; the second contains a choice lot of imported and domestic cigars of the most popular brands; and the third and fourth are devoted to wooden and willow ware of all kinds. They employ five commercial travelers to represent their house, and a satisfactory increase is noted each month.

Mr. Jas. R. Saville is native of Portland, Maine, and was born in 1842. He came to his city in 1866, and has since resided here. He served in the late war, and was a captain in the Third Michigan Infantry. He is now recorder of the Wisconsin Commandery of the military order of the Loyal Legion of the United States. Prior to establishing the present business, he was a member of the grocery firm of Ricker, Crombie & Co. DeWitt C. Butler was born in Geneva, N. Y., in 1824, and came to this city in 1874, and has since resided in the city. Both gentlemen are well known in business circles, and have already established the reputation of their house on a sound basis.

C. CHADBOURNE,
Photographer.
224 and 226 Grand Avenue.

ONE of the oldest and leading photograph galleries in the city is that of C. Chadbourne, at Nos. 224 and 226 Grand avenue. The gallery was started some fifteen years ago, Mr. Chadbourne becoming proprietor in the fall of 1883. This gallery is noted for the excellence and finish of its pictures, which has won for the proprietor a class of patrons of the most desirable character. He occupies the second and third floors of the building at the above numbers, which is most eligibly located. His reception room is situated on the second floor and is attractively and beautifully fitted up with specimens of his work. The operating room is on the third floor, and is complete in every respect. The skylight is large and perfect, and all arrangements are made for the production of first-class work. He enjoys a large and lucrative custom, including both city and State. Mr. Chadbourne is a native of the State of Maine, and came West about twelve years ago. A small circular of information and suggestions is published by the artist, which is of great benefit to those desiring to have their picture taken. It can be had on application, free of charge.

ELECTRO-THERMAL BATHS,
Galvanic, Faradic and Static Treatment, Dan'l T. Coates, Prop.
459 Van Buren Street.

THAT quiet, home-like house at 459 Van Buren street is where Mr. Coates gives his restoring and invigorating electro-thermal baths, and where patients are successfully treated for rheumatism, gout, dyspepsia, neuralgia, nervous debility and general exhaustion. The business was opened by Mr. Coates in 1880, and is now doing, in an unostentatious way, business amounting to more than $5,000 a year. It is the only place in the city where a genuine electric bath can be had, or where it is given as it ought to be given, to do the greatest amount of good. Mr. Coates is backed, as one may say, by many of the leading physicians in the city, who make it a rule to send most of their chronic cases direct to his establishment. One thing that has much to do with the success of Mr. Coates in his important work is that he is more than a mere manipulator, is, in fact, an intelligent, well-read, well-informed man, who looks beneath the surface of things, aiming ever to get at the cause, the root of this thing called disease. The thing is to find the *cause* of a man's ailment, and then begin at once the work of eradication and removal.

Mr. Coates was born in Baltimore, in 1849, and came West in 1860. He has had a great deal of practical experience in the special kind of work in which he is now engaged, and has read and studied the subject so thoroughly that he has come to be regarded as a leading authority on electro-thermal baths. His sister, a lady of much experience also, aids him in his work, and has charge of the ladies' department of the establishment.

Mr. Coates has lately added a Static Battery, at an expense of $800, for treatment of nervous diseases.

GEORGE ZIEGLER,

Manufacturing Confectioner.

235, 237 and 239 East Water Str.

THE representative wholesale candy manufacturer of this city is George Ziegler. The magnitude of this branch of industry in Milwaukee can hardly be estimated, but the importance of this one firm is well known. He is a manufacturing confectioner of great renown, and all his goods are noted for their purity and reliability, over six tons of which are made daily. The business was begun in 1861 under the firm name of Boll Bros., and in 1865 Mr. Ziegler was admitted, the firm being then Boll Bros. & Co. Mr. A. Boll retired from the business in 1870 and in 1873 the other member, John Boll, died, since which time Mr. Ziegler has continued the business alone. It was first located at 315 Third street, where it remained for three years. In 1865 it was moved to the large building at Nos. 3 and 5 Grand ave., where it was burnt out in July of 1882. Mr. Ziegler's energy under such circumstances was soon manifested and in a very few days he established himself at his present large and convenient quarters, Nos. 235, 237 and 239 East Water street. The building is five stories in height, with a large basement, the dimensions of each floor being 55x125 feet. This manufactory affords employment to upwards of 125 hands, both male and female. Being one of the oldest establishments of the kind in the city, its business is consequently very large and extends through New York, Pennsylvania, Missouri, Indiana, Ohio, Kentucky, Michigan, Wisconsin, Iowa, Illinois, Dakota, Kansas and all the Southern States, and aggregates upwards of $300,000 per annum. The latest machinery for this business is in use, which is run by an engine of twenty-five horse power. To provide for the safety of the employés, one of the best fire escapes in the country is used. It is the Holbrook patent, one of the latest and most practical escapes invented. It is the patent of Mr. Holbrook of this city, with the architectural firm of Mix & Co. One of the leading specialties of Mr. Ziegler's establishment is candy ornaments and holiday supplies. He does one of the largest business in this line of goods in the Northwest. His liberal business policy and general enterprise have added much not only to his own success, but also to the advancement of the industrial interests of our city. Mr. Ziegler was born in Bavaria, Sept. 27th, 1830, and came to Milwaukee in 1845. He learned the shoemaker's trade when 18 years of age, and followed it until 1865, when he engaged in his present business.

JAMES B. BRADFORD,

Chickering Piano Warerooms.

No. 422 Broadway.

THIS extensive business occupies two floors, each 22x120 feet. Mr. Bradford established the business in 1872, representing two piano and one organ company, for which he had the agency. Now he is agent for six of the best pianos in the market, namely: Chickering, Sohmer, Gabler, Hallett & Cumston, Kurtzmann and Fouchard, besides the celebrated Loring & Blake Palace organs. These instruments are made in Boston, New York and other leading cities at the East, whence they are shipped directly to Mr. Bradford. What Mr. Bradford says about a given instrument in his comprehensive assortment can be depended upon, so that all who contemplate purchasing a piano or an organ that is thoroughly first-class in every particular, will find it to their interest every way to consult him before closing a bargain at any other establishment.

Mr. Bradford was born in New Hampshire, in 1823, and came to Milwaukee in 1857. He is one of our well known citizens. Personally, and as a business man, he stands high in the estimation of all, having a reputation which is but the natural outgrowth of many years of honest dealing with his numerous customers.

KRUSE & BARKER,

Plumbers, Steam and Gas Fitters, Steam Heating Apparatus.

450 East Water Street. (Market Square.)

THIS institution was founded in the year 1879, and in 1880 Chas. B. Kruse became interested in the firm, its name being then Sloteman & Kruse. It was run thus until 1885, when Charles A. Barker bought out Mr. Sloteman's interest, when the firm took the name it now bears. They occupy two floors and employ twenty-five men, ten of whom are skilled workmen. They do a general business in the plumbing trade, and all repairing is done in first-class style. They make a specialty of steam heating and ventilating, and are sole agents for the Walker & Pratt Manufacturing Co.'s Cast Iron Safety Sectional Steam Heating Appartus, the most perfect of the kind now in use. It has given universal satisfaction, and is now extensively used throughout the city. This house enjoys a good patronage, and is recommended by some of the principal houses in Milwaukee, among them the Milwaukee National Bank, the Republican House, Bradley & Metcalf and T. L. Kelly & Co. They are always prepared to do work promptly. A ten horse-power engine furnishes the force necessary in their fitting and manufacturing department.

Charles B. Kruse, the senior member of the firm, was born in Germany in 1852, and came to Milwaukee direct from that country in 1866. Charles A. Barker was born in Kilbourn City, Wisconsin, in 1865, and came to Milwaukee in 1881. Both are energetic young men and are bound to succeed in their business.

C. F. RINGER,

Architect and Superintendent.

88 Wisconsin Street.

THE rapid growth of Milwaukee during the last few years has created a demand for experienced architects, and among those who have achieved distinction in this line we mention Mr. C. F. Ringer, a young man with years of practical experience as architect and superintendent. He is a native of Germany, and was born in 1851. He came to Milwaukee in 1870, and has since been engaged in his profession. In 1881 he established his present business, and has met with a great degree of success. He designs plans for business houses of all kinds, residences, etc., and superintends their construction, and employs a number of assistants, in order to facilitate operations. Mr. Ringer has erected some very fine buildings in the city and has the recommendations of his many patrons. He has acquired great skill and accuracy in drawing plans of houses, and is sent for from far and near to superintend the construction of various edifices. His buildings are all of the latest styles, conscientiously constructed, and this is probably the reason of his extended popularity.

F. WERNER,

Dealer in Artists' Materials and Manufacturer of Picture Frames, etc.

436 Broadway.

YOU will be surprised, upon entering Mr. Werner's place of business, at 436 Broadway, to see the large and select stock of artists' materials he carries and to learn that he has, within the short space of fifteen years, made for himself a trade that reaches all over the Northwest and even to California. Mr. Werner has two departments for his business on the first floor, a salesroom and a workshop, where picture frames are made and where artists' materials are prepared and put up for use. Mr. Werner was born at Franklin, in this county, thirty-eight years ago. He learned his trade in Milwaukee, and it is but truth to say that he has mastered it in all its details. Mr. Werner is also agent for the "Wisconsin Synodal Buchhandlung," publishers of German books of more or less religious character. He has a full line of the books on his shelves, and is selling them constantly both in and out of the city.

B. J. JOHNSON & CO.,

Manufacturers of Soap and Candles, and Wholesale Dealers in Cheese.

78 and 80 West Water Street.

AMONG the oldest firms to help along the advancement in this line is that of B. J. Johnson & Co. About twenty-one years ago they commenced business on East Water street, and by earnest and persistent effort have steadily advanced along the road to success, till now they are classed with the representative commercial firms of the city. This firm has become very popular with all the households of the State and city on account of the quality and great variety of brands they manufacture. Soon after beginning the soap manufacture, Mr. Johnson bought out the establishment of John Plankinton & Co., at 78 and 80 West Water street, which site he still holds. Of the great variety of brands manufactured by this firm, their specialty consists of the Pure, Galvanic and Badger brands. These varieties have won for them an extended reputation. Their sales extend all over the Northern and Western States. They employ over thirty hands, and their trade outside of the city is looked after by three traveling men. The machinery of the establishment is of the most complete and latest design, and is run by the aid of a large twelve-horse-power engine. The building used as office, store-room and factory is 50x150 feet in dimensions, and four stories high, with a basement. Messrs. Johnson & Co. also do a large wholesale cheese trade. The total sales of this firm in all departments are over a quarter million dollars per year. Mr. B. J. Johnson is a native of the East and came to this city in 1864, and has ever been connected with its business interests and advancement.

G. STRECKEWALD,

Dealer in Grass Seeds, Bags, Twines, etc.

37 West Water Street.

THE enterprise of which we write was founded in 1865 at 222 West Water street by the present proprietor, G. Streckewald. He remained there ten years, when he moved to his present location, 37 West Water street. The building is three stories in height, with a basement, the dimensions of each floor being 25 by 100 feet. The amount of stock kept on hand is generally between $10,000 and $12,000, and consists of all kinds of grass seeds, bags, twines, etc. The seeds are the specialty of the firm, and procured from all parts of this State, Minnesota and Illinois, while in some seasons about $100,000 worth of clover and timothy seeds are shipped to Europe. The aggregate sales will approach $200,000 per annum. The subject of this sketch was born in Hanover, Germany, and came to Wisconsin in 1848, and to Milwaukee in 1863.

CAMPBELL STEAM LAUNDRY.

H. N. Campbell, Prop'r.

514 Grand Avenue.

THIS extensive establishment, which is one of the largest and most complete of its kind in the city, was founded in September, 1880, by the present proprietor, H. N. Campbell. He began business in a small way back of Davidson's steam marble yard, but by his energy and enterprise, with the motto fulfilled "to do all work well," soon advanced to one of the leading positions in this line of business. He now occupies the spacious and commodious quarters at No. 514 Grand avenue, consisting of original building in front 25x100, and premises in rear, which he has lately bought, 50x50 in extent. The business has grown to large proportions, and is systematically conducted in the several departments, each being in the hands of skillful workmen assisted by labor-saving machinery of the most approved styles and designs, including a large steam engine for power. In the various departments of the business six men and thirty-five women are constantly employed, while several wagons are used to facilitate the prompt delivery of orders. Particular attention is devoted to first-class work, especially in shirts, collars, cuffs, and ladies' fine underwear. Orders by mail or messengers promptly attended to, and goods are delivered to all parts of the city. The following branches are established in this city: 68 and 70 Wisconsin street, 145 Reed street, corner Twelfth and Walnut streets, 683 Third street, 427 Chestnut street, 233 West Water street, 600 Mitchell street, 510 National avenue. The State branches are established at Oconomowoc, Manitowoc, Sheboygan, Two Rivers, Waupaca, Waukesha, Ashland, New London, Oshkosh, Darien, Whitewater, Ludington, Fond du Lac, Pewaukee, Stoughton and Palmyra. Everything in this model laundry is under the direct personal attention of Mr. and Mrs. Campbell, and is conducted in the most systematic order. The most reasonable prices rule in all departments. Mr. Campbell was born in Jefferson county, N. Y., and came to Milwaukee in 1879, soon after which he engaged in his present business. Mrs. Campbell is also a native of New York, and was born in Lewis county, that State.

W. H. CUDWORTH,

Dentist.

119 Wisconsin Street.

DR. W. H. Cudworth is one of our popular dentists, and has been established in business at this place since 1882, and formerly occupied rooms on Grove street, moving to his present eligible location in October, 1883. He has had seven years' experience in the profession, and studied in the Philadelphia Dental College. He pays particular attention to fine gold work and teeth without plates. His parlors are comfortably and tastefully fitted up in all their appointments, and his operating room is equipped with all the latest instruments and devices. Mr. Cudworth was born in Shoreham, Vt., in 1860, and came to Milwaukee in January, 1880. Although a young man, he has made his mark in his profession and stands side by side with the older practitioners of our city. He keeps thoroughly posted on all various improvements in dentistry, and is "up with the times" in every respect.

B. F. DEVOE,

Steam Printer and Publisher.

88 Mason Street.

THE "art preservative of all arts" is well represented in the city of Milwaukee, and by no firm more ably than B. F. Devoe, steam printer and publisher. Mr. Devoe established his office in 1881, with a small press and a mere handful of type, but the merit and originality of his work attracted attention and brought him into prominence, until his is now one of the most prosperous establishments of the kind in the city. He makes a specialty of railroad printing and engraved wedding stationery. He also does commercial, show and book printing, and in fact everything that is done in a first-class office. He has the latest styles of presses with all the modern improvements, and everything necessary to do first-class work.

Mr. Devoe was born in Fond du Lac county in 1854, and came to Milwaukee in 1881. He is a practical printer with twelve years' experience in the different branches of the business. He is constantly adding the latest faces of type and machinery.

ANSON BROTHERS,

Jobbers of Fancy Groceries, Sirups, Teas, Spices, etc.

307 East Water Street.

THIS is one of the oldest houses in the trade, having been established in 1868, on the South Side, but for the past eleven years in its present location. The premises occupied consist of four floors, 20x150 feet in area, and well stocked with a full line of fancy groceries, sirups, teas, coffees, spices, soaps, vinegar, tobacco, cigars, etc. The first floor is devoted to sirups, fish, fruits and heavy goods. On the second, canned fruits, tobacco, etc. On the third, nuts, pickles and spices, and on the fourth, a miscellaneous stock of light goods. They make a specialty of green fruits, canned goods, cigars and tobacco, and keep a first-class assortment in these lines. Their goods are drawn from importers and manufacturers, and also from foreign countries, and are sold mostly in the States of Wisconsin, Michigan, Iowa, Minnesota, Dakota and Northern Illinois.

C. H. Anson was born in New York, in 1841, and at the breaking out of the war enlisted as a private in the Eleventh Vermont. He saw a great deal of active service, being in the battles of Spottsylvania, Cold Harbor, Petersburg, Appomattox, and was with Sheridan in his campaign through the Shenandoah valley. He served three years and was promoted by degrees, at the close of the war holding a major's commission, and was aide-de-camp of the Second Division, Sixth Army Corps.

F. A. Anson was born in New York, in 1844, and enlisted in the First Vermont Heavy Artillery during the civil war and served for the twenty last months of the war, participating in the battles of Spottsylvania, North Anna River and Cold Harbor; also, at the capture of Petersburg and Lee's surrender at Appomattox. He was promoted from the ranks, and at the close of the war held an adjutant's position. C. H. Anson came to this city in 1866, and was connected for two years with the firm of B. J. Johnson & Co. F. A. Anson came here two years later, when they together embarked in the present business.

BROWN,

Photographic Studio.

136 and 138 Grand Avenue, Corner Second Street.

"THERE is no school like experience, no stimulus like success," is an old but true aphorism, and is brought prominently to our mind in the preparation of a brief sketch of this enterprise. Brown's Grand Avenue Photographic Studio is situated at Nos. 136 and 138, and consists of reception parlors, which are tastefully arranged, and operating rooms with all photographic apparatus necessary for first-class work. The Brown Bros., Joseph and James, have a complete knowledge of the art, which has been obtained by personal investigation and long practical experience. Photography in all its branches receives the close attention of this firm, who spare no time or pains in making the photograph what it should be, a real work of art. Entire satisfaction is guaranteed, and moderate prices are the rules for all styles and forms of work. Although but lately established in business, they have a reputation and patronage equal to many of the older galleries of the city, and a force of experienced and skillfull artists are employed to keep up with the demands of the business.

THE NATIONAL PARK.

Corner National and Washington Avenues.

WHILE there is a noticeable lack in the public park system of our city, it must be said that the private parks and pleasure resorts in and around Milwaukee constitute one of the main attractions of our city. The most prominent resort of this kind, in extent and attractiveness, is the National Park, at the corner of National and Washington avenues, on the contemplates placing a large steam yacht in the lake for the use of pleasure parties. A fine deer-park is also situated in the western part of the park. Inside the race track a baseball and cricket field is laid out, while at the southern end of the park a shooting range is constructed. All over the grounds are winding walks, beautiful lawns, rustic seats, flower gardens, etc. A large summer dance-hall, 75x100 feet, and dining-hall, 40x80 feet, are located on the grounds. There are also stalls and stable accommodations for about fifty horses. There are ten acres of

THE NATIONAL PARK.

South Side. This delightful place consists of nearly fifty acres, and was laid out and improved in the spring of 1883. The National Park Hotel is a beautiful structure at the main entrance of the grounds. It is three stories in height, finely fitted up with dining-room, dancing-hall, double bowling alley, billiard and pool parlor and sixteen rooms for the accommodation of guests. The park contains as fine a half-mile track as there is in the State, and is a favorite resort for the sporting fraternity and lovers of fast horses. The beautiful artificial lake, of about two acres, is one of the attractions of this place. Five row-boats float upon its surface and next season the proprietor shade trees inside of this park. The genial proprietor, Mr. F. C. G. Brand, gives his closest attention to the wants and wishes of his many patrons not only in the elegant Park Hotel, but throughout the grounds. One of the most novel and pleasing attractions of this park is the roller coaster, which is located near the lake, in the western part of the grounds. It is the latest and most approved pattern, being the patent of Prof. Zealand, of Yale College, and is put up in the most substantial and solid manner possible. It meets with great favor from the public, as is shown from the fact that nearly 15,000 tickets were sold the day of the Scotch picnic. Taking all the attractions and the great advantages presented at this park, the city has cause of being proud of possessing so great a feature as the National Park.

T. H. BROWN & CO.,

Manufacturers of Fine Carriages, Buggies, Phaetons, etc.

182 and 184 Third Street.

PROMINENT among the establishments engaged in this branch of industry, is that of T. H. Brown & Co., at 182 and 184 Third street. This business was founded in 1860, on the East Side, the present firm being organized in 1876, who have had charge of it ever since. They are manufacturers of all styles of carriages, buggies, phaetons, road carts (Brown's patent), sleighs, cutters, delivery wagons, etc. The extensive factory and salesrooms of this firm are situated just north of Grand Avenue, on Third street, and cover an area of 50x150 feet; are three stories in height, with a large basement. The ground floor is used as a blacksmith and wood-working shop, while the first floor is used as a salesroom, in which are arranged the latest styles of vehicles. The other floors are used for workshop, paint and finishing rooms. Only first-class material is used, and the most skillful workmen employed. Fifty hands are employed to meet the demands of the business, this number being greatly augmented during the busy season. A complete and varied stock is constantly kept on hand, and valued at $30,000 to $35,000, while the sales extend to upwards of $100,000 annually. Mr. Brown's patent "road cart," which to-day is without a rival, and very popular, is in all respects the best and most desirable two-wheeled vehicle built. It has now been in use for a number of years by all classes of people, and without exception, all speak of it in terms of highest praise. It is nicely balanced, so that when in use there is no weight on the horse's back. Another specialty is the manufacture of sewing machine wagons, which are lighter than any others built for the same purpose, and in which their general standard of excellence is fully maintained.

Mr. Thomas H. Brown was born in this city in 1839, and with the exception of six years, has always been connected with the business interests of this city. He was elected alderman from the Fourth Ward, serving from 1877 to 1880, when he was called to fill the office of mayor, which he held for two years.

Mr. Louis Dick, the company of the firm, was born in Germany, and was among the first settlers of this city, and is well and favorably known in the business circles of Milwaukee.

STOUT & UNDERWOOD,

Attorneys at Law, and Solicitors of Patents.

66 Wisconsin Street.

A FEW years since nearly all of the patent business of this city, and in fact, the whole State of Wisconsin, was transacted through agents outside of the State, chiefly in Washington, causing no little expense, and much tedious and unnecessary delay. In 1879 Messrs. Stout & Underwood opened an office particularly for this class of business, and devoted their time and attention solely to this branch of the law. They are gentlemen of experience in this line, and since the opening of their office have extended their sphere of labor until more than half of the Wisconsin patents are taken out through this agency, and their cases are increasing at the rate of 40 per cent. per year. During the past year these gentlemen have filed two hundred and fifty applications, and have succeeded to a remarkable degree in securing patents thereon. Patents are mostly taken out by manufacturers, and at least 75 per cent. of them pay a large profit to the inventors or their backers. The widest field for patents now seems to be in milling machinery, electrical apparatus and farming implements, more especially grain-binding and harvesting machinery. Both members of this firm were for many years examiners in the United States Patent Office, and consequently are thoroughly familiar with the intricacies and technicalities of Patent Office practice. Mr. Stanley S. Stout was born in Kentucky in 1850, and came to Milwaukee in April, 1879, when he was soon afterwards joined by Mr. Harold G. Underwood. The last named gentleman is a native of New York, where he was born in 1852. Both members of the firm have had large experience in the practice of patent law and obtaining of patents, registering of trade marks, and every department of this difficult branch of the legal profession in which they have come to be considered experts. They also pay special attention to foreign patents, re-issues, caveats, designs, labels and copyrights, and the prosecution of contested cases and interferences.

BODDEN & HEATH,

Manufacturers of Coffee, Spices, Baking Powder and Wholesale Dealers in Grocers' Sundries.

309 East Water Street.

THE firm of Bodden & Heath take a leading place in this branch of trade, and their business, which was established in 1879, has grown to large proportions. They do only a wholesale business, and manufacture coffee, spices of all kinds, and baking powder, besides handling grocers' sundries. They employ three traveling salesmen and a large force in their mills. The machinery is driven by an eighteen horse-power engine, and their manufactory is equipped with all the latest devices for the proper pursuit of their business. They occupy the whole of the four-story building at No. 309 East Water street, having moved to this place in 1881, their increasing business at that time demanding more room. They manufacture the celebrated brand of baking powder known as "Cream Foam," which is absolutely pure, containing no alum or other injurious adulterations. They also manufacture other well-known brands, such as "Daisy," "Boss," "Standard," and "Pride of the West."

The pepper, cinnamon, allspice, cloves, nutmegs, ginger and other spices are put up under their name, which is sufficient guarantee for their purity. L. F. Bodden is a native of this city and was born in 1857. H. A. Heath was born in New York in 1845, coming to this city a few years later. He enlisted in the 137th Illinois, Co. C, for one hundred days' service in 1864, at the age of nineteen. Both gentlemen are well known in business circles.

OTTO LAVERRENZ & BRO.,

Bookbinders and Manufacturers of Paper Boxes.

428 East Water Street.

IN 1849 a paper box manufactory and bindery was established in Milwaukee by Mr. Otto Laverrenz, father of the present proprietors. Like a large number of other enterprises, it was started on a small basis, and year by year has worked up its trade until it takes rank among the leading industries of the city. Most of its extensive production is used throughout our own city by wholesale houses. So rapidly has trade in this particular line increased, that in the past year the sales of the above firm amounted to the sum of $10,000. Mr. Otto Laverrenz, the head of the house, is a Prussian, and was born in Berlin in the year 1844. He came to this country the same year with his parents, and finally to Milwaukee in 1849. He is a man of known ability and has risen to a high place in the estimation of the people of Milwaukee. He has represented the people of the Second district in the Assembly, and has justly earned their sincere respect. The younger member of the firm, Mr. Charles Laverrenz, is 34 years of age, and is a native of the Cream City. He is also a stirring business man, and ably assists in the work of managing their manufactory. They manufacture paper boxes of every description, and have the largest and most extensive establishment in the city, besides doing bookbinding to order.

MILWAUKEE STOVE WORKS,
J. A. & P. E. Dutcher, manufacturers of Cooking and Heating Stoves and Ranges.
670 Kinnickinnic Avenue.

IN this important branch of industry the old and reliable stove works of J. A. & P. E. Dutcher are the most prominent. The business was originally founded under the firm name of Geo. Williams & Co., but in 1870 was changed to Dutcher, Vose & Adams; ten years later it was again changed to Dutcher, Vose & Co. It continued under this name till September, 1884, when the present firm took charge. From a small local business, it has increased year by year till now it is represented in nearly all the Western States and Territories of the Union. The large plant of these works—foundries, offices and salesrooms—are located on Kinnickinnic avenue. A cut of their works is shown above, which are a regular bee-hive of industry. All varieties of stoves and ranges are turned out and shipped to all parts of the West. The superiority of the products of these works is recognized in the East, the very home of the old-time stove founders, but the greater portion of their stoves is sold throughout the Northwest. From twelve to fifteen hundred tons of pig-iron are used yearly by this firm. Their foundry, molding and mounting shops are large and well arranged for the manufacture of large orders. The latest machinery is used,

MILWAUKEE STOVE WORKS.

and run by an engine of thirty horse-power. The firm are exclusive owners of several important patents, each one possessing merits of great importance in the manufacture of a perfect stove, whether for heating or cooking purposes. Their storerooms are well filled with a large stock of as fine an assortment of stoves and ranges as can be found in the country.

Mr. J. A. Dutcher was born in Salisbury, Conn., in 1829, and came to Milwaukee in 1849, and has always been identified in a prominent manner with the commerce of our city. P. E. Dutcher, his son, is a native of this city, and has early been associated with his father in the business he represents.

J. P. WECHSELBERG,
Manufacturer of Carriages and Wagons.
218 and 220 Wells Street.

THIS business dates back to 1860, when it was established in a small way, on the corner of Milwaukee and Michigan streets. In 1865 it was moved to Second street, and in December, 1881, to the new and commodious building at Nos. 218 and 220 Wells street. The building is four stories in height, and 50x50 feet in dimensions. A force of twelve to fifteen men is employed in this establishment. Only the best material is used and the work turned out is consequently of the most satisfactory kind. The specialty of the house is in ordered work, and in that line its sales extend all over the city and Northwest. Mr. Wechselberg was born in Germany and came to this city in 1848. He is a veteran in the business, and during the many years he has been in the trade he has made many noted improvements, which have gone far to establish his reputation.

FRANZ FALK BREWING CO.,
Manufacturers of Beer.
Milwaukee, Wis.

ONE of the representative brewing establishments of Milwaukee, which by the magnitude of its operations has done much to raise this industry to its present standard, is that of the Franz Falk Brewing Co. (limited). The following are the officers of the company: Franz Falk, president; L. W. Falk, vice-president; Frank R. Falk, secretary and treasurer. The business was founded as far back as 1855, by Messrs. Fred. Goes and Franz Falk, Mr. Falk purchasing entire control of the establishment in 1866, and conducting it on his own account until his death, after which the present company was formed. The brewery is located just outside of the city limits, in the town of Wauwatosa. It consisted at first of only a few small buildings, and only 1,000 barrels were brewed and five men employed the first year. From this small beginning the business has reached its present large proportions. The plant covered by the buildings is over five acres, consisting of a mammoth malt house, with a capacity of over 100,000 bushels, brewery buildings, bottling house, coopering shops, etc. The following figures will be of interest, and show with what rapidity the business increased: First year, 1,000 bbls.; 1866, 3,500 bbls.; 1870, 8,000 bbls.; 1874, 20,000 bbls.; 1877, 22,000 bbls.; 1878, 34,000 bbls.; 1879, 45,000 bbls.; 1880, 60,000 bbls.; 1884, 75,000 bbls. The amount of material consumed annually by this company is as follows: Barley, 200,000 bus.; hops, 160,000 lbs.; ice, 25,000 tons. They have great shops for doing their own coopering, carpenter and machine work, and they own all the cars used in shipping their beer throughout the country. A force of 125 hands is constantly employed at the brewery, while about the same number of agencies are founded throughout the Union. The sales of this brewery extend all over this country and to the East Indies, Sandwich Islands, Mexico and South America. In 1877 the bottling department was established, and over 25,000 barrels of beer are put up every year in this department alone. The beer produced by this company has a great reputation for purity and quality. The city offices are located at the southwest corner of East Water and Mason streets, and have direct communication, by means of the telephone, with the brewery, city and suburban towns. This is truly a home concern, as all the officers are native Milwaukeeans, who, by their enterprise and liberal business policy, are certain of not only retaining their position already acquired, but of advancing their business to an influence and power equal to any other establishment in the city.

GRAND CENTRAL DRUG STORE,

A. v. Trott, Proprietor.

No. 471 East Water Street.

AMONG the large number of firms engaged in the drug business, there is none that has a higher standing in commercial circles than that of August v. Trott, proprietor of the Grand Central Drug Store. The business was begun nearly twenty years ago, although Mr. von Trott has only had charge of it since 1873. During that time the business has increased to a large and valuable patronage. His store is admirably arranged and equipped for the business. The shelves contain a choice and carefully selected stock of the purest drugs and chemicals, besides a full line of patent medicines usually in demand by the public. Prescriptions are filled with accuracy and promptness. He also carries a full line of toilet and fancy articles and other goods found in a first-class establishment of this kind. Mr. von Trott is a skillful apothecary and chemist, graduating as pharmacist from the University of Marburg, in 1866. He came to Milwaukee in 1867, and in 1869 began the drug trade with Mr. Lotz. Mr. von Trott was elected alderman from the Fourth Ward for the years 1880 to 1882, and is now supervisor of this county from the Fourth Ward.

GOODYEAR RUBBER CO.,

W. W. Wallis, Manager.

372 and 374 East Water Street.

AMONG the many business establishments of the Cream City whose resources and facilities have been sketched in this review, that of "The Goodyear Rubber Company," at Nos. 372 and 374 East Water street, claims more than ordinary attention. Their main office is in New York city, with F. M. Shepard, president, and J. A. Minott, Secretary. Branch houses are established in Boston, Washington, Buffalo, Chicago, St. Louis, Kansas City, St. Paul, Minneapolis, San Francisco, Montreal, Can., and in this city. This company are the largest manufacturers and distributors of rubber goods in the world. They are owners of valuable patents in rubber goods and make the best line of boots and shoes offered to the trade; nothing but pure rubber is used in their manufacture, no "shoddy" or old rubber ground up being used. Their store was established in this city ten years ago. Mr. W. W. Wallis, who has been with the company for ten years, took charge of the Milwaukee branch last year, and from his long experience is thoroughly posted in every feature of the business. The premises occupied at Nos. 372 and 374 East Water street consist of a splendid five-storied building, admirably arranged with every facility for the display of the valuable and extensive assortment of rubber goods. The stock consists largely of druggists', stationers', railroad and sporting supplies; boots and shoes, weather strips, clothing, leather belting, packing and hose, jewelry, toilet cases, toys, gossamer clothing for men, women and children, etc. They are the only manufacturers of "crack proof" ribbed and "coasting" sole boots and shoes. This company are also agents for the Union India Rubber Co., Rubber Clothing Co., National Rubber Co., Union Tubing Co. and Rubber Footwear Co.

JAS. E. PATTON & CO.,

Manufacturers of White Lead, Zinc, Colors, etc.

268, 270 and 272 East Water Str.

THE firm of Jas. E. Patton & Co. is engaged extensively in the manufacture of white lead, zinc, colors and varnishes, and as dealers in linseed and lubricating oils, putty, window-glass, brushes and artists' materials are among the largest in the Northwest. The house was first located at the corner of Grand avenue and West Water street, under the name of Patton & Williams, but the latter retired in 1870, since which time it has borne its present name. As the business increased, the demand for more room decided Mr. Patton to erect a building especially for the business, and accordingly the present structure was reared and ready for occupancy in 1875. It occupies three numbers—268, 270 and 272 East Water street, is four stories in height, being 50x219 feet in area, and is supplied with all the latest machinery and a 50 horse-power engine with a boiler of equal proportions. A large force of workmen is employed in the establishment, the most of them being skilled in the business. Three traveling salesmen represent their goods in Michigan, Wisconsin, Minnesota, Iowa and Dakota. Mr. Patton was born in Lewiston, Penn., in 1832, and came to this city in 1855. Being thoroughly familiar with the business in which he is engaged, and taking an active part in all its practical details, he has placed his house on a substantial basis, and developed it into its present proportions. He deals in plate and sheet glass of every variety, and offers substantial advantages to the trade in every line.

J. E. SINGER & CO.,

Woolens and Tailors' Trimmings.

372 and 374 Broadway.

THE above firm is one of our representative houses in its particular line of business. Mr. J. E. Singer, the head of the firm, was born in Austria in 1841, and came from thence to the Cream City in 1864. He was, until 1872, with Adler, Mendel & Co., as salesman in their clothing establishment, and then started in business as senior partner in the firm of Singer & Benedict. He continued in this firm until 1883, when the present business was founded. The premises occupied are large, elegant and commodious, five stories high, being thirty-four feet in width and one hundred and twenty in depth, and are located at No. 372 and 374 Broadway, in wholesale portion of the city. They do an exclusively wholesale trade, and have a large force of well trained and efficient employes, who thoroughly understand their business. They deal in both domestic and imported goods, the latter being selected and brought to this country by the head of the firm. Six commercial travelers are employed on the road, and the trade of the house extends through Wisconsin, Minnesota, Iowa, Illinois and Michigan. The present business is based upon true business principles, and on a cash basis, and their systematic methods of transacting affairs have given them an excellent repute with the trade throughout the State, and builded them a reputation second to none in the business.

FRED. ANDRES & CO.,

Contractors of Cut and Sawed Stone.

Office, 779 North Water Street.

FOR a firm who began operations with nothing at all, as one may say, Fred. Andres & Co. have done remarkably well during the five years of their business existence at No. 779 North Water street. They employ regularly thirty-five men and do a yearly business amounting to $65,000. They run by steam, using a thirty-five horse power engine. They are agents for and handle the Berea, Ohio, sandstone, the Bedford, Indiana, sandstone, and what is known as the Vert Island stone, from Nipicon Bay, Ontario. As contractors of cut and sawed stone and wholesale and retail dealers in all kinds of lime and sandstone, their business extends throughout the State and even reaches into neighboring States. Their office is at No. 779 North Water street, their yard and mill corner Broadway and North Water streets.

Among the more prominent buildings in this city for which Fred. Andres & Co. furnished the cut stone may be mentioned the following: The Conro Block, the Police Station, Best Brewing Co.'s malt-house and brew-house. Fourth and Fifth District School buildings, Val. Blatz's residence, W. W. Coleman's residence, Armory (Light Horse Squadron), and County Jail. Outside of the city they have had among others the following contracts: Fond du Lac, Court House, German Bank; Sheboygan, Sheboygan Insane Asylum; Elkhorn, Insane Asylum; Engine House and City Hall at Beaver Dam; and Engine House and City Hall at Chippewa Falls. Fred. Andres was born at Bridgeport, Conn., in 1856, and came to this city at the tender age of two months. He has always lived here, and of course learned his trade here.

LEBEAU & SCHUHMAN,

Dentists.

325 Chestnut Street.

THE enterprising firm of young dentists, Lebeau & Schuhman, situated at No. 325 Chestnut street, although but just launching out upon the sea of business, already take a leading position. They are thoroughly conversant with all branches of dental surgery, are skillful operators, and are graduates from the famous Rush Medical and Dental College, of Chicago. Their location is all that can be desired, in a populous and business part of the city, with street cars passing their door every few minutes for all parts of Milwaukee. They occupy three large dental parlors, which are furnished and fitted with taste, and contain all the latest scientific and modern appliances used in their profession. Their office hours are from 8:30 A. M. to 1 P. M.; 2 to 6 P. M.; 7 to 8 P. M.

WM. BOOTH,

Merchant Tailor.

418 Broadway.

AFTER doing a large and successful business in Albany, N. Y., for eighteen years, Mr. Booth came to Milwaukee in 1866 and began at once to do a large and lucrative business here. He now employs from eight to ten first-class workmen, and besides his regular city work, has orders from various places in the State, as well as from Iowa, Minnesota and Dakota. His yearly business now amounts to some $6,000. Now, Mr. Booth says, he is making a little money, while formerly, though doing ten times as much business, he was losing money right along. Wherefrom, he rightly concludes, that what the country needs is more cash and less business. Pay as you go, ought to be the rule with everybody—with the producer no less than with the consumer. A business experience of fifty years has taught Mr. Booth many valuable business maxims, which he carries out in his business system, prominent among them being the cash basis for all transactions, thus enabling him to give good material, good work, perfect fit and entire satisfaction to all.

WM. S. GUY,

Dealer in Fancy and Staple Groceries.

94 Martin Street.

THE growth of Mr. Guy's trade has been so rapid since his store was opened, at No. 94 Martin street, that he contemplates putting up a larger building, arranged within with special reference to the retail grocery trade. Mr. Guy is a man of large business experience. He established his present store in 1880, and the trade already amounts to nearly $20,000 a year. Mr. Guy is a native of England, where he was born in 1835. He crossed the ocean with his parents in his infancy, going to Canada where he lived seven years, or until 1842, when he came to Milwaukee. Mr. Guy is a quiet, unassuming sort of man, who doesn't go much on mere show and noise in business. He is content to keep a good, full stock of the best and freshest groceries, and to give all who come the full worth of their money, and thus build for himself a reputation for fair dealing not only for his own satisfaction but because it is a natural characteristic of the man in business matters, and gives a pleasure merely to do right.

MATH. SCHWALBACH,

Manufacturer of Tower Clocks.

1002 Galena Street.

THIS clock is an improvement on Church and Tower Clocks. The invention greatly simplifies the construction of this kind of clocks, and correspondingly cheapens the price, and at the same time increases the reliability of the clock and durability of the work. Any one can keep this clock in good order. The clock is seven feet high, four feet wide, and three and one-half feet long. The striking part pulls a hammer from thirty to forty pounds; the quarter striking part from twenty to thirty pounds. Pendulum ball scales one-hundred and twenty-five pounds.

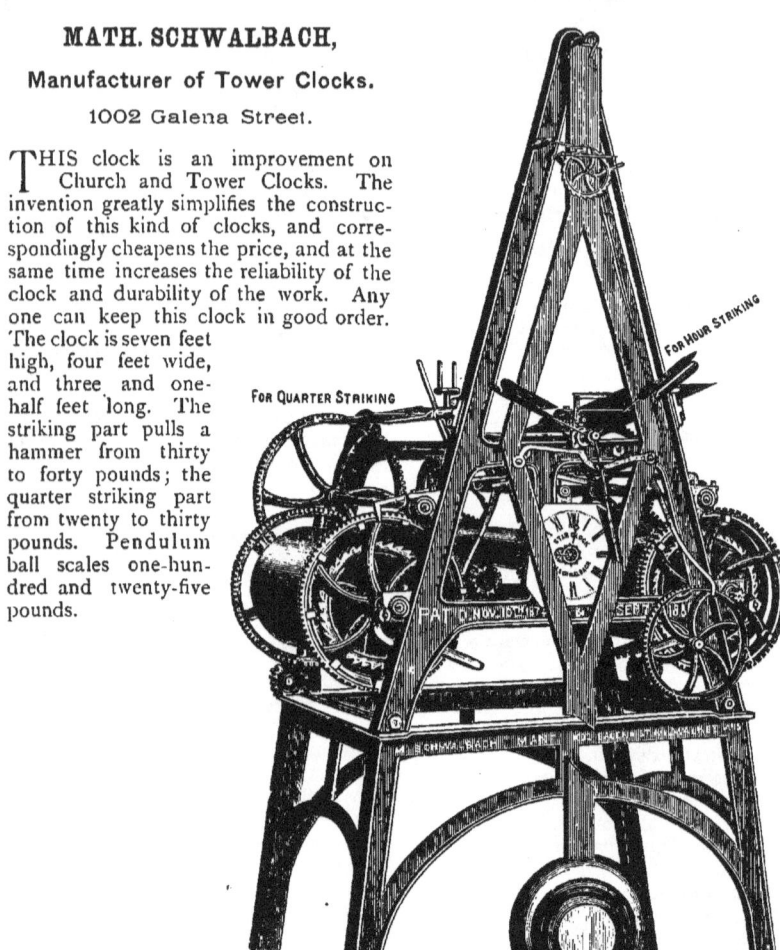

JULIUS FRIEDMANN.

Restaurateur and Caterer.

465 Market Square.

AN object of interest to the hungry visitors to Milwaukee is the European and American Restaurant of Mr. Julius Friedmann, at No. 465 Market Square, just opposite the St. Charles Hotel. It occupies a leading position in the city, as a place *par excellence* at which to invigorate the inner man. The location is the most central and convenient in the city, and is furnished in the most tasty and attractive manner.

Inviting tables, laden with the best the market affords, and capable of seating over 100 persons, are arranged about the room. The promptness and politeness with which the business is conducted, and the faultless *cuisine* and splendid sideboard presented by this restaurant render it one of the most popular resorts of the kind in the city. It was established by the present proprietor about two years ago, and he has already won a patronage of large proportion. A corps of twelve assistants is employed in attending to the wants and comforts of his numerous guests. His display of artificial supplies, embracing all varieties of vegetables, meats, fruits, etc., is worthy of note, as it is the best of the kind in the United States, and was imported directly from Nürnberg, Germany, at his special order. Mr. Friedmann is ready at all times to give prompt attention to orders for ball and wedding suppers; lunch being served at all hours of the day. Mr. Friedmann was born at Vienna, Austria, in 1847, and came to Milwaukee in 1865, and has always been closely identified with the business interests of this city.

ROSE HILL PARK.

Wm. Miller, Proprietor.

ONE of the well planned and beautiful pleasure resorts of the Cream City is that of "Rose Hill Park." This site was formerly occupied by the famous Dunlap nursery and was purchased in 1881 by Mr. Wm. Miller who, in the spring of 1882, opened the beautiful Rose Hill to the public. The beautiful winding walks, terraces and flower gardens show them to be under the skillful management of artistic hands. There is over a mile and a quarter of finely graveled walks, leading all over and around the hill, and across the plateau on the east. Rose Hill Park is situated near the southwestern limits of the city, and is conveniently reached by two prominent street railway lines—the Milwaukee City railway and the Cream City line. It consists of six acres, and has accommodations for over 15,000 people, its seating capacity being greater than any two parks in the city. The large and handsome dwelling on the summit of the hill is occupied by the proprietor, and it is so arranged that the entire lower floor can be thrown into a mammoth dining-room. Near the residence is situated the large pagoda, or band stand. A pavilion, 60x100 feet, is also located near by, and can be used for either dining or dancing purposes. Surrounding these is a profusion of evergreens, shrubbery and flowers, presenting as beautiful a scene as can be found around Milwaukee. Near the eastern base of the hill is situated the large covered dancing pavilion, 55x86 feet in dimensions, with a reception room 22x40 feet. The southern part of the park is laid out into an extensive parade ground, around which are arranged seats in amphitheater style, capable of seating over 3,000 people. One of the attractive features of Rose Hill Park is the fine collection of wild animals which amuse the young folks and interest the larger ones, and not least worthy of mention are the large sheds capable of sheltering over 100 horses. Concerts and various attractions are given at the park all through the summer season. It is also leased to societies, parties, etc., on special terms. Meals are served in the best style, and with a promptness to suit all. Mr. Miller was born in Germany and came to this city over twelve years ago.

MRS. B. KUMP.

Mattress Manufactory.

137 Second Street.

NO establishment in this line in Milwaukee excels that of Mrs. B. Kump, which is situated in the large two-story brick building at 132 Second street. This business was started in a very moderate way, by the present owner, at 177 Second street in 1873. By her energy Mrs. Kump has built up a trade of not only the best custom in this city, but also through various parts of the State. She moved to 146 and 148 Second Street in 1880, where she remained for four years and then took up her present location. Mrs. Kump manufactures different kinds of hair, husk and cotton mattresses, which have gained a reputation for quality and durability surpassed by none. Hair mattresses and featherbeds are cleaned by steam process; old mattresses made over as good as new, chairs re-caned, and, in fact, everything belonging to this special line of trade is satisfactorily attended to at the most reasonable terms. All the latest and most approved machinery requisite for the successful operation of this business is in use.

DR. LOUIS R. ESAU,
Dentist.
128 Wisconsin Street.

THE dental rooms of Dr. Esau, at 128 Wisconsin street, up stairs, are tastily furnished and provided with all the best modern appliances and instruments used by the most successful practitioners of the important art of dentistry. There is, in the first place, a reception room, well lighted, neatly carpeted and hung with rare and carefully selected pictures; then there is the operating room and several smaller apartments, where the various kinds of mechanical work are executed. Dr. Esau is a young man of intelligence and enterprise, and deeply devoted to his chosen profession. He is a graduate of the dental college at Ann Arbor, Mich., and is fast building up a large and lucrative practice among the best people of the city.

A. NEUMANN,
Merchant Tailor.
439 East Water Street.

AMONG our city tailors who have achieved notoriety by virtue of the first-class work turned out, by long continuance in business and honorable dealings, we call the attention of our readers to the establishment of A. Neumann at No. 439 East Water street. He has been located in this city since 1864, and has built up a large and profitable trade. His yearly sales amount to the splendid sum of $25,000, thus conclusively showing the estimation in which his skill is held by an appreciative public. Mr. Neumann was born in Austria in 1843, and came to Milwaukee in 1864. He is eminently qualified to conduct such an establishment, having long been engaged in the trade. He also keeps a stock of men's, boys' and youths' clothing on hand, but his specialty is the manufacture of suits to order. His goods are first-class in every way, and in fit, style and workmanship are unequaled.

AUGUST SPANKUS,
Blank Book Manufacturer, Binder and Ruler.
234 West Water Street.

ONE of the most experienced and practical book binders and blank book manufacturers of Milwaukee is Mr. August Spankus, who has followed this enterprise all his life and is thoroughly acquainted with every department of the business. He began for himself about three years ago at 320 Chestnut street, where he remained a short time, as the business grew so rapidly as to demand a more commodious situation. With this in view he obtained his present favorable location, on the second floor at 234 West Water street. The establishment has dimensions of 22x100 feet, and contains all the requisite machinery necessary for the work, and of the latest improved make, and is run by a gas engine of ten horse-power. This firm, by superior workmanship, and the manufacture of superior articles in this line, have attained a widespread reputation with a correspondingly large trade. From fifteen to twenty hands are employed to keep up with the demands of this steadily increasing trade. Special attention is given to Art Binding, and persons having anything of this kind will do well to consult this firm before going elsewhere.

MILWAUKEE GARDEN.

Pius Dreher, Proprietor.

State and Prairie Streets, between 14th and 15th.

THE Milwaukee Garden is one of the oldest and most popular summer resorts in the city. It was established as far back as 1850 by H. Kemper, but was sold to the present proprietor, Mr. Pius Dreher, in 1855. For years it was the out-of-town park, visited by those taking drives about the city, but the rapid growth and extension of the city of late years has placed it almost in the heart of the city. Mr. Dreher has improved it from time to time, until now it is as commodious and beautiful a park as can be found in Milwaukee. It covers a large block, 315 by 416 feet, or about three acres, between Fourteeth and Fifteenth, and State and Prairie streets. It is easy of access by three of the principal street railways of the city. A few of the principal features of the park are the large residence and mammoth hall and theater at the corner of State and Fourteenth streets, the summer theater and large dancing pavilion in the center of the park, the large bowling alley and shooting galleries, two fountains near the center of the park, swings, refreshment stands, etc. The south end of the park is fitted up for the use of Turning societies, and accommodation is afforded for 15,000 persons, the park being illuminated with over 300 gas lamps. Over thirty persons are employed to keep the park in repairs and look after the comforts of its patrons, and is altogether one of the most perfectly equipped pleasure gardens in Milwaukee or the Northwest. Its patronage is from the best ranks of our German population.

B. H. HELMING & CO.,

Manufacturers of Collars, Riding Saddles, Halters, etc.

173 Second Street.

ONE of the representative firms of this city for the manufacture of harness, collars, saddles, halters, bridles and fly-nets is that of B. H. Helming & Co., at 173 Second street. Mr. Helming commenced to learn his trade in the city of St. Louis, Mo., and came to Milwaukee in 1855 and established himself in business on Second street. The business at first was very small, only calling for the services of himself and one boy. His ability as a collar maker soon became known to the trade and his business increased, so that inside of two years and a half he had to move to the more extended quarters at 189 Second street, in the same block he now occupies. He remained here for over twenty years, during which time his trade increased to very large proportions, which called for still greater facilities. So, in 1882, he took charge of his present convenient and commodious quarters at 173 Second street. The building is four stories with the basement, 25x80 feet in dimensions. A large workshop of three floors, 25x50 feet in dimensions, is situated in the rear. The choicest of leather, materials, fittings and mountings only are used in the production of their goods, thus establishing a reliability of all goods leaving the house. The stock carried is valued at from $20,000 to $30,000. The establishment, when in full operation, employs upwards of seventy-five men, including two traveling salesmen, who are constantly looking after the interest of this firm throughout the Northwest. The sales aggregate $75,000 a year. Associated in business with Mr. Helming is Mr. Casper M. Sanger, who has had large experience in this branch of manufacture and is well and favorably known to the trade throughout the West.

H. STERN, JR., & BRO.,
Wholesale Jobbers of Dry Goods Notions, etc.
335, 337 and 339 Broadway.

THE above establishment is a good example of what energy, enterprise and perseverance will do, if directed in their proper channels. Its inception dates back thirty-five years, when the business was started under the name of Goll & Stern. In 1852, this firm dissolved, it being then conducted by H. Stern, Jr. In 1853, the name again changed to H. Stern, Jr., & Bro., and thus it has since remained. The first building occupied by the former firm was at No. 79 East Water street, up stairs. From there they removed, in 1851, to Market Square, and the firm of H. Stern, Jr., in 1852, to the corner of East Water and Mason streets; then to a store at No. 349 East Water street, which was purchased by the firm. Business increasing, they finally made arrangements for the construction of a much larger building, and selected the site now occupied by their imposing and commodious structure, which they occupied in 1868. It consists of five stories, including the basement, and presents a front of sixty feet, with a depth of one hundred and twenty. It contains one of the largest stocks of dry goods and notions in the city. They employ four traveling salesmen to represent them among the retail trade, and have built up an enormous trade throughout the entire West, their annual sales reaching not less than one million dollars.

The pioneer member of the firm, Mr. Henry Stern, was born in Bavaria, in 1825, and came to this country in 1848, and two years later to Milwaukee. Herman Stern was born in Bavaria, in 1826, and came to Milwaukee in 1853, entering the firm the same year. Both gentlemen are prominent members of society, and occupy a high position in the business community.

CITY STEAM LAUNDRY,
J. P. McCarty, Proprietor.
332 and 334 Broadway.

THE above is one of the pioneer establishments of the kind in this city, and is an old landmark, having been established in 1870 by Mrs. McNelly, and met with immediate success. The establishment was conducted by Mrs. McNelly until this present year, when she disposed of it, with good will, to Mr. J. P. McCarty, who is now carrying on the business, with every late improved facility required for turning out neat and artistic work. That this establishment gives universal satisfaction is evidenced by the fact that it numbers some of the best people in society among its customers, and never fails to satisfy the most critical. Mr. McCarty was born in this county in 1857, and has resided the most of his life in Milwaukee. Previous to entering into business for himself, he was for several years a traveling salesman. He is thoroughly posted as to the wants of his customers, and all work placed in his hands will receive prompt attention.

J. A. STAPLETON,

Wholesale Tobacconist.

121 West Water Street.

MR. J. A. Stapleton, wholesale tobacconist, is situated at 121 West Water street. He began business about twelve years ago, dealing in cigars at his residence, delivering them himself to his few customers in the city. From this small beginning he has advanced to his present large business. He occupies an office and salesroom 20x40 feet, which is comfortably and pleasantly fitted up. Mr. Stapleton is a clear-headed, discerning business man, and justly popular among his customers, and in mercantile circles, and in social life. Most of his goods are purchased in the large Eastern cities, but Mr. Stapleton takes advantage of the market in all parts of the country, buying close, and selling cheap to all his customers. Mr. Stapleton is a native of Prince Edward county, Ontario, and came to Milwaukee in 1862, residing here since that time, putting all his time and attention to his present live business.

JOHN H. NARAMORE,

Dentist.

407 Grand Avenue.

FOUR years ago Dr. John H. Naramore established himself in the dental business in this city, and since then has won a prominent position in his profession. He occupies two fine dental parlors, which are located at 407 Grand avenue, up stairs, opposite the Library block. He has in use all the latest appliances necessary for the practice of dentistry. He is a skillful operator, and enjoys a large and lucrative practice all over the city and vicinity. Special attention is given to preserving the teeth, and gold plate work is done as well and at as moderate prices as anywhere in the city. Dr. Naramore was born in the State of New York and came to this city in 1880, and has become well known to members of the profession and the public in general.

THE FILER & STOWELL CO.,

(Limited.)

Cream City Iron Works.

Corner of Clinton and Florida Sts.

THIS is one of the large and representative manufacturing establishments that has become a part of the industrial history of Milwaukee and is known wherever the name and fame of the Cream City extends. The business was established in 1865 by J. M. Stowell and after several changes in name finally organized as at present in 1882. The plant of this business occupies about six lots at the above location, where are erected buildings and equipments of various kinds, consisting of machine shops, foundry, wood-working department, etc. All the latest and most improved machinery and labor-saving devices are in use here. A sixty horse-power engine furnishes the necessary force to run the machinery, and from 150 to 175 people here find remunerative employment, a large proportion of them being skilled workmen in some special branch of the business. A specialty is made of the manufacture of saw mill machinery. Their gang edgers to saw flooring from cants, their gang bolters, gang lath mills and the "boss dog" are well and favorably known wherever lumber is made in the United States. Particular description of their numerous machines, such as their new Twin engine, steam feed new patent head blocks, saw guide, shingle mills and their splendid new circular saw mill, is outside the province of this work, but their business is large and rapidly increasing in all these lines, besides jobbing, repairing and steamboat work, including flour-mill machinery of all kinds. Mr. J. M. Stowell, the president of the company and surviving member of the old firm, is a native of New York State, and has been a resident of Milwaukee for thirty years. He has been Mayor of our city for one term, serving in that honorable capacity from 1882 to 1884 and was also a member of the State Legislature for a number of years, besides holding other positions of honor and trust. Mr. Stowell is president also of the Milwaukee Savings and Investment Association, which is filling so happily a long-felt want among the working classes of. Milwaukee. T. B. McDonald, the secretary of the company, is a native of the State of Georgia and is well known to the business public since his connection with the house two years ago, and has done much to forward the interests of the company since that time. Mr. Walter Read, the treasurer, is a nephew of Mr. Stowell and has, as it were, grown up in the business, learning every detail and being thoroughly conversant with every department of the vast manufacturing interests of the house. He is a native of Cleveland, O., and came here and entered the business when a mere boy. Mr. T. J. Neacy, a large stockholder, represents the house as commercial agent and is very popular wherever he goes, as every reader of these lines will attest who has ever met him in a business or social way. Not a little of the rapid upbuilding and success of this institution is due to his judicious and untiring efforts. His connection with the firm dates back some fifteen years. All in all, this is one of our standard concerns and richly deserves the large patronage bestowed upon it. Any particulars can be learned by addressing the house as above.

H. R. JOHNSON,

Dentist.

136 and 138 Grand Avenue.

THE Grand Avenue Dental Parlors, conducted by Dr. H. R. Johnson, at Nos. 136 and 138 Grand Avenue, were opened in 1881, and by able management and a thorough conception of every feature of the profession, built up a practice and attained a standard position. His dental departments are recognized as among the largest in the Northwest, and the doctor, by his scientific attainments, and adoption of the various modern helps, has done much to advance the profession. His convenient and commodious parlors embrace six rooms. The reception parlor is handsomely furnished and presided over by polite and courteous assistants. On the west side of the parlor is the extracting room, which is under the doctor's personal supervision. This room is light and airy and possesses all those desirable and complete appointments which bespeak more emphatically than anything else, FIRST-CLASS WORK. In this department is used Hurd's Vitalized Air, for which Dr. Johnson has the exclusive right of city and State. The operating rooms are three in number, accessible by double entrances, and contain double windows, which afford clear, bright light for the use of the operators. Operating-room No. 1 is under the immediate control of Dr. Purinton. Here the finest and most skillful dental operations are performed—gold and silver filling, fitting of teeth, regulating of natural teeth, and in fact, *fine* general work of every description. One special feature of work of this room is the use of Dr. J. E. Low's no-plate method, which is meeting with such great favor by the public. This patent method does away with the extraction of teeth, restores all firm, decayed teeth and broken roots to their original usefulness and beauty, and gives the wearer teeth without plates. This new method supplies all lost teeth without covering the roof of the mouth. Operating-room No. 2 is presided over by Miss Annie Thon, whose practical experience and years of careful study have fitted her for the position she ably occupies as principal assistant to Dr. Purinton. Operating-room No. 3 is chiefly used for taking impressions. Its general adaptation for this purpose, in the way of light and arrangement, is at once noticed. Work in gold, silver, rubber and celluloid is here given its initial introduction. A portion of the laboratory is fitted up for gold and silver work, and a part is devoted to rubber and celluloid work. Under charge of these rooms we find Dr. Wm. Brown, a gentleman possessing great skill and inventive faculties in every branch of his profession. The practice of Dr. Johnson extends all over the Northwest, and aggregates upwards of $15,000 yearly.

F. W. ERBACHER & CO.,

Wholesale Cheese, Fancy Groceries, Etc.

83 West Water Street.

THIS business was begun January 1, 1885, under the firm name of C. A. Kurth & Co., but was changed to F. W. Erbacher & Co., January 1, 1886. They occupy commodious and convenient quarters at No. 83 West Water street. The two floors and large basement are well filled with a new and fine stock of cheese, canned goods, fish, and fancy groceries of every description. Their specialty is in the cheese trade, in which line they are building up a large and successful business in this State, Minnesota and Michigan. This firm are also city agents for the Mosler Safe and Lock Company fire and burglar proof safes. This safe is the only one constructed of one continuous plate, with rounded corners, and filled from the bottom, making it not only stronger and much more secure, but causing the fire-proof filling to be hermetically sealed. The bolts and locks are placed on the inside instead of on the outside flange of the doors, making them much more secure against burglars, and preventing their being affected by heat in case of fire. The Mosler safes have taken the lead in every exposition in which they have been shown, so incontestable is their superiority over all others. F. W. Erbacher & Co. are to be congratulated in having so worthy an article in connection with their thriving business.

H. ELLINGHAUSEN & CO.,

General Commission Merchants.

Office, 156 West Water Street.

THIS firm opened business at their present site, No. 156 West Water street, in 1876. The store is 20x110, besides which they occupy two floors and a large basement. Their general supply is received from all parts of Wisconsin and some parts of Michigan, the greater part of which is re-shipped to Eastern and Southern points, as they do business in Boston, New Orleans and various parts of Texas. A great portion of their trade is with the retail merchants of the city, and such is the local trade that, with the exception of speculative produce, their large salesrooms are emptied every evening, only to be refilled during the early hours of the next day. Mr. H. Ellinghausen was born in Bremen, in 1842, and came to Milwaukee in 1870 and his name soon became associated with the enterprising business men of this city, from whom he receives the greatest confidence and support.

JOHN CLARK,

Wholesale Manufacturer of Harness.

210 West Water Street.

THE wholesale harness manufactory of Mr. John Clark is situated at 210 West Water street, and an enterprise which adds much to the business prosperity of Milwaukee. The commodious building consists of two floors 24x60 feet, and is divided into a workshop, salesrooms and office. The business was begun in

1880 by Mr. Clark. It was then located at 230 Grand avenue, being removed to the present site in 1884. The specialty of this firm is hand-made harness of all descriptions. Mr. Clark is a practical and skillful workman himself, and he sees to it that nothing but the best work is presented to the public. He also deals in horse clothing, trunks, valises, etc., of which he carries a large and complete stock. Besides enjoying a large city trade he has patrons all through the Northwest, his sales aggregating upwards of $25,000 per annum. Mr. Clark was born in New York State and came to Milwaukee in 1863, and has ever since been connected in various ways with the harness business.

D. A. MARTIN,
Grain Dealer.
63 and 65 Second Street.

THIS business was established under Pennock and Martin in 1879, but has for some years past been under the sole proprietorship of Mr. D. A. Martin. The store-room and mill is three stories in height, with a large basement, and has a frontage on Second street of 40 feet, and a depth of 65 feet. In the rear are two store-rooms 25x85 feet in dimension. An engine of twenty-five horse-power is used to run the various machinery used in the operation of this business. The specialty of this house is in handling damaged grain, which is received in large quantities from all the wheat-growing States of the Union. The grain when received is cleaned, separated and put through a process which renders it good for the market again, and it is sold to the malt and grain men all over the country. With one exception, this is the only enterprise of the kind in the Northwest. All grains damaged in wrecks, fire, water, etc., are purchased by this firm. Mr. Martin was born in Weston, Vt., and came to Milwaukee in 1874, soon after which he entered into his present business. He served during the late war in the Fourth Vermont Infantry, from 1863 to the close, in the Army of the Potomac.

ESTABLISHMENT OF MUELLER & ILHARDT, 449 and 451 East Water Street.

SHERMAN, BELL & CO.,
Auctioneers and Commission Merchants.
212 and 214 Grand Avenue.

A LEADING house of this line is that of Sherman, Bell & Co., at Nos. 212 and 214 Grand avenue. This firm sells on commission for parties from all parts of the United States. They hold regular trade sales of Boots and Shoes, Clothing, Dry Goods, Carpets and General Merchandise every week during the year, with sales of Crockery, Glassware and Cutlery at frequent intervals, and find customers to attend their sales from all parts of Wisconsin, from Michigan, Minnesota, Iowa and Dakota. They also attend to sales of Real Estate, Household Furniture, and in fact all branches of legitimate auction business, holding sales of household furniture and second-hand goods regularly every Saturday at their salesrooms. This house makes liberal advances on all classes of goods entrusted to them for sale, when desired, prompt sales and quick returns being a peculiar characteristic of this house. Their large business aggregates over a quarter million dollars annually, and consignments are received from all parts of the Union. The auctioneering department of this business is conducted and managed by Mr. Sherman, while the financial management of the firm is under the charge of Mr. Bell. Liberality and promptness have ever characterized all the transactions of this house, and the success which has attended it since its inception is but the natural result of a sound commercial policy.

ware, and due attention is paid to repairing of wares. Mr. Gross is ably assisted in the business by his son, Arthur E. Gross, and his son-in-law, Chas. E. Mueller. The trade of this house ex-

PHILLIP GROSS,
Hardware Merchant.
110 and 112 Grand Avenue and 195 West Water Street.

A REPRESENTATIVE and leading house in this branch of trade is that of Phillip Gross, at 110 and 112 Grand avenue and 195 West Water street. The whole store room is arranged expressly for this business and is filled with an immense and complete stock of foreign and domestic hardware, including every kind of mechanics' tools, builders' hardware, shelf goods, heavy hardware, house furnishing goods, fine cutlery and plated ware, and all articles pertaining to this branch of trade. He is also dealer in ranges, filters, refrigerators, etc., besides the exclusive agencies for the Colby Clothes Wringers, Adams' Westlake Oil, Gas and Gasoline Stoves, Bismarck Stoves and Ranges, Aladdin Heaters, Norton Door Checks and Springs, Peck & Snyder's American Club Skates, Alaska Refrigerators, Lily Wrought Iron Ranges. The site occupied by this firm is one of the oldest and most convenient in this city for this branch of trade. This house manufactures all forms of tin-

tends all over the State and is of a strictly permanent and first class character, and the sales are large and annually increasing. This store is the headquarters and distributing point of the Northwest for all kinds of roller rink goods. A complete illustrated catalogue and price list of these goods has been published by this firm free for the trade, and reflects great credit upon them. Mr. Gross is a native of Germany and came to Milwaukee over 33 years ago, and this city's industrial advancement owes its progress in no small degree to this firm.

CREAM CITY PRESERVING WORKS,
N. M. Klein, Prop.
131 and 133 Sycamore Street.

THE Cream City Preserving Works, Mr. N. M. Klein, proprietor, were established in 1874. This firm manufactures fruit butter, pure fruit jellies, cranberry sauce, preserves and mince meat. Meeting success on every hand, Mr. Klein was able to erect a factory of his own at his present location, 131 and 133 Sycamore street. The building is three stories high, with a large basement. The newest and latest machinery is used in this factory. The trade of this house extends to all parts of the country, and the annual sales of the firm amount to nearly $75,000. Mr. Klein is a native of Prussia and came to this country in 1853, but resided at Laporte, Ind., until 1874, when he came here for the sole purpose of establishing the Preserving Works.

struction," that brought him into favorable notice and established his reputation as an artist of no mean merit even at that period. At the opening of the first art gallery of the Cold Spring Course in Wisconsin, in 1873, at the time of the agricultural fair, Mr. Lydston was assistant superintendent, and continued to act in that capacity for two years, and afterwards for one year he filled the office of superintendent. He is largely in request among people of refined taste and the most wealthy members of society, and his pictures are pronounced to be among the best.

J. C. WELLES,
Dealer in Guns, Revolvers, Ammunition, etc.
428 East Water Street.

THIS is one of the oldest houses in Milwaukee, in this line, having been organized by Mr. Welles in 1855. The stock is complete. Revolvers of all the best makes, single and double barrelled shot guns, breech and muzzle loaders, rifles of all the latest improved patterns, game bags, cartridge belts, gun cases, shooting jackets and, in short, everything in this line can be found in his store, and all at satisfactory prices. His house is one of the solid institutions of East Water street, and is so well known an extended mention in these pages is not necessary.

J. H. H. LANDWEHR,
Dealer in Groceries, Cigars, etc.
467 East Water Street.

THE grocery house at No. 467 East Water street is an old stand, having first been opened in 1844 by Hilgen & Schroeder. They continued until 1847 when the business was sold to August Ehlebracht. In 1857 the firm became Winner & Landwehr, and in 1876 Mr. Winner retired, leaving Mr. Landwehr sole proprietor. He was born in Germany in 1836, coming to America in 1854, stopping one year in New York, and from there coming direct to Milwaukee. He now has a nice business, and keeps a fine line of groceries, provisions, cigars, etc.

F. A. LYDSTON'S
Art School and Studio.
94 Wisconsin Street.

AS an artist, Mr. Lydston needs no words of commendation in these pages. His name and fame are known throughout the entire country, and what little we could say would not add to his known popularity. He was born in Massachusetts in 1819, and came to Milwaukee in 1861. Just before the outbreak of the civil war he painted a very fine and expressive picture on the situation, entitled, "Re-union, Contention and De-

H. ZWENGEL,
Manufacturing Jeweler.
79 Wisconsin St. (Iron Block).

THIS popular Wisconsin street jeweler has had a long experience in the business, which gives him a prominent position in his field of effort. For ten years he has devoted himself to the jewelry manufacturing business, and the extra quality of his work has gained him a reputation throughout the city and country. He manufactures jewelry of all kinds, but gives special attention to diamond settings. He does a wholesale and retail business, but is confined mostly to Wisconsin and neighboring States. He makes all kinds of ornaments in the jewelry line to order, and handles precious stones of all kinds. His shop is fitted up with all the mechanical contrivances and facilities for the furtherance of his work, and all work is supervised by him personally, and he uses the most painstaking care to give satisfaction to all customers. The quality of his work is first-class, and his services are largely in demand. He was born in Milwaukee in 1860, and has since resided here. He is a young man, well liked for the enterprise he has exhibited in establishing and carrying on his trade, and has many friends among the leading citizens of Milwaukee.

senior partner withdrew, when Mr. J. G. Flint became sole owner. Since the inception of this business on Spring street, now Grand avenue, it has increased so rapidly that repeated improvements had to be made to meet the demands of trade. After occupying the Reese Block for a number of years the present site was purchased in 1872, and the large, handsome block, represented in the cut below, was erected. It covers an area of 80x200 feet. The firm carry an extensive stock, and the product of these mills is shipped to all parts of the country. Besides the coffee roasters, and large grinders, they have other necessary machinery of the latest and most

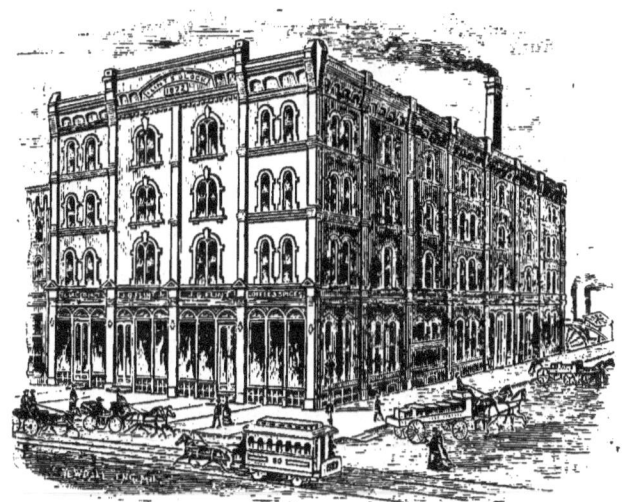

J. G. FLINT'S "STAR" COFFEE AND SPICE MILLS.

J. G. FLINT,
"Star" Coffee and Spice Mills.
Cor. West Water and Clybourn St.

THE largest coffee and spice manufactory in the Northwest, is situated on the corner of West Water and Clybourn streets, and is known as the "Star" Mills. These mills were established by the Flint Bros., under the name of W. & J. G. Flint, in the fall of 1858, but in 1880 the

perfect pattern, all of which are run by two engines aggregating 60 horse-power. The goods are of all varieties of coffee, spices, teas, baking powder, etc., of the best and purest quality in the market. No household in the Northwest but what is familiar with the "Star Crystal Baking Powder," which is so popular wherever sold, and one of the specialties of this firm. Mr. Flint is also proprietor of the extensive and well-known establishment, the

"Star" Tobacco Factory,

which he established in 1870, in partnership with M. B. Kneeland. After the death of Mr. Kneeland in 1875, Mr. Flint purchased his interest and has since conducted the business under the firm name of J. G. Flint, Jr. The various brands of this house have become popular all over the Union, and established the name and reputation not only of the firm, but also of the city, as a tobacco center. The favorite brands of smoking tobacco consist of "Floating Cloud," "Climax," "King Bird," "Staple," "Bobtail," "Uncle Tom," "Royal," and a dozen others. In chewing tobacco we specially mention "May Queen," "Star" and "Diadem," all first-class productions. The fine cut chewing tobaccos are manufactured entirely from the Kentucky leaf, while the smoking tobaccos consist of Virginia and North Carolina leaf. The capacity of this factory is upwards of 1,000,000 pounds annually. Nearly 200 hands are employed in the Spice Mills and Tobacco Factory, and from 15 to 20 traveling men represent this house in all parts of the country. Mr. Flint is a native of New Hampshire and came to Milwaukee in 1858. He is Vice-President of the Commercial Bank of Milwaukee, and also holds a similar office with the Albion Marble Company of Vermont.

EDWARD BARBER,

Real Estate Agent and Business Broker.

79 Wisconsin Street.

MEN are constituted roaming creatures, always on the lookout for new locations, and it is right they should be, for if it were not so, one part of our universe would be over-populated, whilst the rest would be a howling wilderness. This desire for change has made such men as myself a necessity, for it requires as much tact and wisdom to cater to the wants of a community who buy and sell the land upon which we live, as it does to traffic in any other commodity, and in this line I have had over thirty years' experience in Wisconsin. It is the pleasing part of our occupation to point out the pleasant places to live in, the good locations to do business upon, the choice bits of land to speculate with, and we can advise our friends to look at the "Industrial History of Milwaukee," and assure them that the half is not told. Come and see Milwaukee, for seeing is believing. I shall take great pleasure in showing the readers of this book and all who may call, the beautiful scenery depicted in its pages, and also to advise them in making investments. Very truly yours,

EDWARD BARBER.

THIELE BROS.,

Pork and Beef Packers.

385 and 387 Third Street.

IN 1884 Thiele Bros.—Fred., Jr., and John C.—succeeded their father, Mr. Frederick Thiele, in the extensive pork and beef packing business which he established in 1852. They are located at Nos. 385 and 387 Third street, in a commodious building, where they are now doing their retail business. Following the trade in this city for the past thirty years, they have naturally a large local trade, besides which they also have a large railroad and marine trade. A large ice-house, that will hold over 300,000 pounds of meat, is connected with their retail market. Their packing house, between Third and Fourth streets, is arranged with the most modern steam improvements. They are extensive manufacturers of refined lard, all kinds of sausages, and are curers of the celebrated mild sugar-cured hams, bacon and shoulders. Heavy regular consignments of their noted cervelat sausage are shipped to the East and South as far as Texas and Matamoras, Mexico. All their meats are shipped in their improved ice-boxes to summer resorts and hotels, assuring arrival in good condition. They have facilities for cutting 200 lbs. of sausage meat every five minutes, and there is a large three-storied smoke-house in the rear of their packing house, where they can smoke 25,000 pounds of sausage at one time. They also have two other large smoke houses to smoke hams, bacon and shoulders. In conclusion, we heartily commend this house to our many readers, feeling assured that they will receive entire satisfaction and the best the market affords at the most reasonable prices.

OSCAR ZINN,

Druggist and Apothecary.

432 Chestnut Street, Cor. Fifth.

THE neat and attractive drug store, at No. 432 Chestnut street, northeast corner Fifth, is kept by Oscar Zinn, who is well-known as an able druggist and apothecary. He is a graduate of the Philadelphia College of Pharmacy, and after pursuing the business for eight years in Chicago, came back to his native city and established himself at his present quarters about one year ago. His store is filled with a large and well-selected stock of pure drugs, patent preparations, chemicals, surgical instruments, toilet and fancy articles, perfumery and druggist's sundries, and all appliances found in a first-class store of this kind. He bestows his personal attention to his large and growing prescription trade, and possesses the confidence and esteem of the medical profession in an eminent degree.

WILLIAM R. KNELL,

Dealer in Paper Hangings and Shade Goods.

403 Grand Avenue.

ONE of the representative firms in this line of trade is that of Wm. R. Knell, at No. 403 Grand avenue. His handsome salesrooms are always filled with a choice selection of wall papers of every description, in the latest designs and best qualities. Paper hanging, ceiling decorations, window shades and fixtures are kept in stock, and frescoing done, and in fact, everything pertaining to the business can be secured at this house. Ten skilled workmen are employed, and during the busy season double this number are required to meet the demands of trade. The decoration of ceilings is a feature of the business to which special attention is devoted, and in which special line Mr. Knell has few equals and none who are superior in point of execution.

Mr. Knell has been established in business for over four years, being located in his present location for the past three years. Mr. Knell is a professional lithographic engraver and designer, which adds much to his knowledge of decorative work. All desiring work of this kind can be suited at this house with work done in the highest style of the art.

ST. CHARLES HOTEL.

Chr. Fernekes & Bro., Proprietors.

Market Square.

MILWAUKEE hotels have a good reputation which is fully deserved, and which in a measure accounts for this city fast becoming such a popular summer-resort. One of the representative establishments of this kind is that of the St. Charles Hotel on Market Square, at 458 to 466 East Water street. This favorite hotel was built by Captain D. Upman in 1857, who had charge of it until 1862, when Christian Fernekes and his brother Valentine purchased it. In 1870 Mr. Valentine Fernekes died, his brother continuing the business since that time under the same firm name. It is a large imposing brick structure, five stories in height, with a frontage of over 155 feet on Market Square and a depth of 150 feet. Its halls are wide, and its rooms cheerful and inviting. The parlors are tastefully and elegantly furnished, and everything is fitted up in modern style. The dining-room is large, well ventilated and its tables admirably arranged. The *cuisine* of the St. Charles Hotel is perfect in every respect, and surpasses most of the large hotels in variety and quality. Their improved passenger and baggage elevators render all the floors easy of access. Bathrooms and closets on each floor, electric bells, steam laundry, barber shop, elegant billiard parlors, and bar are some of the attractions found here. The house can accommodate 200 persons or more, as it contains upwards of 125 rooms, which are supplied with every convenience for the comfort of the guests. The popular proprietor and manager, Mr. Christian Fernekes, adds the two needful things—able management and courteous attention, which transforms hotel-life into home ease, without its care. One feature worthy of note is the perfect provision and arrangement made for the safety of guests in case of fire. Mr. Fernekes is a native of Germany and came to this city in 1853, and by his successful connection with this hotel has become closely identified with the business interests of this city.

TURPIN & CO.,

Great 5, 10 and 25 Cent Store.

136 Grand Avenue.

AMONG the novel industries which demand consideration in this work, is the great five, ten and twenty-five cent store of Turpin & Co., at 136 Grand avenue. A most select, complete and varied stock is carried, consisting of dry goods, toys, stationery, picture books, tinware, crockery, glassware, notions, lace, etc. It is safe to say that nowhere else in the city can such great bargains be had in this line as at Turpin & Co.'s. It was established just one year ago last May, and has met with great success. Strangers to our city will fail to see what advantages Milwaukee presents in a cheap line of household articles if they do not call on this firm. Residents of Milwaukee will also do well to bear in mind the great inducements offered by Turpin & Co., and call with their friends and give them a trial. There are seven branch houses of this business in as many different cities, which are as follows: Washington, D. C.; Baltimore; Cleveland; Bridgeport, Conn.; Columbus, O.; Indianapolis, and Milwaukee. The headquarters and distributing point for all these branches is in New York City, under the able management of Mr. S. T. Turpin.

EDWARD E. BORGNIS,

Manufacturer of Models, Dies, Small Machinery, etc.

318 State Street.

THIS shop manufactures scales, yet the main work is that of the finer and more particular work, such as small machinery, models for patents, also dies, seals, presses, branding irons, baggage checks, brass labels, etc., and all manner of repairing. The business was originally founded in 1852, and has been recently known as the Phenix Scale Company. Mr. Borgnis purchased the business in 1876 and in 1882 moved into the premises at 318 State street. The machinery consists of drill-presses, turning lathes, punches, etc., and is impelled by an Otto gas engine of four horse-power. His specialty is the manufacture of the Phenix Scale. The shop is neat and tidy in all its details, and the location is convenient. Mr. Borgnis was born in Germany in 1842. He spent seventeen years in New York City where he learned the trade of a machinist, Milwaukee becoming his home in 1867.

E. LEIHAMMER,

Manufacturer of and Dealer in Harness, Saddles, Collars, etc.

265 Third Street.

THIS business was started by the present owner and his father. The son entered the business with him in 1857, on the corner of Cedar and West Water streets, where the business was conducted until 1881, when it was removed to the present location. The senior partner retired from the concern in 1878. From the inception of the business it has prospered until it now enjoys as fine and extensive a patronage as any of its kind in the city. The greater amount of business is in the way of manufacturing to order. Potsdam, Germany, is the place of Mr. Leihammer's birth, and in 1852 he came to New York City, where he followed his trade of carriage trimming. In 1856 he came to this city and continued in the prosecution of harness-making and trimming carriages up to the time of the establishment of the business we have just described.

THE REMINGTON STANDARD TYPE-WRITER.

Chas. H. Welch, Manager.
395 East Water Street.

THE writing machine called the type-writer was invented at Milwaukee, Wis., in 1867, by C. Latham Sholes, Samuel W. Soule and Carlos Glidden. It embodies the fundamental principles of writing machines, and embraces patented devices which are essential to the construction of a successful and practical type-writer. It is the nearest approach to perfection that has yet been reached. It meets the demand, and everywhere throughout the world is being used with the utmost satisfaction. The average

speed of the type-writer is from forty to eighty words per minute. It is a simple, strong, compact machine, and is easily portable. The No. 2 Remington type-writer contains seventy-six types, which, with certain simple combinations, print about eighty characters, including the letters of the alphabet (both capitals and small letters), punctuations, figures, marks of reference, commercial signs, etc.; in short, everything required for any of the principal modern languages. These eighty characters are printed by the manipulation of only thirty-nine keys. Messrs. E. Remington & Sons have the sole right to manufacture the type-writer, and the material, workmanship and finish of the machines are such as to fully sustain the enviable reputation of their world-renowned establishment. In August, 1882, the firm of Wyckoff, Seamans & Benedict, of New York city, were appointed sole agents for the sale of the machines throughout the world. Since May, 1882, Charles. H. Welch, at 395 East Water street, has represented the machines in this State. Among the prominent users of machines in Milwaukee are the C. M. & St. P. R'y, W. C. R'y, M. L. S. & W. R'y, E. P. Allis & Co., R. G. Dun & Co., Bradstreet Agency. Nearly all the leading corporations, firms and business and professional men are using one or more of these valuable instruments. The sale of these machines has increased to such an extent that the Remingtons have been compelled to add to their buildings—already the largest of the kind in the world—and increase the force of skilled artisans. Important improvements have just been put upon the machine, increasing its durability and value. The type-writer is adapted to write the different languages, and is being sold in all parts of the world.

JOSEPH WECKERLE,
Practical Jeweler.
308 Grand Avenue.

MR. Joseph Weckerle, the practical Grand Avenue Jeweler, established his business in this city in 1867, coming to his present quarters, 308 Grand avenue, two years later. He is manufacturer and dealer in watches, clocks, jewelry, silver and plated ware, etc. Mr. Weckerle is a native of Germany, coming to Pittsburg in 1854 and to Milwaukee in 1867 to follow his trade, which he had learned in his native country. He gives particular attention to repairing watches and jewelry of every description. Also diamond setting, engraving, and chasing done in the neatest style and at the shortest notice. A full and varied stock is constantly kept on hand, great care being taken in his selections. This policy has led to the standard reputation of this house, which extends all over the city and State.

KIPP BROS.,
Manufacturers of and Wholesale Dealers in Mattresses, Spring Beds, Cots, etc.

208 to 220 South Water Street.

AN industry of no small magnitude is that of the firm of Kipp Bros., manufacturers of and wholesale dealers in mattresses, spring beds, cots, feathers, comfortables, bedding supplies, curled hair, excelsior, etc. Their large and commodious factory and salesrooms are situated at Nos. 208 to 220 South Water street. It consists of a large, four-story brick building, covering a surface area of 100x200 feet. It is fitted complete in every respect, and furnished with the most modern machinery used in a factory of this kind. A large Corliss engine of 125 horse-power is used to run the extensive machinery. Upwards of seventy-five hands are employed in the various departments, and the factory is a regular bee-hive of labor during working hours. The business was established about five years ago under the firm name of Milwaukee Mattress Co., but recently taken charge of by Chas. M., Frank J., Wm. J. and Geo. W. Kipp. Their trade now extends all over the Union, and aggregates over $200,000 annually. Their goods have a reputation second to none in the country, and are much sought after by the trade.

FACTORY OF KIPP BROTHERS.

frame structure, which was used both as a brewery and a dwelling house. It was located on Thirteenth street, between Cherry and Galena streets, and the business was only carried on during the winter months, the beer being stored in a large cellar. The property was sold in 1860 to John Beck and Stephen Weber; two years later Mr. Beck purchased Mr. Weber's interest and continued the business alone. Mr. Beck sold out the business in 1877 to Wm. Gerlach, and on May 1st, 1879, the Cream City Brewing Co. was organized, with Wm. Gerlach, president; Chas. Worst, secretary; Jac. Veidt, superintendent. The officers of the company were changed in September, 1882, to Wm. Gerlach, president; Louis P. Best, secretary; Jacob Veidt, superintendent. In 1883 both Mr. Gerlach and Veidt died, when in September, 1884, the company was reorganized and the following officers and directors were elected: John Meiners, president; Adolf H. Meyer, vice-president; Louis P. Best, secretary and treasurer. The breweries are situated at Nos. 500 to 510 Thirteenth street, and on the northwest corner Eighth and State streets, with general offices at 501 Thirteenth street. They also have a large branch-depot and offices at Nos. 12, 13 and 15 West Ohio street, Chicago, Ill. Their main plant on Thirteenth street has dimensions of 150x200

CREAM CITY BREWING CO.
Office, 500 Thirteenth Street.

THE Cream City Brewing Company dates its origin back to May 1st, 1879, but the business was begun in 1853, when Geo. Wehr, his brother Conrad, and C. Foster built a two-story feet, where besides the large brewery and malt house is situated the bottling department, where nearly 5,000 bbls. of beer are bottled annually. The area of ground covered on Eighth street is 100x100 feet in dimensions, and contains malt houses and large cellars. From a business of very small proportions the company has grown to its present magnitude amounting to over 30,000 bbls. a year, and with yearly sales of $250,000. They make about 50,000 bus. of malt every year, besides purchasing nearly 30,000 from the various malsters in this city. The beer of this company is in such demand that they are increasing their facilities for a larger production. A force of nearly fifty hands is employed, also twelve wagons and twenty-five horses. All the best and latest improved machinery is in use at their brewery, which is run by a steam engine of 120 horse-power. They have just put up a second large improved ice-machine, built by Weissel & Vilter. In quality their beer is equal to any in this city. All orders are promptly filled and satisfaction guaranteed.

M. McCANANY,

Printing House.

303 Grand Avenue.

THE enterprising printing house of M. McCanany has had a successful run of business for over three years. The printing office is situated at 303 Grand avenue, where, besides the stock of printing material, he has four steam presses, and a paper cutter. The steam power of six horse, with other facilities, enables him to turn out the most satisfactory book, job, and miscellaneous printing at moderate prices, and of the most improved style of execution. His trade is chiefly located in the city, and includes many of the large mercantile firms, as well as jobs from the C., M. and St. P. Railway, and M., L. S. and W. Railway. A force of six hands, besides the proprietor, is constantly employed. Mr. McCanany is a practical printer and conversant with all the details of this business, having had an experience of many years in all departments of printing. He is a native of Ireland and came direct to Milwaukee with his parents in 1852, and with the exception of a period of ten years—1865 to 1875—has always resided in this city.

MR. & MRS. C. G. SEVERANCE'S

Dancing Academy.

No. 421 Milwaukee Street.

THE leading and most beautiful dancing academy in the city is that of Mr. and Mrs. C. G. Severance, at No. 421 Milwaukee street. The dancing hall has a surface area of 50x60 feet, and is one of the largest and most beautifully decorated ones in the Northwest. The season is from September to June of each year. Upwards of 500 students are enrolled at this academy each season, and the sociables given at the opening and closing, and during the holidays, have a wide reputation, and are looked forward to with great pleasure. Prof. C. G. Severance was born in Vermont in 1829, and came to this State in 1837, with his parents, who settled near Whitewater. He came to Milwaukee in 1860, and for five years was connected with the musical profession. Besides his Milwaukee patronage, Prof. Severance gives instructions and has classes in the various large cities of the State.

D. FISHER & CO.,

Manufacturers of Flavoring Extracts, Perfumes, etc.

110 and 112 Huron Street.

THIS is a business requiring the most consummate skill as well as great care and natural aptitude for the business. These qualities are all combined in the person of Mr. D. Fisher, who has since May, 1879, been engaged in the manufacture and sale of flavoring extracts, perfumes and grocers' sundries. His warehouse and laboratory is situated at Nos. 110 and 112 Huron street, and is completely filled with a large and varied assortment of goods in his line. His laboratory is most complete in its appointments in labor-saving appliances. Mr. Fisher is a graduate from several scientific colleges, both in this country and Germany. He first studied chemistry in scientific schools at Troy, New York, and Cambridge, Mass. From here he went to Germany in order to complete his education, and studied at Munich under Liebig, and under Bunsen in Heidelberg, where he took the degree of Ph. D., in 1854. He then returned to America, and was for four years Professor of Chemistry at the United States Naval Academy. Mr. Fisher was born in Boston in 1832, and came to Milwaukee in 1865. In addition to his acquirements as a manufacturer, Mr. Fisher has had a long experience and very complete education as analytical chemist, and practices in this profession quite extensively in the same building he occupies for the main business.

SAMUEL F. PEACOCK.

Undertaker.

431 Broadway.

IT is now eight years since Mr. Peacock first started in the undertaking business at his present location, and during that time has won a leading place among the representatives in this branch. He is a graduate of the Cincinnati embalming school, and was the first to practice that science in this city. Mr. Peacock has one of the largest establishments in the city, and always keeps on hand a full line of coffins and caskets of the most approved style and make, as well as everything else connected with the trade. Mr. Peacock is a native of England, having been born at Leeds in 1847. He came with his parents to this country in 1850, and later to Milwaukee in 1853, being one of the old settlers. He is a gentleman of the highest practical business experience in his profession and well adapted to his business. Carriages, flowers, hearses, shrouds, etc., furnished on application. His residence being over his place of business, renders night calls sure of prompt attendance. He is president of the Wisconsin Undertakers' Association and was also president of the city and county Undertakers' Association until a year ago last September, when he resigned, and about the same time he was elected one of the vice-presidents of the United States Undertakers' Association which met in Chicago.

Mr. Peacock has lately fitted up beautiful parlors where strangers in the city can hold services over their dead, and also nice waiting rooms for visitors or strangers in the city.

H. H. MARTIN & CO.,

Manufacturing Jewelers and Watchmakers.

410 Chestnut Street.

IN 1882 H. H. Martin & Co. opened, at No. 410 Chestnut street, an establishment which is certainly one of the neatest and best arranged in this or any other city. They are manufacturing jewelers and watchmakers, and carry everything usually found in a place of this kind. There are watches, clocks, rings, pins, bracelets, lockets, chains, and things of that description in endless variety. The Elgin and several other equally popular kinds of watches are kept in stock and sold as low as at any other reliable house. Mr. H. H. Martin was born in Milwaukee in 1858, and his partner, Mr. A. Hassman, was born here also and about the same time. Though young in years, comparatively, they are old in experience and in knowledge of their business.

MRS. M. JACOBI,

Dealer in Embroideries and Fancy Goods, etc.

125 Grand Avenue.

THE Ladies' Bazaar at 125 Grand avenue is so well and favorably known to all devotees of fashion, that an extended description is unnecessary. Mrs. M. Jacobi is proprietress, and has had charge of the business for over four years. The store is centrally located and is 25x40 in dimensions. Mrs. Jacobi deals in embroideries and fancy goods. The specialty of the firm is art embroidery, which is taught in large classes throughout the city, and proves the means of popularizing the "Bazaar." Mrs. Jacobi employs the assistance of four skilled art-workers, besides giving out employment to various parties in the city.

F. W. SCHNECK,
General House Furnisher.
255 and 257 Third Street.

THE career of the subject of this sketch is a fitting illustration of one of the many cases of success wherein the son has followed in the footsteps of the father. The business conducted by Mr. Schneck is one of the most extensive of its kind in the city, complete in all its

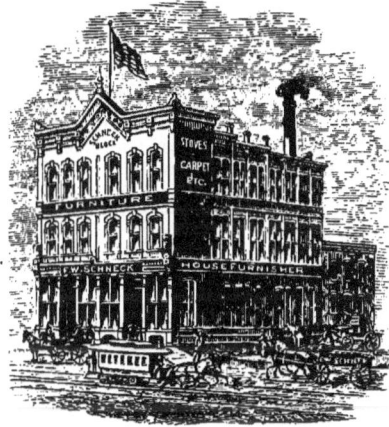

details, and managed in every way in a strict business manner. The establishment was originally founded by Jacob Schneck, the father of the present proprietor, in the year 1842. The father was a native of Germany, but the son was born in Milwaukee. Jacob Schneck first purchased the lot, which is 50x150 feet in dimensions, and erected two frame structures, in one of which he carried on the business. These were afterwards moved back on the rear part of his premises and the site was rebuilt, consist-

ing of a four-story tenement house, the ground floor being devoted to business —one occupied by the owner. At that time this building was considered one of the largest on the north side of what was then known as Spring street—now the beautiful Grand avenue. In the year 1868, Mr. Schneck found his business of too great a magnitude for himself, and he associated with him his two sons, F. W. Schneck and John Schneck. In 1874, Jacob, the father, retired, leaving the two boys to the continuance of what proved to be a very successful course. In 1881, the two brothers dissolved their co-partnership, dividing the stock and real estate. During the same year they razed the monument of their father's labor, and each, upon his respective property, erected an emblem of his own honesty and ability. The gentleman with whom we are now concerned is one of the young business men of our city. He has on hand an average stock of $15,000 and upwards, and the yearly sales amount to about $50,000. He has just constructed upon the West Side a residence worth $7,000. The building erected and occupied by him is twenty-five feet front and one hundred and fifty feet in depth, consisting of three stories and basement, the latter being used as the stove department, the first floor for second-hand furniture and for crockery; upon the second elevation is kept new furniture and carpeting, and the third floor is used for storage. Altogether, the establishment of F. W. Schneck is one of the representative ones of the Cream City.

HOFFMANN & BAUR,
Tin, Copper and Sheet Iron Workers.
146 Clinton Street.

AMONG those industries contingent upon, or springing from the iron trade, may be classed the enterprise of Messrs. Hoffman & Baur, tin, copper and sheet iron workers. Their office and factory is located at No. 146 Clinton street. The business was established seven years ago by Kleser & Hoffmann, and two years ago the present firm was organized. Six skillful and experienced workmen are constantly employed in the various branches of this business. Special attention is given to tin jobbing and furnace work, while their mill buckets and elevator work has a fine reputation. All class of copper, tin and sheet-iron work is done in a prompt and most satisfactory manner, and at moderate prices. Specimens of work performed by this firm are found throughout the entire city and surrounding country, and the business aggregates over $12,000 a year. Both members of the firm are natives of this city, and recognized as business men of merit and ability.

G. W. WALTERS,

Dealer in Family and Fancy Groceries.

657 Jackson Street.

THIS gentleman has a good stand for the grocery business at No. 657 Jackson street, and it is pleasing to note that his business is rapidly increasing. He opened the place in November, 1884, and the business, which was fair at once, has shown a steady increase ever since. He carries a full line of fancy and family groceries, keeps all the choicest fresh fruits and vegetables in their season, and, in fact, has as complete and as attractive a store of the kind as can be found in the city. Mr. Walters is a native of the good old State of Virginia, where he was born in 1846, and has resided in Milwaukee about ten years. Like every other man and boy in the South at that time, Mr. Walters was in the Confederate army, and saw a great deal of hard service.

THEODORE GROSSKOPF,

Importing Wine Merchant, Cigars, etc.

107 Grand Avenue.

ONE of the noted importing houses of wines and cigars in the city is that of Theodore Grosskopf, at No. 107 Grand avenue. Although he has been deceased for over ten years, the business has been ably conducted by his wife. This house imports direct from Cuba the best of Havana cigars, while their liquors consist of the best brands. A large stock of the best Kentucky and Pennsylvania whiskies are also kept on hand. Some of the oldest Port and Madeira are found among the selections. This house takes great pains in choosing its stock of goods which has given it a standard name in the trade.

H. J. BAUMGAERTNER,

Sign Painter.

66 Wisconsin Street.

MR. Baumgaertner occupies a high position among the representative artists of this class, and is the only painter in the city who does exclusive sign painting. This he does in first-class style, and includes all the various kinds, such as gilt-glass signs, silk and cloth banners, and everything in the way of fancy painting. He employs several skilled workmen who are adepts at the brush, and is kept continually busy. Mr. Baumgaertner is a native of Germany, but has resided in this city since 1852, and is highly respected among all classes, and has been alderman from the Tenth Ward for the past six years, and has just been re-elected for another term of three years. He has been president of the Council for two years, and in that capacity won golden opinions for the just and upright manner in which he conducted the details of business.

PETER GOEBEL,

Manufacturer and Dealer in Tobacco, Snuff and Smokers' Articles.

55 Oneida Street.

TO be a good cigarmaker one must have had years of practical experience at the business. The "P. G." and "High Life" brands of cigars made by Mr. Goebel have been long before the public as candidates for favor

INDUSTRIAL HISTORY OF MILWAUKEE. 171

and have met with unqualified success. He deals mostly in imported goods, the best quality of his material coming from Havana. Mr. Goebel established this business in 1865, at his present location. He was born in Germany in 1834, and came direct from thence to Milwaukee in 1845. During his long residence he has gained the confidence of the public by his straightforward dealings and strict integrity. His business is steadily increasing as his goods continue to attract attention, and have gained a leading place among the first ranks of standard brands.

TSCHANK'S,

Ladies' and Gent's Restaurant.

138 Grand Avenue.

TSCHANK'S Ladies' and Gents' Oyster Parlor and Restaurant at 138 Grand avenue, northeast corner Second street, is one of the most popular enterprises of this kind in the city. It is open day and night, and being centrally located is serviceable to those whose occupation keeps them late down town. This restaurant was established in 1879 at his present quarters. The restaurant is conducted entirely on the European plan, so that a meal can be procured at any price desired. The genial proprietor and manager attends personally to all the little details of his business, and places before his customers nothing but the very best in the market. He employs from eight to ten persons to assist him in the business, which averages throughout the year 250 persons a day.

SULLIVAN, HAUF & CO.,

Champion Horseshoers.

110 and 112 Clybourn Street.

THE champion horseshoeing establishment of this city is that of Sullivan, Hauf & Co., at 112 Clybourn street, where it has been located since 1865, although the present firm has only been organized a few years. Mr. W. H. Sullivan, the head of the firm, commenced the business in the year stated, and so proficient has he become in the business, that he is the acknowledged champion of horseshoers, which title he has successfully held for years, and in all contests for supremacy has met with signal victories. The shop is 20x80 feet in dimensions, with three forges in use, and four men employed to meet the demands of the trade. Mr. Sullivan has won his reputation by close study of horses and persistent application to every feature of his trade. Mr. Sullivan treats all ailments, such as flat feet, quarter cracks, split feet, seedy toes, lamanites, stumbling, forging, cutting corns, bruised heels, sore tendons, knee-sprung, etc. He has published a very neat and attractive circular to horse owners, setting forth some ideas of practical utility, which is valuable for all horsemen to possess.

W. D. BROCK,

Manufacturer of Hydraulic, Steam and Hand-Power Elevators.

Corner Clybourn and Third Sts.

ONE of the leading manufacturers in Milwaukee of hydraulic, steam and hand-power elevators is Mr. W. D. Brock, whose establishment is situated at 219, 221, 223 Clybourn street. For a number of years this gentleman has been engaged in constructing and perfecting what is known as Brock's Safety Worm-geared Elevators, for use in stores, warehouses, factories, etc., and it has the reputation of being the best elevator in use for the purpose for which it is intended. Mr. Brock also manufactures spur-geared factory elevators, and deals extensively in wire rope. He had patented in July, 1884, the friction-clutch pulley, for use on all elevators. Twenty-five skilled workmen are constantly employed in the several departments, and the aggregate sales are upwards of $100,000 a year. The erection of elevators by this firm extends throughout all parts of the Northwest, and from a small beginning but a few years ago, has grown to be one of the important industries of the Cream City. Mr. Brock's native State is Illinois, and he came to Milwaukee in 1872, associating himself with the business interests of this city.

F. P. ADLER,

Dealer in Fine Confectionery, Fruits, etc.

250 West Water Street.

ONE of the most enterprising firms on this thoroughfare is that of F. P. Adler. He began business at his present site in 1873, but with only about one-fourth the room he now occupies. Mr. Adler keeps as varied and complete a stock as may be found in the city, and his numerous customers always find him ready for any emergency. The specialty of this house is the manufacture of ice cream, and last season the production of this article was over 2,000 gallons. His ice cream parlors are attractively fitted up in the latest style and complete throughout. The aggregate sales are over $12,000 per year, and the business is widening and extending itself rapidly. Mr. F. P. Adler was born in Germany, but came to Milwaukee with his parents when he was only four years old.

CHAS. H. CLARKE,

Letter Cutter, Engraver and Die Sinker.

Cor. East Water and Wisconsin Streets.

MR. CLARKE is most successful in this line of business, and has added to his facilities in order to supply the increased demands, until it has grown to large proportions, and extends throughout the entire country. He was born in Boston in 1835 and resided there until the breaking out of the civil war. He served three months in the Union army as adjutant, and was a participant in the disastrous battle of Bull Run. In 1862 he came to this city and opened up in his present quarters, at the corner of East Water and Wisconsin streets. He manufactures marking plates, rubber stamps, seals, burning brands, advertising plates, flour brands, steel letters and figures, badges, door plates, checks, type, stencil dies, outfits, etc. He has invented a changeable rubber stamp that works to perfection. It is so arranged that letters can be taken out, and others substituted, such as changing an address or name. The patent is now pending. Mr. Clarke is president of the Wisconsin State Musical Association, and in that capacity has a large acquaintance throughout the State.

J. JOSTEN,

House and Sign Painter.

209 Second Street.

ONE of the first-class shops on the West Side at which to get any kind of work in this line done neatly and expeditiously, is that at No. 209 Second street. The business was established in 1882 and has met with very great success, attributable to the personal attention and ability of Mr. J. Josten, the proprietor. Prompt attention is given to the filling of all orders in the line of house and sign painting, graining, glazing, calcimining and paper-hanging. Fourteen to eighteen skilled journeymen are employed during the season, with competent foremen, to meet the wants of this trade. This house is every way worthy the success which it has achieved. Mr. Josten was born in Milwaukee, learning and pursuing his trade here.

GEO. HAYS,

Proprietor Second Street Planing Mill and Box Factory.

Nos. 145 and 147 Second Street.

THIS business was established at its present quarters, 145 and 147. Second street, some twenty years ago. After passing through various hands, it was taken charge of by Mr. Hays, in 1870. The premises occupied are central and commodious, having a frontage of 100 feet on Second street, with a depth of 150 feet. This establishment is known as the Second Street Planing Mill and Box Factory, doing all kinds of turning, planing, re-sawing and scroll-sawing, besides manufacturing all styles of boxes for tea caddies and packing boxes of every description. Banisters and newel posts constantly on hand, and stair railing made to order. Constant employment is given to twelve men; the force is greatly increased during the busy season. The machinery consists of two planers, two cross-cut, one scroll and one band-saw, all of which are run by a 35 horse-power engine. Mr. Hays is a native of the North of Ireland, and came to Milwaukee in 1865. He is a thoroughly practical business man, fully acquainted with every detail of his successful and growing trade.

WM. BOYLE,
Practical Horseshoer.
49 Second Street.

MR. Wm. Boyle commenced business for himself in this line in 1875, at 123 Clybourn street, where he remained for eight years. Increase of business enabled him to erect a fine, commodious brick shop, 25x75 feet in dimensions, at 49 Second street, where he enjoys the reputation he has acquired in his trade in a large patronage. He employs five or six hands to assist him with his work, and three forges are kept running constantly. Mr. Boyle is a native of Wisconsin, and came to this city in 1865, since which time he has been connected in various ways with this branch of business. He is known by all as a straightforward, experienced workman, an honor to his trade, and worthy the liberal patronage he receives.

HENRY W. MOTT,
Druggist.
138 Grand Avenue, Corner Second Street.

ONE of the neatest and most attractive stores in this line on the West Side is that of Henry W. Mott, 138 Grand avenue. He occupies a large and handsome store, 22x75 feet in dimensions, which is tastefully fitted up and presents an attractive appearance. He carries a large and well-selected stock, averaging $5,000 in value, consisting of pure drugs and medicines, all popular and reliable patent preparations, chemicals, surgical instruments, toilet and fancy articles, perfumery, druggists' sundries, and all such goods as are to be found in well-conducted establishments of this kind. The store is admirably located, and is doing an annual business of upwards of $10,000, and it is rapidly increasing. Mr. Mott is a thoroughly skilled and practical druggist and pharmacist, and bestows his personal attention on his large and growing prescription trade.

Mr. Mott is a native of New York State, and came west to Wisconsin in 1865. He entered the First New York Light Artillery, Battery D, serving two years and ten months in the Army of the Potomac.

CLEMENTS BROTHERS,
Practical Steam-Heating and Ventilating Engineers.
445 Jefferson Street.

IN this climate the people must have their houses comfortable and well-warmed in the winter, and the skilled services of men like the Clements Bros. are, therefore, in constant requisition. That they understand their business thoroughly is shown by the fact that the heating apparatus in the splendid new Chapman building came from their establishment, as did the apparatus in the Northwestern Insurance building, and in many other similar structures here and elsewhere. The brothers were born in Scotland, where they received the best mechanical education the best schools of the land afforded. They came to Milwaukee in 1878, and were for a time interested in the management of the steam heating company then in operation here. They have all the work they can attend to, not only in the city, but also throughout the cities and the larger towns of Wisconsin and of Michigan. They are agents for Bates' patent self-feeding boiler for low pressure. Negotiations for work to be done can be arranged by mail or by calling in person at their place of business.

DR. FRED. S. HADLEY,
Dentist.
Corner Milwaukee and Mason Streets.

OF all the neat and well arranged dental parlors of this city, for light, ventilation and location, those of Fred. S. Hadley, in the new and elegant Colby & Abbot Block—room 54—are among the most attractive. Although a young man, he has by skillful operations and prompt attention established a reputation and practice of no small proportions. He makes no specialty of any particular branch of his profession. Dr. Hadley is a graduate from the dental department of the State University of Michigan, situated at Ann Arbor. He is fast advancing towards the front rank of his chosen profession, and it is easy to predict for him great success.

J. LANGENBERGER,
Contractor and Builder.
146 Third Street.

AMONG the most extensive contractors and builders in this city is J. Langenberger, whose large and commodious shop is situated in the rear of 146 Third street and 217 Grand avenue. This business was started over thirty years ago, and in 1874 the present proprietor took charge of the business. Mr. Langenberger constantly employs upwards of twenty-five hands, and sometimes has as high as seventy-five men on his pay-roll. He is constantly engaged in large building contracts throughout the city and country. A 20-horse-power engine is used at the shop to run the necessary machinery for the business. All work turned out is first-class in every particular, and entire satisfaction is guaranteed. Mr. Langenberger received the contract for the carpenter work on the Exposition Building, Conro Block, Evening Wisconsin, and is just finishing the Light Horse Squadron's New Armory. He is a native of Bavaria, and came to this city in 1846. He is a practical mechanic and possesses good business qualifications, which have added so materially to his success.

C. W. ST. JOHN,
R. R. Employment Agency.
Corner East Water and Mason Streets.

AN employment agency is a necessity in a city the size of Milwaukee. There are times when a large force of men are needed for some particular work, and the most ready way to procure them is through an agency, whose business it is to keep posted in that respect. For the past six years Mr. St. John has been in this business at his present location, and has found employment for thousands of people. His chief line is the employment of railroad laborers for the South and West, and yearly furnishes these companies, on an average, twenty-five hundred men. He is a native of Milwaukee, having been born in this city in 1849, and is well-known for his enterprising and persevering character. He can be found at his place of business, always ready to transact any business in his line.

H. WEDEN,
House and Sign Painter, Dealer in Wall Paper and Window Shades.
601 Jackson Street.

THE neat, attractive business appearance of the place makes you feel at once that Mr. H. Weden, at No. 601 Jackson street, is capable of doing first-class work in his line, which is painting, glazing, paper-hanging and fresco-painting, and that his large force of skilled assistants must be kept pretty busy throughout the house-building and house-renovating season. The salesroom, office and paper department is large and airy and well lighted, being 22x40 feet in extent. The basement is used as a paint-shop, and it is there that the fine sign and other ornamental painting is done. Mr. Weden carries one of the finest stocks of paper in the city, and gets his supplies largely from the East—from Philadelphia and New York. His paints he buys mostly in Chicago and in this city.

Among the many residences and other buildings in this city on which Mr. Weden did the painting and glazing may be mentioned the First Ward School building, St. Mary's Day School, the Effingham residence on Grand avenue, the Campbell residence on Twenty-fourth street, Judge Mallory's house, the houses of A. E. Inbusch, of Mr. Benjamin, of Edwin Reynolds, of C. H. O'Neill and of P. B. Mann. Mr. Weden was born in Germany in 1848, and came to Milwaukee in 1854. He has resided here ever since.

PETER EHR,

Custom Tailor.

No. 393 Broadway.

THE above is an old established business, and dates its inception from 1861, Mr. Ehr becoming proprietor in 1881. He does all kinds of custom tailoring, but makes a specialty of the repairing of clothing, and has built up a large business in this branch of the trade, and employs three practical assistants in the work. He was born in Prussia, Germany, in 1862, and was brought by his parents to this country the same year, settling in Columbia county. He came to Milwaukee in 1870, and has since resided here. He turns out work of the first quality, and guarantees satisfaction.

J. T. WALLIS,

Manufacturer and Dealer in Harness, Saddles, Bridles, etc.

290 and 292 Broadway.

THE above is one of the oldest establishments of the kind in the city, having been founded by its present proprietor in 1845. It was started on rather a small scale, but has increased steadily with the growth of the city. Mr. Wallis manufactures harnesses and trunks, and carries a stock of about $3,000, and his annual sales reach nearly $15,000. Having had forty years' experience in the trade, he is thoroughly adapted to his business, and this is probably the reason of his uniform success. At his salesrooms can be found a most complete stock of trunks, valises, harnesses, whips, robes, saddles, bridles, collars, etc., all exhibiting superior workmanship. Mr. Wallis was born in England in 1827, and came to this city in 1844, since which time he has been actively and prominently identified with the business interests of our city.

GRAND AVENUE HOTEL,

H. M. Merryman, Proprietor.

909 Grand Avenue.

THE best family hotel in Milwaukee is the Grand Avenue House, between Ninth and Tenth streets. Mr. H. M. Merryman is proprietor, and adds the two needful things—able management and courteous attention—which renders this house so popular to pleasure-seekers, and those desiring large and pleasant quarters away from the noise and bustle of business. The location is all that could be desired—at the center of the widest part of the avenue, through which the monument-park runs. The hotel site covers an area of 180 by 200 feet, and is just opposite the palatial residence and grounds of Hon. Alex. Mitchell. The house is commodious and attractive, and contains all the modern improvements for the comfort and safety of the many guests. The parlors are tastefully furnished, and the guest-chambers elegant and comfortable. The dining-room is large, well ventilated, and its tables admirably arranged, and the bill of fare could not be improved. Throughout the house everything is done to transform hotel life into home ease without its care. Summer guests enjoy spacious apartments, wide halls, the freedom of parlors, broad verandas, and elegant lawns. Street cars pass the door every few minutes, thus enabling guests to conveniently reach the center of the city, depots, and the various places of amusement. Mr. Merryman is a native of

Maine and has resided here since 1879, and has thoroughly identified himself with this city and her interests, and spares neither time, money nor pains to make all who seek the Grand Avenue Hotel as comfortable as possible.

FRED. ZANDER,

Undertaker and Dealer in Coffins, Caskets, etc.

509 Broadway and 482 Eleventh Street.

FRED. Zander, the undertaker, at No. 509 Broadway, has carried on the business in this city since 1840; first on Martin street and then on East Water, and then in the fine new quarters occupied to-day. He has also a branch establishment at No. 482 Eleventh street, with a large, well-stocked livery stable in the rear. Mr. Zander's father was the first undertaker in Milwaukee. He deals in coffins, caskets, shrouds and habits, and has some of the finest hearses and carriages in the city. Carriages for parties and weddings are also furnished, and all orders receive prompt attention. Math. Franzen is the embalmer of the establishment, and has been with Mr. Zander seventeen years. He is thoroughly skilled in his work, and gives satisfaction in every case entrusted to his care. Mr. Zander is a gentleman so well fitted for his work naturally, that "the right man in the right place" may be truthfully said of him.

J. BINNEY,

Agent for Platt & Company's Baltimore Oysters.

310 East Water Street.

THE house of Platt & Co., of Baltimore, Md., ranks among the foremost establishments of this kind in the United States. Their business covers the whole range of oyster, fruit and vegetable packing, and their goods are sold in every quarter of the civilized world. The transactions of this firm are enormous, and constitute an important element in the packing trade of the United States. Mr. J. Binney is their agent at this place, and does a wholesale trade through Wisconsin, Michigan, Iowa and Minnesota. He established the business in 1874, and since that time his business has more than quadrupled, his sales last year amounting to $40,000. A specialty is made of the famous "Tiger" brand of oysters, which have been favorites of long standing with epicures all over the country. They are selected with the greatest care, and are unsurpassed for size and flavor. Mr. Binney occupies premises at No. 310 East Water street. He is a native of Boston, and was born in 1835, and came to this city in 1857.

GEO. E. POTTER,

Livery, Boarding and Sale Stable.

100 Detroit Street.

THE building occupied by Mr. Potter is two stories in height, and is well fitted with all the modern conveniences. He has some most elegant turn-outs, which are furnished with or without drivers, at reasonable rates. Every step to insure the comfort of patrons is taken. The stable, although recently established, has built up a good business on a solid foundation and its success is assured. The proprietor, Mr. Geo. E. Potter, is a native of this city, and was born in 1864. He takes horses to board by the day, week or month, and has a number of fine horses in connection with the establishment, and is always prepared to suit customers in every instance.

GURNEY BRICK MACHINE WORKS,

T. C. Gurney, Proprietor.

97 Wisconsin Street.

THE Gurney Brick Machine was invented by Gaylord Martin, and patented in 1883 by T. C. Gurney, since which time some important improvements have been added, on which a patent has been granted during the present year. It is now considered the most perfect brick machine in use, having been gotten up under the supervision of Mr. Martin, who is a practical brick-maker, and knows the wants of manufacturers.

Mr. Gurney, the proprietor, has been connected with the manufacture of brick machines for a number of years, having given a good deal of attention to the matter, and has examined the machinery in use both in the East and West, and has visited the large yards where the brick are manufactured in all the large cities of the Union. The Gurney machine has been a development from stage to stage of improvement, till it has grown into a machine which will work any clay and meet the wants of any locality.

Lumps of clay and stones this machine disposes of in short order by means of crushers, which are inside of the machine.

Mr. Gurney is a native of Western New York, but has been a resident of this city over thirty years, during which time he has been connected with her manufacturing interests.

SPENCERIAN BUSINESS COLLEGE.

CORNER WISCONSIN ST. AND BROADWAY.

Established 1863.

FOR almost a quarter of a century the "Spencerian Business College" has been in successful operation under the direct management of Robert C. Spencer, son of Platt R. Spencer, founder of the Spencerian system of penmanship. The efficient corps of able instructors in the various departments of this school give the pupils thorough drill in all the studies pursued.

The design of this Institution is to qualify youth and middle-aged men and women to transact business intelligently, honorably and successfully for themselves or others.

The Spencerian Business College makes a specialty of business education, to which it confines itself, and for which it affords to both sexes superior advantages.

The experience of its thousands of students in the various departments of private and public life, has proven beyond question the efficiency and value of its instruction and training.

This College aims to develop business talents, awaken and direct business energies, inculcate sound business principles, cultivate the best business qualities and character, and lay the foundation of practical usefulness in the business acquirements, habits, and thoughts of young people.

The benefits arising from the teaching, training and influence of the Spencerian Business College, are equally important to all classes. They tend greatly to improve the condition and prospects of those who are dependent upon their own exertions, by furnishing them the means of earning a living and gaining a competence. They also afford the best safeguards against losses and reverses of fortune, so liable to overtake those whose business education is defective. They enhance the prosperity of individuals and communities, and avert evils and misfortunes arising from ignorance and inefficiency in business affairs.

The *course of study* in the Spencerian Business College meets the requirements of business life by the combination, adaptation and practical application of the following, viz: 1. *Book-keeping and Business*. 2. *Business Writing*. 3. *Business Arithmetic*. 4. *Commercial Law*. 5. *Civil Government*. 6. *Business Practice*. 7. *Banks and Banking*. 8. *Office Work*.

The foregoing furnishes a fair outline of the design, claims, scope and methods of the Spencerian Business College, as at present conducted. They are accepted and approved by the better judgment and progressive sentiment of the business community to which they appeal.

The students and graduates of the Spencerian Business College during the past twenty years and more, numbering many thousands, have been absorbed into the business life of all portions of our own and foreign countries, and constitute a body of useful, honorable and sterling men and women, inferior to none. In fact, they comprise a most enterprising, able and influential body of people whose average prosperity is greater than that of any other equal number of persons, due largely to the benefits derived from the education and training received in the Spencerian Business College, Milwaukee, Wis., where students are received any time.

JAMES MORGAN,

Importer and Dealer in Dry Goods, Millinery, etc.

386 and 388 East Water Street.

ONE of the largest wholesale and retail dry goods and millinery establishments in this city is that of Jas. Morgan, located at Nos. 386 and 388 East Water street. The business was established in 1874 in a comparatively small

way, having a force of less than a dozen people, but now upwards of 200 persons are constantly employed, and the trade extends all over the Northwest. The location is in the most central portion of the city, and easily reached by the three lines of street railways from the depots, steamboat wharves, and all parts of the city. The building is four stories in height, with a large basement, all the floors having dimensions of 40x150 feet. Here is made as fine a display of dress goods, cloaks, shawls, flannels, curtain laces, blankets, shoes and millinery as can be found in the Northwest. A special feature is the perfect lighting and ventilation, beside the perfect mode of transit from one floor to another by means of the large passenger elevator. Mr. Morgan's maxim in business has always been to sell the best materials at popular prices and not to keep any old stock on hand. His special, season and remnant sales draw large crowds and meet with great favor from the shopping public. He gives his close personal attention to every feature of his large business, and is ably assisted by his brother Thomas, who entered the establishment in 1874. Mr. James Morgan is a native of Perthshire, Scotland, and came to this country in 1863, but followed the dry goods business in Illinois for ten years before coming to Milwaukee, and is closely related with every enterprise that adds to our city's advancement. Mr. Thomas Morgan is also a native of Scotland, and came direct to Milwaukee in 1874, since which time he has had charge of the financial department of this large establishment.

RUNDLE, SPENCE & CO.

Nos. 63 and 65 Second Street.

THIS business was established in a general way by the senior member of the firm, J. P. Rundle, on Milwaukee street, in 1867, and is one of the most prominent houses in this line in the Northwest. In 1870 Mr. T. Spence was admitted as partner, and in 1881 the present company was organized by the addition of Mr. E. C. Smith. The firm occupy a five-story brick building, which they own, on Second street, between Clybourn and Fowler streets. The structure has ground dimensions of 50x150 feet, and cost about $20,000. The basement and first and second stories are used as a store, in which the large wholesale business of the firm is conducted. The third floor is fitted up as a brass and iron finishing shop; the fourth floor as a brass foundry and the fifth floor as an iron foundry. The firm manufacture all kinds of brass and iron goods for plumbers, steam and gas-fitters. Their trade extends to almost every State in the Union, but is principally confined to the Northern and Western States, and is steadily increasing. They employ from 100 to 150 experienced workmen for the various departments of their establishment, and traveling men are kept constantly on the road. This establishment has machinery of the latest device for their use, and is run by a fifty-horse power engine. Mr. J. P. Rundle is a native of the State of Connetticut, born at Hartford in 1842. He came to Milwaukee in 1858, and has ever been connected with the commercial interests of this city. Both Mr. Spence and Mr. Smith are natives of Milwaukee and are widely known as pushing business men.

WM. ROHLFING & CO.,
Milwaukee's Largest Music House.
Cor. Broadway and Mason St.

ONE of the largest and most popular musical emporiums, not only in this city, but in the Northwest, is that of Wm.

Rohlfing & Co., on the corner of Broadway and Mason street, extending from Nos. 102 to 110 Mason street. This house was established in Milwaukee in 1878, and has a trade which extends over all parts of the Northwest. The leading pianos manufactured are sold by this firm, the Steinway and Knabe being their specialties. Organs, too, are handled in large variety and sold at prices and on terms not easily duplicated. Their large stock of sheet music and musical merchandise is complete in every respect. Importing of foreign music is their specialty in this line, and they are agents for the United States for several European music publishing houses. They are also publishers of the prize cantata—"Columbus," for which Mr. John Plankinton donated $1,000, and which was awarded by the judges, Prof. E. Catenhusen, Dr. F. L. Ritter and Dr. L. Maas, to Mr. C. Joseph Brambach, musical director at Bonn on the Rhine. It was chosen from forty competing composers from all parts of the world, and will be sung at the 24th National Sängerfest to be held in this city next July, from the 21st to the 25th. Wm. Rohlfing, the enterprising head of this establishment, was born in Quackenbruck, Province of Hanover, Germany, December 17th, 1830. He came to America in 1852, after having acquired a thorough knowledge of the business in the extensive piano manufactory of his father. He immediately entered the house of Wm. Knabe & Co., of Baltimore, where he remained for twenty years, and where he achieved such remarkable success in his chosen line. He came to Milwaukee in May, 1878, and began business in a small way, but through his energy and experience it soon developed into the large establishment we see to-day. He is ably assisted by his three sons, who are a tower of strength to this enterprise. The great secret of this firm's prosperity is due largely to the fact that they are practical piano makers and can thus judge of the quality of the instruments which they handle, giving their customers the benefit of this experience. The firm consists of Mr. Wm. Rohlfing and his three sons, Wm. Rohlfing, Jr., Charles and Albert. They are all practical musicians, having been brought up in the business under the tutelage of their father, who is acknowledged to be the best judge of musical merchandise in the country. This firm has long been highly esteemed by the musical circles of the country, the latest compliment being their representation in the leading committees of the Sängerfest which is to be held in this city next July.

JOHN ESCH & SON,
Manufacturers of Esch's Patent Platform Truck.
58 and 60 Second Street.

WE call attention to the patent platform truck of John Esch & Son, which to-day stands without a rival, and is the best, strongest, easiest handled and most convenient of any in the market. This truck fills a want long felt, doing away with the reach, enabling the driver to safely make a short turn. Can be built with either thimble-skein or iron axle. The above cut fully represents the truck. Parties wishing to manufacture trucks with patent improvements, on royalty, will, for terms, etc., please address the above firm. The following parties are using these trucks in Milwaukee, to whom reference can be made as to utility and general practical value: John Plankinton & Co., packers; Layton & Co., packers; Ph. Best Brewing Co.; Board of Public Works city of Milwaukee, for sprinkling wagons, now using twenty; Milwaukee Harvester Co., Hoffmann & Billings Mfg. Co., Shadbolt, Boyd & Co., Suelflohn & Seefeld, and many others.

FLINT & PERE MARQUETTE R. R.
L. C. Whitney, General Western Agent,
Milwaukee, Wis.

THE Flint & Pere Marquette Railroad and Steamboat Line is becoming the most popular passenger and freight route between this city, Ludington, Manistee, and all Eastern points. The large and magnificent steamers of this line, Nos. 1 and 2, were built expressly for this Company, the cut on the inside front cover being an exact representation of these steamers as taken from the official draft. They are new and well arranged for the accommodation of passengers. One of these steamers leaves Milwaukee every evening, except Saturday, at 8:15 o'clock, from their dock on West Water Street, west end of Buffalo Street Bridge, arrives at Ludington at 5 A. M., and at Manistee at 8 A. M., connecting with the steamer Geo. D. Sanford, Jr., for Frankfort, and at Ludington with the fast day express for the East. This is the only direct line to Saginaw, Bay City and Toledo, and its steamers are the strongest, safest and newest on the lakes, of about 1,000 tons burden each. This line was established in this city about three years ago, Mr. A. Patriarche being General Western agent then, but about two years ago he resigned and Mr. L. C. Whitney, the present General Western Agent, took charge of the business and by his liberal policy and perseverance, has built up a first-class business for this line. The boats run winter and summer, and have been very successful thus far.

Mr. Whitney is a native of N. Y. State, but has been in the service of the F. & P. M. R. R. Co. for seventeen years.

ORMSBY LIME COMPANY,
Manufacturers and Jobbers of Lime.
395 East Water Street.

AN important branch of commercial activity, and one of the leading business interests of Milwaukee, is that of the "Ormsby Lime Company," with works at Grafton, Hayton and Brillion, this State, and headquarters at No. 395 East Water street. The business was established, with only four small kilns, in 1876, by the present company, which has at its head the following officers: J. W. Ormsby, president; O. W. Robertson, secretary and treasurer, and George Nicholson, Jr., superintendent of the works. The entire plant of the company, including their timber lands, consists of over 600 acres. The Grafton plant is twenty-five miles, and the two at Hayton are seventy-seven miles from Milwaukee, on the M. & N. R. R., while those at Brillion are on the M., L. S. & W., just 100 miles north of here. Their plant consists now of eighteen large kilns, which give them a capacity of turning out 2,200 barrels per day. They employ all the way from 100 to 250 men, according to the season of the year. In 1885 they manufactured 218,000 barrels of lime, shipping nearly 2,000 carloads to different parts of the country. Two large steam Ingersoll rock drills are used at these works to facilitate operations, and upwards of 500 cars of supplies and material were received at their works during the year. This company are proprietors of "The Ormsby Patent Lime Bin," which preserves lime from air slaking. They also have a patent process for preserving bulk lime from air-slaking while in transit, a necessary feature in transportation to long distances. We call special attention of the trade and of consumers of lime in general to the statement of the chemical analysis of their Brillion and Hayton limestones, which is submitted as *the only correct and scientific test of quality*. This analysis shows that their Hayton lime is nearly ninety-nine per cent. pure, while their Brillion lime is *over* ninety-nine per cent. pure. This fact places the Ormsby lime at the head of all other limes produced in the Northwest, and consumers can feel perfectly confident in its working qualities for stone and brick work, and especially for *fine white finishing*. It is only just to say, in conclusion, that under its present able management this company is certain to retain the ascendency in the future which it has acquired in the past, and that it will continue to exert a healthy influence among the important industries of this city's commerce.

MILWAUKEE SCHOOL OF MUSIC,
John C. Fillmore, Director.
Corner Milwaukee and Mason Sts.

THIS school is most centrally located in the imposing and handsome Colby & Abbot building, on the corner of Mason and Milwaukee streets. This institution was founded in the beginning of 1884 by the present director, Prof. John C. Fillmore, and immediately met with favor from the music-loving people of Milwaukee and the State. This school gives first-class instruction in all departments at the lowest prices. The special results aimed at are to secure in its pupils: a solid, well-grounded technic; musical intelligence, and artistic interpretation. The general plan of the school is that of the famous conservatories of Europe and America, and looks toward producing intelligent musicians of broad culture, as well as skillful executants. Special attention is paid to the elementary instruction of children in playing the pianoforte. They will be taught in classes of *four*, and will receive three lessons, forty minutes in length, every week. One feature of this school is the concerts—six in number—given during the year by the pupils and teachers. They are well attended and highly appreciated by the musical circles of the city. The instructors are: John C. Fillmore, pianoforte, organ, theory (harmony, part writing, counterpoint, form and composition), and history of music; Max L. Laue, vocal culture, Italian, German and English singing; C. G. Muskat, violin playing; Cornelia T. Stayner and Anna R. Robinson, pianoforte (primary department); Ernst Beyer, violoncello; N. D. W. Ainsworth, flute (Boehm and common); J. B. Hoffmann, guitar, cornet and all brass orchestral instruments; P. Chapek, clarinet; H. W. Mueller, zither. Prof. Fillmore is a graduate of Oberlin College, Ohio, and has also spent two years at Leipzig, Germany, making a specialty of theory, under Prof. Richter. Prof. Fillmore is well known to the music world as the author of "The History of Pianoforte Music," with biographical sketches and critical estimates of its greatest masters. It is a 12mo. volume of 245 pages, bound in cloth and costs $1.50. All information regarding this work, or terms of tuition and calendar of school will be freely and gladly given by calling on or addressing Prof. John C. Fillmore.

MILWAUKEE TYPE AND ELECTROTYPE FOUNDRY,

Francis Keehn, Proprietor.

128 Second Street.

MR. Keehn founded this establishment in 1869 and has since been sole proprietor. He commenced business in a moderate way at 416 East Water street, where he remained for about four years, when he moved to his present location, 128 Second street. The dimensions of the foundry are 35x50 feet, in the fore part of which he has fitted up a salesroom. Two machines are run and six to eight hands employed. His specialty is in manufacturing newspaper type of the very best quality, though he is besides a dealer in all kinds of printers' material, and can furnish, on short notice, complete outfits for newspaper and job offices. His trade, which is large among the various newspapers of this city, is also extended through this and other States. Mr. Keehn is a native of France, born 30 miles from Metz, in the department of Moselle, March 7th, 1826, coming to this country when but five years old.

THE THOMAS & WENTWORTH MANUFACTURING CO.,

Manufacturers of Brass and Iron Goods.

170 and 172 West Water Street.

THE representative and leading house in the manufacture of brass and iron goods in this city is the "Thomas and Wentworth Manufacturing Co.," at Nos. 170 and 172 West Water street. The business was originally founded by Mr. R. J. Thomas, with a capital of less than $500, in 1872, and was located on Ferry street, South Side. Mr. D. O. Bebb was associated with Mr. Thomas for a number of years, and the business carried on by them was very successful. The trade increased so rapidly that greater facilities were required, so the present company was incorporated, with Mr. R. J. Thomas, president; W. S. Wentworth, treasurer, and A. B. Pursell, secretary. Their large and beautiful building, which is four stories high, 40x100 feet in dimensions, is well stocked with plumbers', brewers', railway and engineers' supplies; Babbitt metal, steam, gas and water fittings; wrought and cast iron pipe; belting, packing and hose; in fact, a complete assortment of everything in the line of brass and iron goods. They employ a large force of skilled workmen, who turn out a most superior class of goods. This firm are inventors of various specialties in the brass trade, such as oil-cups, bearings, gauges, etc., which they ship to all parts of the world. Their establishment contains the most improved machinery, for the running of which a forty-horse power engine is used. The home dealings of this company are very large, and their trade also extends to almost every State in the Union, and they even ship to some of the European countries, so that the house adds much to the commercial reputation of this city.

THE NEW HAMPSHIRE BLOCK.
Grand Avenue, between Sixth and Seventh Streets.

THE large number of fine buildings erected during the past few years has done much to beautify the city, and none has added more in this respect than that of the "New Hampshire Block." It is designed as a business and dwelling block, and meets these requirements perfectly. The building has a frontage on Grand avenue of 150 feet, and a depth of sixty-five feet, being four stories in height, with six tiers of bay-windows extending from the second to the fourth floor. There are six large stores on the gound floor, each having a frontage of twenty-four feet, and a large office on the Sixth street side. Four commodious stairways extend from the street to the fourth floor. The second and third floors are arranged into twelve flats of six rooms each. The ceilings are high, and each flat is furnished with a large range, steam chests and gas. The fourth floor contains about fifty rooms divided into twenty-four apartments. These are also rented to individuals or families. The entire building is heated throughout by steam, and the most perfect arrangement is made for light and ventilation. For comfort and convenience these flats and rooms are unsurpassed by anything of the kind in the city. The building is entirely fire-proof and erected in the most substantial manner, and is an ornament to the city. Strong balconies and stairways are constructed in the rear, so that every flat and suite of rooms has an outlet in that direction, and can receive all groceries and supplies in the same manner. The New Hampshire Block was begun July 16th, 1882, and completed for occupancy Feb. 10th, 1883. Mr. E. D. Holton, the owner of this block, is one of Milwaukee's representative men, and by his wealth and position has done much to forward the general interests of this city.

CARPENTER & UNDERWOOD,
Manufacturers of Crackers and Fancy Biscuits.
518 and 520 Grand Avenue.

THIS firm are extensive manufacturers of crackers and biscuits of all varieties, and also fine bread for the city trade, and is the largest exclusive cracker bakery in the State. Their salesrooms, offices and workshops occupy their new and handsome block, 518 and 520 Grand avenue, erected in 1883. They have the

latest and best machinery invented for this business, and they manufacture upwards of 200 barrels of crackers daily, using from forty to fifty barrels of flour. Forty hands are employed, and five wagons are kept busy delivering to the retail trade throughout the city. A large trade has been established all over the Northwest as far as Washington Territory, and is rapidly increasing and extending itself. Mr. Michael Carpenter, the senior member of this firm, is a native Milwaukeean, and has always been connected with the cracker business. Mr. H. W. Underwood was born in Massachusetts, and came to this city in 1868, and soon afterwards entered this business.

LOUIS LACHMAN,

Merchant Tailor and Men's Outfitter.

429 East Water Street.

MR. Lachman is a German by birth, is thirty-one years of age, and settled in Milwaukee many years ago, and first assumed the proprietorship of the clothing parlors at 429 East Water street in 1867. He has been very successful in trade, and has succeeded in attracting a large and valuable patronage. His customers have always been pleased with the prompt manner in which he fills their orders, turning out neat suits, cut in the latest style and always a perfect fit. He employs ten men to assist him in filling the large number of orders daily received.

I. SILBER,

Manufacturer of Suspenders, Trusses, Shoulder-Braces, etc.

593 East Water Street.

THE Northwestern Suspender Factory, at No. 593 East Water street, is a busy place and turns out goods to the value of $40,000 to $50,000 a year. Premises 20x75 are occupied, the salesrooms being in front and the factory in the rear. S. Silber is the business manager, while his brother, I. Silber, superintends the factory. From fifteen to twenty skilled workers are employed, and the goods manufactured embrace suspenders of all kinds, shoulder-braces for both ladies and gentlemen, trusses which find a large sale throughout the Northwest, in Wisconsin, Illinois, Iowa, Nebraska, Minnesota and Dakota, and school-bags. The factory was opened in 1875 by Mr. I. Silber, father of the present proprietors, and the business is still carried on in his name, although he is now deceased. The Silber Brothers were both born in Prussia, but came to this country at an early age. They are enterprising, intelligent business men, who have an exceedingly good thing in the way of trade and know just how to handle it. Their line is manufacturing and jobbing, and they are doing both on a large and profitable scale.

HENRY HERMAN,

Real Estate and Loans.

No. 97 Wisconsin Street.

MR. Herman, though one of the youngest men in the real estate trade in the city, has been connected with the business for years, there being few men now in the trade who have been in it longer than he. He is thoroughly acquainted with the property of the city and is considered one of the best informed men in Milwaukee on real estate questions as to value, etc. While he deals in real estate and owns a large amount, he makes a specialty of attending to the business of others, and taking charge of estates of parties both in and out of the city, in which business he has been for some years, and has gained the confidence of those with whom he deals, both for judgment and reliability.

Mr. Herman was born in Maine and came to Milwaukee when quite young, and has long been actively identified with the business interests of the Cream City.

MRS. E. J. PETERS,

Dealer in Watches, Diamonds, Jewelry, etc.

318 Chestnut Street.

MRS. Peters has been in the jewelry line in Milwaukee since 1861, leasing a fine establishment at No. 318 Chestnut street. The business has shown a gratifying increase from the beginning, and the stand is now as well known and as well patronized as any similar concern on the West Side. Mrs. Peters employs competent workmen to repair and clean watches and jewelry. She makes a specialty of the Springfield, Ill., watches, the best watch made, and deals in diamonds and jewelry of all descriptions, solid and plated silver-ware, and keeps a full line of clocks, spectacles, etc. Mrs. Peters is an accomplished lady and a native of Westphalia, Prussia. She first came to this country in 1844 and lived in New York a number of years before coming to Milwaukee.

JOHN B. REITER,
Manufacturer of Soda and All Mineral Waters.
193 Jackson Street.

ONE of the representative and leading firms in this branch of business is that of Mr. John B. Reiter, at No. 193 Jackson street. He is manufacturer of all kinds of soda water, seltzer, root and ginger beer, and bottler of the Waukesha mineral waters. He began business in a very small way in 1876, at No. 110 Huron street, but moved to his present quarters about three years ago. His factory has a capacity of 600 doz. bottles per month, consisting of one large generator, containing over fifty gallons, two large fountains, fillers, and all the latest appliances in use. The specialty of Mr. Reiter is ginger ale, which has won for him a large reputation and lucrative custom. A brand of soda water, worthy of mention, is his "Little Daisy," which for flavor and pleasantness constitutes as fine a cool drink as can be obtained. Mr. Reiter was born in Germany, and settled in Milwaukee in 1869, soon after which he began the business already described.

RICHARD BEER,
Livery, Sale and Boarding Stable.
141 and 143 Second Street.

THE livery, sale and boarding stables of Mr. Richard Beer, 141 and 143 Second street, have the reputation of being the oldest in the city. Six to eight men are constantly employed, while on some occasions from twenty-five to fifty are hired. Forty-five horses, twenty-five buggies and carriages and fifteen sleighs constitute the stock of this firm. Mr. Beer gives special attention to the buying and selling of fine horses, and being centrally located and having every facility for this branch, he has a large business in this line. Mr. Beer is a native of Germany and came to this city in 1863, soon afterward entering into the livery stable business, which he has since successfully pursued.

THE JOSEPH SCHLITZ BOTTLING WORKS,
(LIMITED).
Milwaukee, Wis.

THE Jos. Schlitz Bottling Works (limited) is composed of the following officers: Christopher Voechting, president; Aug. Uihlein, vice-president: C. E. Meyer, secretary and treasurer; C. Uihlein, superintendent. The company was established in 1877, under the firm name of Voechting, Shape & Co. Their establishment was located at the cor. of Third and Galena streets, where the first year they put up over 1,000,000 bottles of beer, which has increased until now they bottle over 10,000,000 per annum. This rapid increase necessitated great improvements and more room, which requisites are all met within their new quarters, consisting of eleven acres on South Bay street, between the tracks of the C., M. & St. P. Ry. and the C. & N. W. Ry. Their main building is 76x340 feet in dimensions, with an adjoining building

62x320 feet. Numerous large sheds are also erected for storage purposes. The manufacturing and shipping facilities are better than any similar concern in the Union. The capacity of these new works is 500 barrels per day of ten hours. The latest and best machinery is in use throughout this establishment, the time required to bottle a barrel of beer being just four and a half minutes. Over 220 persons are employed, their weekly payroll averaging $2,000. Shipments are made throughout the United States as well as to Central and South America, Cuba, the Pacific islands, Australia, China and Japan, and inquiries for prices and samples are received almost daily from all parts of England, Germany and other European countries. During the past year, 1885, they bottled over 36,000 barrels, or about ten million bottles, and worth about eight hundred thousand dollars. This company are sole bottlers of Joseph Schlitz Brewing Co.'s Export Pilsner Milwaukee beer.

MRS. JEAN KAVANAUGH,

Artist and Teacher.

Room 29, Iron Block.

IN this laudable industry mention is made of the establishment of Mrs. Jean Kavanaugh, who has taught this branch in this city for the past twelve years, and has attained great proficiency and popular favor. She teaches all branches of the work, oil and water colors, crayon, flower, landscape and portrait painting. Her long experience and the wide range of subjects she has gained during her travels at home and abroad, render her particularly competent to give lessons to those desirous of learning the profession. She has taught in the Milwaukee College for several years, and has been very successful with her school, which is attended by pupils from all parts of the country. Her studio is elaborately furnished and contains all the essentials for doing the work required in the highest order of the art, as well as assisting pupils to a better idea of the requirements necessary to the development of an artistic taste. Her work is beyond question among the most meritorious in the city, and has established a fine reputation in this line. Mrs. Kavanaugh also has a branch school at Wauwatosa, and so well known is she as an artist, that students from at least sixteen cities of the Union are represented in her classes and more are constantly applying.

B. CASSEL,

Dealer in Stoves, Ranges, etc. Paper and Paper Stock.

600 East Water Street.

THE specialty of this house is repairing all kinds of stoves and furnaces, and putting in broken or worn-out parts of stoves wherever they may be needed. Mr. Cassel is the only man in town doing such work and is, therefore, specially prepared to do it, promptly, neatly and at low figures. Mr. Cassel established the business in 1879, in a small way, and by industry and close attention to business he has worked up a fine trade, which consists of a general trade in stoves, ranges, paper and paper stock, in which he has a large and growing patronage. Mr. Cassel was born in the town of Polk, Washington county, Wisconsin, in the year 1850. He came to Milwaukee in 1865, and has resided here pretty constantly ever since. While attending strictly to his own business, he yet takes a deep interest in the general business prosperity of the city.

HALLASKA & CO.,

House Painters, Graining, etc.

154 Fourth Street.

THE above named firm began business in 1880 at their present quarters, 154 Fourth street, two doors south of Grand avenue. They employ from eight to ten men in their industry, although during the busy season the force is greatly increased. In house and sign painting this firm has had very large experience, and is always careful to employ and keep steadily engaged only such workmen as thoroughly understand their business.

The business of this firm consists of house painting, graining, glazing, paper hanging, etc., and is confined to this city, and aggregates over $10,000 annually. Mr. A. P. Hallaska, the senior member of the firm, was born in Austria and came to this city in 1859, while his partner, Mr. J. Elias, is a native of Holland and settled in Milwaukee in 1862. They have both been closely connected with the painting business in this city for over twenty years, and are deserving the large support and patronage they are receiving. Specimens of this firm's work can be found in the following blocks: Marquette College, Belvidere Block, Harvey Williams, T. L. Kennan's residence on Prospect avenue, and many others.

DR. A. E. NEUMEISTER,

Turkish, Electrical and Medical Institute.

457 and 459 Milwaukee Street.

DR. Neumeister's Turkish and Electrical bath establishment and medical institute is located at 457 and 459 Milwaukee street, between Mason and Oneida. Two floors, each 20x60, are occupied, and two separate departments for the two sexes are elegantly maintained. Dr. Neumeister opened his institute in 1876, on Mason street, and in 1880 he established himself in his present location. Dr. Neumeister is a regular physician, with a large and general practice among the best classes of Milwaukee society, and people from all parts of the State come to his institute for treatment. All kinds of chronic diseases are treated, such as rheumatism, neuralgia, paralysis, spinal irritation, spinal tenderness, Bright's disease, dropsy, general debility, catarrh of the head, lungs, stomach or bladder, consumption, asthma, dyspepsia, etc. Dr. Neumeister was born in Saxony, Germany, in 1842, and came to America in 1848, direct to this city. He is a graduate of one of the best homœpathic medical colleges in Chicago, and may be said to hold a secure place in the front rank of the best practitioners in the city.

J. J. HOF,

Land Office.

117 and 119 West Water Street.

MR. J. J. Hof, the subject of this sketch, came to America in 1865, from his native land, Norway. After visiting various portions of the United States in search of lands, he finally purchased large tracts in Wisconsin, in the Fox River Valley, near Green Bay and Appleton, which lands are renowned for their rich soil, and freedom from floods, and lie in a good climate. After holding these lands many years he decided to colonize them, which he did slowly, only locating a few families on them each year and carefully watched their progress. During the years of '83, '84 and '85 he located large numbers of families, expended large sums in improving the lands by sub - surveying, and build ing roads bridges, etc., and has been very fortunate in procuring a thrifty class of settlers, mostly Poles. They are good farmers and are happy and contented in their new homes. They are well cared for by Mr. Hof, who makes weekly trips to look after their interest and welfare. They have a small church and school of their own, and they have in process of erection a larger house of worship. A large sawmill has been erected by Mr. Hof in the centre of the colony, which is rented and run by them. For further information, maps and circulars address Mr. J. J. Hof, who will promptly furnish any facts desired.

E. R. PANTKE & CO.,

Manufacturers and Dealers in Hats and Caps.

390 East Water Street.

AMONG those who have established an excellent reputation for doing good work, and keeping a fine stock of goods in this line is the firm of E. R. Pantke & Co., at No. 390 East Water street. Mr. Pantke established the business alone in 1857, in a store at his present quarters. At first the business was small, but increased with the demand, until at present it is one of the largest stocks in the city. In 1865 Mr. Lebeau came in as partner, but in 1873 disposed of his share to Adam Fink of St. Paul, who now represents the "Co." Besides hats, this firm manufactures a fine quality of seal-skin sacques, caps, robes, gloves, coats, mitts, etc. They make furs, silk and cassimere hats their specialties, and do a large trade in this line. They employ twenty persons in manufacturing their goods, and are kept constantly busy in filling orders. Mr. Pantke was born in Prussia in 1836, and was brought to this country by his parents in 1848, coming direct to Milwaukee. He is a practical hatter with years of practical experience, and never fails to give the utmost satisfaction.

PETER SCHMIDT,

Stone and Marble Works.

679 & 681 Market Street.

ONE of the most prominent men in Milwaukee in the stone and marble contracting business is Peter Schmidt, whose stone and marble works are located at No. 679 and 681 Market street. All kinds of building work is furnished and set in any stone desired. He makes a specialty of cemetery work, such as monuments, head-stones, fonts, etc., and in this line he has done some very fine work, which can be seen in all the prominent cemeteries in and around Milwaukee. An ample force of skilled workmen is employed the year round in the various departments of his business. A great variety of monuments and head-stones is kept in stock, and can be seen at the yards, and it will pay any who contemplate purchasing anything in this line to call at Mr Schmidt's works and make an examination into styles and prices. As a stone contractor Mr. Schmidt is well known, and has furnished all the material for many of the most prominent structures in Milwaukee and throughout the Northwest, and has special facilities for furnishing all kinds of stone and marble for building and other purposes at rock bottom prices, and asks all builders and contractors throughout the country to give him a chance to bid for furnishing any and everything in this line.

HASSENTEUFEL & WAECHTER

Dealers in Lamps, Glassware, Chinaware, etc.

602 East Water Street.

A FULL stock of fine goods is carried in this establishment, including lamps of all kinds, glassware in the latest styles and varieties, and some of the finest China tea and dinner sets to be seen in the city. The rule is, good wares and low prices, and all who go there to trade are sure to get the worth of their money. Mr. Hassenteufel was born in Prussia in 1831, and has been in America some thirty years and in Milwaukee six years. He is thoroughly familiar with the business, having been in the same line of trade elsewhere in the city. Mr. Waechter is also a native of Prussia, where he was born in 1840. He came to America when he was quite young, and saw a great deal of this wide land before coming to Milwaukee thirteen years ago.

MILWAUKEE STONE YARD.

Cook & Hyde, Proprietors.

Office, 97 Wisconsin Street.

THE firm of Cook & Hyde is the largest and the oldest firm in the stone business in Milwaukee, and has furnished the cut stone for many of the finest buildings in the city. They are identified with at least the later history of the growth of the place, having been in business as a firm since 1858, and having furnished material for such buildings as the Plankinton House, the Plankinton Block, the Chamber of Commerce Building, the Club House and St. Paul's Church. Mr. Cook was born in England and came to this country when quite a young man, and has been an active business man and large real estate owner in Milwaukee for many years. Mr. Hyde was also born in England and came to this country at a later date, and while being an active business man, has held a number of important public offices, having been in the city council, the Legislature of the State and the State Senate.

MRS. LYDIA ELY,

Artist and Art Teacher.

Rooms 25 and 27, Iron Block.

THE fine arts are liberally patronized in Milwaukee, and the city boasts of some artists who rank first in their profession. The lady mentioned above has been engaged in the above work for many years, and by hard labor and close application to study has gained a wide reputation as an artist, and especially as an able teacher. She first opened a studio in the city in 1872, but had been engaged in the work previous to that time. She teaches the art in all its branches, oil and water colors, crayon work, landscape painting, etc., and makes drawing a specialty. She is thoroughly in love with her art, and has traveled throughout this country in pursuit of her studies, as well as having spent a great deal of time abroad for a like purpose. Her genius has been recognized by our citizens, and she has been appointed superintendent of the art department of the Exposition. She is most thorough in the course of studies given to pupils, and has a large class, which occupies most of her time and attention.

GERMANIA PUBLISHING CO.,

Geo. Brumder, Proprietor.

286 and 288 West Water Street,
84 and 86 La Salle Street,
Chicago.

THIS is the leading German publishing house in the Northwest. They have the best and cheapest list of German advertising mediums, comprising secular, political and agricultural publications, their weekly circulation running as follows: The "Germania," Milwaukee, 65,000; "Haus- und Bauernfreund," Milwaukee, 75,000; "Deutsche Warte," Chicago, 25,000; "Erholungsstunden," Chicago, 20,000; "Deutsches Volksblatt" Buffalo, N. Y., 10,000, making a total weekly issue of

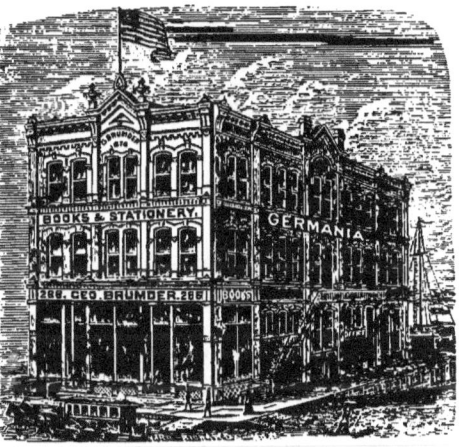

195,000. This house also issues the "Germania Kalender," an illustrated annual of 250 pages issued in October, with a circulation of 30,000 copies. They also issue the "Home Library," including 20 volumes, and the Germania Youths' Library of 25 volumes, and publish a large number of school and miscellaneous German books. The house also do all kinds of blank book and edition binding, book and job printing in all modern languages, besides ruling, numbering, perforating, stamping, edge gilding and stereotyping.

They also do a large trade as stationers and booksellers and make a specialty of stamping in gold, silver and inking in all colors, and in case-making. Mr. George Brumder, the proprietor of this house, is a pushing business man and is well and favorably known throughout the country, in his line of business and has done much toward bringing Milwaukee into prominence as a publishing center.

GERBER & GRAM,

Pianos, Organs and Musical Merchandise.

437 and 439 National Avenue.

AMONG the enterprising and reliable firms of our city, none are more worthy of mention than that of Gerber & Gram, wholesale and retail dealers in pianos, organs and musical merchandise at Nos. 437 and 439 National avenue. Their tastefully arranged music parlors are stocked with as fine a class of instruments as can be found in the city. They hold the sole agency for the leading pianos of of the world, including the celebrated **DECKER BROTHERS'** piano, an instrument too well known to require words of recommendation. It has been awarded numerous first-class prize medals and received the endorsement of all the leading music composers and singers of the age, such as Theodore Thomas, Julia Rive King, Adeline Patti, Emma Abbott, and many others. They are also sole agents for the Lindeman & Sons' pianos, whose factory was established in Dresden, Saxony, in 1821, and in New York in 1836. It is a first-class instrument in every respect. They also hold exclusive right in the Northwest for the popular Bauer & Co.'s pianos, Harrington and Bent & Co.'s pianos, and also have manufactured in their name the "Opera" piano, which is much sought after by the trade. The Bauer & Co. piano is one of great celebrity among noted musicians throughout the country, and the sales of this instrument through the agency of Gerber & Gram have reached favorable results. The Clough & Warren Orchestral organs, for church and parlor use, are also handled by this firm. They carry a large assortment of band instruments and musical merchandise of all kinds. Their grand display at the Exposition last fall was worthy of note, and was one of the principal attractions in the musical line. Although these gentlemen have been in the business but a few years, they have made many friends, built up a large trade and won a reputation equal to the oldest houses of this kind in the city. They can be strictly relied upon in the representation of their goods, and will be found most pleasant gentlemen with whom to deal.

JOHN GRAF,

Manufacturer of White Beer, Soda Water, etc.

Milwaukee, Wis.

ONE of the popular establishments manufacturing mineral waters, soda water and weiss beer, is that of John Graf, at No. 530 National avenue. From eight to fifteen hands are employed during different seasons of the year, while all the latest machinery is in use. He carbonates the mineral water for the White Rock Springs at Waukesha, which has an average of from fifty to sixty thousand bottles per month. Mr. Graf has two of the largest generators in the Northwest, and four large fountains and eight large washers. He moved to his present site in 1877, and year by year has added various improvements to his large establishment. The amount manufactured during the summer months is 200 cases per day, while less than half that much is put up in the winter months.

Mr. Graf was born in this city in 1852, and has always been engaged in this class of business, with which he has been very successful.

E. C. BOWER,

Cash Grocery Store.

338 Clinton and 83 Fifth Streets.

THE retail grocery trade of our city is ably represented by the house of E. C. Bower, at 338 Clinton and 83 Fifth streets. He keeps constantly on hand a choice stock of staple and fancy groceries, teas, coffees, and general family supplies, which he delivers free of charge to all parts of the city. Mr. Bower commenced this business in a small way in 1881, but his honorable business methods, and the superior class of goods carried, soon won for him a large and desirable trade, which has been constantly increasing and extending itself, until it has reached its present large proportions, his patrons being found in all parts of the city and State. He does business strictly on the cash basis, which enables him to present his customers not only with a superior class of goods but at the lowest possible cash prices. Mr. Bower is a native of Indiana, and is a self-made business man in every respect, and has always been active in any movement tending to promote the best interests of the Cream City.

G. PODOLL & CO.,

Photograph Studio.

333 Third Street.

THE name of Mr. Podoll on all kinds of photographs is pretty well known in this city and in the surrounding country, and it is therefore interesting to learn something about his work and his place of business. The gallery is at No. 333 Third street, and is most admirably equipped and arranged for doing all kinds of photographic work. This studio makes fine work in photographs without a doubt, and does everything in this line in the highest style of the art. Their $3 cabinets are marvels of cheapness as well as excellence, and cannot be duplicated for the money elsewhere in the city. They employ a number of skilled assistants, and all work is quickly and artistically disposed of. The rooms are elegantly furnished and fitted up and visitors are always welcome, whether they come on business or not. Mr. Gustave Podoll, the head of the firm, has had large experience in fine photography, and was for twelve years in Chicago, where he did a large business, and has followed the business actively for over a quarter of a century, and has always closely studied his art from the standpoint of an artist, which accounts for his fine work in this line.

HEUEL & ULLMER,

Artists.

115 Wisconsin Street, Room 12.

OUR city is possessed of a number of first-class artists who have built up a large local patronage, which speaks well for the character of our citizens by their appreciation and support of our local painters. Among those who have achieved a reputation for doing excellent work, we mention Messrs. Heuel & Ullmer, at 115 Wisconsin street. They have been located in this city since 1883, and were formerly at 221 Grand avenue. They do all kinds of artist work, such as crayons, India ink, pastels, water colors and oil. A specialty is made of pastels, and the best of satisfaction in every instance is guaranteed. Great attention is also paid to portrait painting, and enlarging and finishing old pictures. Mr. Heuel was born in Germany, in 1858, and came to this country in 1880, and in 1883 to Milwaukee. He has had several years experience in the business, in Hartland, Iowa, and at Chicago. Mr. Ullmer is a native of this State, and was born in

1860. He is a first-class artist, and has been long a resident of this city. Postal orders to this firm will be promptly attended to.

"STANDARD PAPER CO."

IN the front rank of the paper houses of the Northwest will be found the Standard Paper Company of Milwaukee. This young and enterprising corporation is well known in nearly every city and town in Wisconsin, Iowa, Minnesota, Dakota, in fact throughout the entire Northwest. The officers of the Standard are all young men of ability, energy, push and enterprise, who have not only succeeded in building up a large business, but are constantly increasing it, so that the spacious store which they now occupy is crowded to overflowing with the various kinds of paper stock which the necessities of their trade demand. A glance through their large and well-kept stock will convince any one in want of goods in their line, that what is not found at the Standard Paper Co. will be difficult to find anywhere else, as they aim to supply the trade with everything in the way of paper that can be obtained at any house in the East or West. Here we find paper in rolls, in large quantities, for building purposes; straw wrapping paper, manillas, heavy and light, in all sizes. These papers can be purchased from a roll or bundle to a car load, as their warehouse is kept constantly supplied. Here also will be found tier upon tier of print, book and cover papers in all the various weights and sizes. While the amount of papers in these lines shown in their stock is large, it is small compared to the amount which is shipped direct from the mills to consumers; in fact, the paper upon which most of the leading dailies and weeklies in the Northwest are printed, is supplied by the Standard Paper Co. We find also large quantities of flat papers for printers' use, in all grades, weights, and sizes, from the thin French folios to the finest linen and heaviest record and ledger papers. Their shelves are always well stocked with ruled goods, such as note and letter heads, bill heads, statements, etc., and any form of ruling can be done at this establishment.

Envelopes by the millions and thousands of sheets of card boards, such as wedding bristols, tinted bristols, railroad ticket tough check, circus board, chinas, blanks, etc., are here seen. In their miscellaneous stock we find glazed papers, bond papers, tag board, straw and cloth boards, tags, twine, paper bags, etc., too numerous to enumerate, while their stock of wedding goods, invitations, ball programmes, steel engraved folders and novelties, visiting cards and ladies' fine stationery, is not excelled by any house in the West. If close attention to the details of business, prompt consideration of the wants of patrons, first-class goods, low prices, and straightforward, honorable dealing, are standards whereby success is achieved, this company is on the high road to prosperity.

JUNG & BORCHERT,

Manufacturers of Lager Beer.

Broadway, Ogden, Milwaukee and Knapp streets.

THIS brewery was erected in 1848, by Henry Stoltz, and was conducted by him under various changes until his death, which occurred in 1865. After this the brewery passed into various hands and gradually lost prestige, until the fall of 1874, when the property and business was purchased by Ernst, Charles and Fred Borchert, who put it on a good basis and continued under the firm name of F. Borchert & Son. For five years they conducted a successful business, when, in 1879, Phillip Jung purchased a one-half interest and the firm was known as Jung & Borchert, under which name it has since continued. Under this firm the production has increased from 500 barrels in 1874 to about 75,000 barrels in 1885. They employ a force of about 100 men in all departments, many of them skilled in this branch of business.

Chas. S Van Duyn, *President.*

Chas. L. Blanchard, *Secretary.* Fred. A. Cary, *Treasurer.*

They also have nine beer trucks, seven box-wagons, four bulk wagons, five spring wagons and six buggies, used in the transaction of their business. Over thirty horses are in use for delivering, and their large city trade is recommendation for the purity and quality of beer produced. The various brands are Pilsner, Culmbacher, Export and Lager beer, which meet with great favor from the public. A short time ago a bottling department was established, which is under the direct management of N. A. Root. The main plant of Jung & Borchert's brewery is located on Ogden street, where it extends 300 feet, with 180 feet on Broadway and Milwaukee streets. They also occupy 150 feet on Knapp street. On this site is located their large brewery, mammoth malt house and extensive cellars, besides their large malt house at the corner of Eighth and State streets. They have extensive plants at Fond du Lac and Chilton, this State, each of which covers an area of about 5 acres. Their Chicago branch is situated at the corner of Union and Olive streets.

LITT'S MILWAUKEE MUSEUM,

Jacob Litt, Proprietor and Manager.

ONE of the most popular family resorts in the city is that of the "Dime Museum," under the proprietorship and management of Mr. Jacob Litt. The building is four stories with a large basement, all departments of which cover a surface area of 50x125 feet. The large and beautiful auditorium is situated on the ground floor, and consists of a well-arranged stage, furnished with the latest and best improved scenery and fixtures. The best artists are engaged in this department, and performances are given every hour, and oftener, as business may require. Over twenty-five persons are employed in the various departments of this establishment. The Milwaukee Dime Museum is one of the finest of the kind in America. It is well ventilated and brilliantly illuminated, and contains hot and cold water, and toilet rooms on every floor. The stairways are broad, and every egress is carefully arranged for use in case of fire or panic. The auditorium has wide aisles, and all the modern inprovements. Mr. Davis, the assistant manager, looks after the interests of all. The attendance last season consisted of an average of 3,000 persons daily, and is still increasing, which attests to the favor in which it is held by the public.

"THE NEW ACADEMY."

THE great majority of the people who reside in cities demand and expect more or less in the line of amusements, and the thousands of people around the State and the country who visit a city, or nearly all of them, do so with the expectation of being able to devote more or less time to being amused. Milwaukee is now fast advancing to the front rank in amusements, and to no one person is she more indebted for this fact than to Mr. Jacob Litt, manager and lessee of the New Academy of Music, proprietor and manager of the popular Dime Museum, and manager of the Summer Theater at Schlitz Park. Through his untiring efforts and ability he has raised the standard of Milwaukee's reputation as an amusement center, and given to the citizens as fine a theater as can be found in the country. He took charge of the old Academy last season, which had barely closed ere he began the transformation which produced the new and beautiful amusement parlors opened to the public last August, with John T. Raymond as the initial attraction. From the stage to the gallery everything has been made as cozy and attractive as money and art could make it. Four elegantly constructed proscenium boxes have been introduced, which are decided novelties in the way of private boxes. They are designed to represent Moorish pagodas, and stand in full relief on either side of the proscenium opening, in the corners of the auditorium. They are built out from the wall and the effect is very beautiful. All these changes have been made not only with an eye to the comfort, but also the safety of the many patrons, and no theater is better provided with means of egress for use in case of fire or panic. Not only has Mr. Litt produced a fine theater, but has also provided it with the best attractions traveling, which accounts in a measure for the large attendance during the present season. Another point, which adds much to Mr. Litt's popularity with Milwaukeeans, is his generosity in tendering the New Academy for public, charitable and religious purposes. For the benefit of strangers we would say that the New Academy is located on Milwaukee street, between Wisconsin and Michigan.

FRED. MILLER,
Brewer and Malster.

THE drink known as Lager Beer was probably known in some form as far back as the time of the Egyptians, and Tacitus speaks of it as being in common

MENOMONEE VALLEY BREWERY.

use among the Germans of his time. Mr. Fred. Miller, the subject of this sketch, has been in the brewing and malting business for over thirty years, being classed among the oldest representatives of this industry in the city, and by his experience and liberal business policy has built up a large and profitable trade. The bottled beer of this brewery has a wide notoriety, as Mr. Miller never bottles any beer that is not sufficiently old to give it the best taste and flavor. It must be well fermented, and as he uses only the very best materials, and has special brewings for his own purposes, he succeeds in producing a beer which for pureness and quality has a reputation unsurpassed by any other firm of the kind in the city. His brewery is in the town of Wauwatosa, just west of the city limits, and has been known since 1878 as the "Menomonee Valley Brewery." It was originally founded by Chas. Best and others, in 1848, and called the "Plank Road Brewery," but after a few years the business failed and the property lay idle for over a year, when, in 1855, it was sold to Mr. Miller for $8,000. The brewery then only had a capacity of 1,200 barrels per annum. The plant occupied by the numerous buildings now consists of eleven acres. The brewery has one of the best locations of any in the country for cellars, which are made in the large bluff, at the side of which the brewery is located. They have a storage capacity for over 15,000 barrels. The large brewery now standing was built by Mr. Miller in 1870. He has a large ice house in Chicago, one in Waukesha and two in Milwaukee, besides eleven surrounding the brewery. He uses annually over 15,000 tons of ice. The following figures show the rapid increase in the production of this brewery: 1855, 1,200 bbls.; 1880, 30,000 bbls.; 1884, 60,000 bbls. Mr. Miller uses annually 150,000 bushels of barley and over 125,000 pounds of hops. In 1883 a bottling department was founded and over 5,000 barrels are bottled yearly. Over twenty agencies are located throughout the United States, to which his beer is shipped direct. To better facilitate these shipments, arrangements are being made to put in a spur from the C., M. & St. P.

railroad, that cars may be loaded right at the brewery, thus saving a great amount of time and trouble. Nearly one hundred hands are employed in all the departments, while forty wagons and upwards of fifty horses are used to facilitate the prompt delivery of all orders. There is a summer garden near the brewery, well patronized by the various societies, schools and private clubs of Milwaukee, for picnics and socials. The whole side of the bluff is laid out with winding paths, rustic benches, level lawns and high swings, making it a beautiful resort. From these gardens a fine view of Lake Michigan and the Menomonee valley is had. Beautiful shade trees cover the whole place, making it a delightfully cool and pleasant resort during the hot and sultry summer days.

HERMAN VOSS,

Blank Book Manufacturer and General Book Binder.

Nos. 372 to 376 Milwaukee Street.

ONE of the oldest and largest establishments of this kind is that of Herman Voss, in the *Evening Wisconsin* Building. His large and well-arranged quarters are perfectly equipped, and he receives work from all parts of the Union, which aggregates upwards of $25,000 annually. Machinery of the latest patent for use in this line is found here, notable among which is the wire-stitcher and book-trimmer, the only one in use in the State. Upwards of 50 hands are constantly employed to meet the demands of the large business. The special line is in edition work, the facilities for which are so great that nearly 25,000 pamphlets have been folded, stitched and trimmed in one day. This large establishment was begun in 1874, by the present proprietor, with only two boys and one girl in a small room in Prentiss' Block on East Water street. Business increased until he was compelled to seek more commodious quarters, which he found in his present location in 1880. Mr. Voss has been ably assisted by Mr. Geo. Seelman, bookkeeper and manager, who attends to all outside business. Mr. Voss is a native of Germany, where he learned his trade, and worked in all the larger cities before coming to this country.

H. O. PARKS,

Licensed Bill Poster and Distributer.

Office, 116 Grand Avenue.

IN 1868 the first Bill Posting Company was formed in Milwaukee, under the firm name of Treyser & Higgins. The firm of Parks & McLaughlin succeeded them in 1871, but the latter withdrawing soon after, a Mr. Walters took his place, and remained in partnership until his death in 1878, when Mr. Parks took entire control and has retained it up to the present. Mr. Parks has added much to the advancement and general standing of this business and was the only licensed bill-poster in the city for a number of years. He has secured the principal and finest stands in the city, and has over 100,000 feet of lumber in sixty-five large bill boards and nearly 500 three-sheet boards. Mr. Parks was born in Vermont, and came to this city in 1857. He is a practical printer by trade, and was formerly foreman of the *Sentinel* job room. He is also a successful real estate dealer, and has in various ways added to the progress of the Cream City's commercial interests.

THE CONTINENTAL RESTAURANT AND OYSTER HOUSE,

S. J. Eldridge, Proprietor.

No. 392 East Water Street.

ONE of the standard institutions of our city is the Continental Restaurant and Oyster House at 392 East Water street, just four doors south of Wisconsin street. This model eating house was opened last May, and has had a successful career, being patronized largely by the business men and clerks in the neighborhood. The obliging proprietor, Mr. S. J. Eldridge, looks personally to the general arrangement of the establishment, so that all his patrons may rest assured of not only receiving a first-class meal, but in having it served in as satisfactory a manner as at their own homes. The restaurant is elegantly fitted up with all that adds to the comfort and pleasure of their patrons, while the meals consist of the best the market affords, and served in a style to satisfy the most fastidious. As an oyster house it is becoming eminently popular and well deserves the large patronage it receives.

ST. MARY'S INSTITUTE,
Cor. Knapp and Milwaukee Sts.

THIS Institute, which is under the direction of the School Sisters of Notre Dame, was founded in 1850, guages, needlework, music, drawing or painting. These branches may be exclusively pursued. Differences of religion form no obstacle to the admission of such as are willing to conform outwardly to the established routine, satisfactory references being invariably required. The scholastic year commences on the first Monday in September, and ends on the third Thursday in July. The terms for board and tuition in English, French, German, plain needlework, embroidery and vocal music, per annum, are $180, and after the third year, $100. Connected with the institute is a day school, for pupils residing at home, with entrance on Jefferson street. For terms, inquire

St. Mary's Institute.

making it one of the oldest institutions of the kind in the Northwest. The buildings, a cut of which is given above, are situated on one of the most elevated and healthy localities of Milwaukee, and command an extensive view of the city and its environs, while the pleasure grounds adjoining the buildings afford ample advantages for healthful exercise. The system of education embraces every useful and ornamental branch of art and science suitable for young ladies. Special time and attention will be paid to pupils whose friends desire their proficiency in the lan- at the school. Letters of inquiry must be addressed to
SISTER DIRECTRESS,
St. Mary's Institute, Milwaukee, Wis.

MILWAUKEE ELECTROPATHIC INSTITUTE

For the Treatment of All Diseases.

No. 168 Mason Street.

THE Milwaukee Electropathic Institute was established by Dr. J. McGuffin in 1879, for the treatment and cure of all curable diseases, by the different modifications of electricity, galvanism and magnetism. The doctor has labored with untiring energy for many years in this department of therapeutics, for the purpose of establishing this system of practice on a reliable, scientific basis. His highest hopes have been realized, judging from his success in controlling diseased conditions. The imponderable agent in his hands is mild and pleasant even to the most delicate and sensitive persons, producing no painful or disagreeable feelings.

Dr. McGuffin was engaged in the regular practice of medicine for a number of years when he began to investigate the subject of electricity in its various modified forms as a curative agent. He finally became convinced that electricity, electro-magnetism and galvanism, when scientifically used, were superior to any other mode of treatment for all the various diseases of the human system. He at once gave up a large medical practice and commenced a full course of study in electro-therapeutics and graduated in that school. He is the discoverer of the new and improved method of treating diseases of the eye without the use of drugs and entirely painless. The doctor has cured diseases of this delicate organ which have baffled the skill of some of the leading oculists in the United States. He has hundreds of letters and testimonials in his office from patients he has cured, who had given up all hope until they took electrical treatment. The doctor treats with success all the various diseased conditions of the human body, as electricity can always be relied upon, when scientifically applied, in the treatment of any disease. In a few years this new system of treatment has become so popular that applications for treatment are being made from nearly every State in the Union.

There are many who formerly looked on electrical treatment with suspicion, who now acknowledge its superiority in the treatment of all chronic diseases. Electricity can only be depended upon in the cure of disease just so far as the electrician is skillful and scientific. This hint may be deemed necessary, as many persons use electricity in a kind of random way who have never made electrical science a special study, and are therefore not qualified to be successful electricians. Persons who have not investigated this system of treatment, if they will take the trouble to do so, will find that it is founded on scientific principles and sound philosophy, the correctness of which is demonstrated in the many wonderful cures the doctor has made during the past ten years.

JAMES SHERIFFS,
Manufacturer of the Best Propeller Wheels in the United States; Steam Engines, Boilers, Mill Machinery, Iron and Brass Castings, etc.
124 to 130 Barclay Street.

FOR over thirty years the large establishment of James Sheriffs has exerted a large influence in the manufacturing circles of this city. This is not only the oldest, but also one of the largest and most important foundries in Milwaukee. Commenced in a small way in 1854, it has grown to its present large proportions, a good illustration of the works being given on the opposite page. From the first job, one ton of grate bars for the tug Tifft, the business has extended to almost every State in the Union, and products of this establishment have been sent to points so distant as Australia and Cuba. The plant now covers an area of 180x220 feet and contains all the latest machinery necessary for the construction of the largest steam engines and propeller wheels in use, the latter being probably the best made in this country and in which he has a great reputation. Mr. Sheriffs also makes boilers, mill machinery and iron and brass castings, etc. From sixty to seventy men are employed in the various departments, while the business aggregates upwards of $100,000 annually. Mr. Sheriffs is a native of Scotland and came to Milwaukee the year he began business, 1854, and has been closely identified with all interests tending towards the improvement and commercial advancement of our beautiful city.

Vulcan Iron Works—Jas. Sheriffs, Proprietor.

MARKHAM ACADEMY,
Milwaukee, Wis.

MARKHAM ACADEMY.

ONE of the popular institutions of Milwaukee is the Markham Academy, which was established here almost a quarter of a century ago.

This school is designed to furnish the choicest educational advantages for a limited number of boys and young men. Its work consists in preparing students for the universities, or in giving them such a course of study and discipline as shall qualify them for the more immediate occupations of business. For the accomplishment of these aims, the institution carries on two wisely-planned and comprehensive courses of instruction, in either of which facilities are offered which are unsurpassed.

The school possesses a valuable collection of philosophical apparatus, and a variety of other well-selected appliances, designed to aid in illustrative teaching. Encyclopædias and other works of reference are at all times accessible to the students.

This Academy is recognized as one of the leading and most efficient college preparatory schools in the State, and has always received a liberal local patronage from our city, besides the State at large and throughout the Northwest. Graduates from this school have, from year to year, been admitted with high honors into the very best colleges of our land, and many of the leading business and professional men of Milwaukee are graduates of this school.

The Academy is centrally and most eligibly located, on the corner of Van Buren and Oneida streets, within one block of the Court House Park, and easily accessible by street cars from all parts of the city.

The Academy building, in all the studied details of its interior arrangements, is admirably adapted to its purpose. Its system of warming and ventilation is thoroughly scientific, and hardly susceptible of improvement. The study rooms are spacious, and rendered exceptionally cheerful by an abundance of light.

The building throughout is supplied with the most approved patterns of school furniture, and in all its appointments it bears evidence that the health, comfort and convenience of the pupils have been carefully considered.

Prof. Albert Markham, principal and proprietor of this Academy, is a thorough educator and disciplinarian, and looks personally to the welfare of all the students, and he has associated with him as competent a corps of instructors as can be found in any of the colleges.

Copies of the Annual Catalogue, giving in detail the courses of study, etc., may be obtained from the principal on application.

DAVIS OMNIBUS LINE.
Davis & Baird, Proprietors.
Office, 305 Milwaukee Street.

THE Davis Omnibus Line has a history almost identical with the city. It was first started in 1850 by Brown & Davis, as a stage line to outside towns. Later on, as business increased and the town grew to be a city, they turned into a regular bus line. There have been various changes in the firm name through the years up until 1883, when the establishment was purchased by Mrs. K. C. Davis and Mr. J. C. Baird. It is now owned by them under the firm name of Davis Omnibus Lines. They own ten buses and five express wagons, and have thirty-five horses in their stables, employing twenty men in connection. They have a large two-story brick stable, with a comfortable and well-equipped office, at 305 and 307 Milwaukee street. Their conveyances are all of the latest style, and admirably adapted for the work for which they are designed. The fare charged is very low, and the firm should receive the commendation and support of the public.

Mr. J. C. Baird and J. A. Cochran are the managers of the business, Mr. Baird being a native of Wisconsin, having been born in Walworth county in 1851. He has been a resident of this city for the past 15 years. Mr. Cochran was born in Troy, New York, and came to Milwaukee in 1848, and had long been connected with the C., M. & St. P. R'y before taking charge of this line with Mr. Baird.

GEO. GEBHARDT,

Manufacturer and Dealer in Confectionery Articles.

491 East Water Street.

ONE of the important and leading concerns in this business is that of Geo. Gebhardt, at No. 491 East Water street. He is a manufacturer, wholesale and retail dealer in all kinds of confectionery, gum paste, ornaments and toys, consisting of brides and grooms, cupids, hands, lacepapers, Easter eggs, flowers of all sizes and colors, ornamenting paper, tubes, rubber bags, foam confects, gold and silver leaves, and all ornaments for weddings, parties and Christmas trees; in fact, a full supply of everything in this line. Mr. Gebhardt commenced the business over seventeen years ago on the South Side, in a small way, but it has gradually increased until it has reached its present large proportion. He moved to his present commodious quarters one year ago and now employs from nine to twelve persons to assist in the business. His sales extend throughout the city and State and reach about $10,000 per annum. Mr. Gebhardt is a native of Mayence, Germany, and came to Milwaukee in 1867. He is a practical confectioner, having learned the business in his native country. Sound business principles have characterized all his transactions and no better quality of goods can be procured anywhere in the city or State.

SPALDING BROS. & CO.,

Publishers and Booksellers.

Nos. 157-163 LaSalle St., Chicago, and No. 119 Wisconsin St., Milwaukee.

ONE of our most extensive houses in this line is that of Spalding Bros. & Co., who began business here in 1884, by purchasing the good will of an older firm. Since they assumed control, success and prosperity has attended them because of good management and the superior grade of works they represent. They deal both on the installment and cash plans, and do an extensive business throughout all parts of the Northwest. They handle all the popular works, embracing science, history, religion and fiction; and also deal largely in albums and pictures. They are making a specialty of "The Modern Family Physician and Hygienic Guide," which is having remarkable success, and is invaluable to all classes of people. They also handle Gaskell's Compendium for 1886, which is a most valuable and instructive work. Chambers' Encyclopedia, The World, Historical and Actual, Webster's Unabridged Dictionary, and a fine edition of the Pictorial Bible are among their most important works. Mr. Chas. T. Elliott has just been admitted as a partner, and arrangements have been perfected for enlarging their rapidly growing business by establishing headquarters at Chicago. This firm have had years of experience in this line, and are prompt and reliable business men.

JEWETT & SHERMAN CO.,
Merchants Coffee and Spice Mills.

AN important branch of commercial activity, and one that adds in no small way to the renown of Milwaukee as a manufacturing center, is the Merchants Coffee and Spice Mills, owned and man-

aged by the Jewett & Sherman Co. This business was begun in a small way in 1867, at No. 222 East Water street. Increased patronage demanding increased facilities, they found more commodious quarters at Nos. 90, 92 and 94 Huron street, but still being hampered for room, they decided to build the fine block which they now own and occupy on the corner of Broadway and Detroit street. It consists of an elegant brick building, which, for its architectural beauty and design, is the most conspicuous in that part of the city. It is 60x125 feet in dimensions and four stories in height, with a large basement. Every story is well arranged and fitted in the most perfect manner. The first floor is occupied by the offices, shipping room, coffee-roasters and mills. The second floor is used exclusively for the manufacture and packing of baking powder, cream tartar and spices. The third floor is set apart for dry and prepared mustards, and the fourth floor to the manufacture of Hummel's coffee essence, which now has a national reputation and use. Besides the articles mentioned above, this company are the sole manufacturers of the celebrated self-rising buckwheat flour, known as the "Magic," and in great demand throughout the entire West and Northwest. They also manufacture all varieties of flavoring extracts and bluing. The general trade of this company now embraces every State west of the Alleghanies. Besides the large number of resident agents, they have fourteen traveling salesmen to look after their interests. The latest and best machinery is in use and run by an engine of 40-horse power, forty to fifty experienced hands being employed in the various departments. The officers are representative business men in the best sense of the term, and have done much to forward the business interests of the Cream City. Liberality and promptness have always characterized all their transactions, and the success which has attended them during the past is but a natural result of a broad and systematized commercial policy.

WILLIAM A. FRICKE,
Dentist.

NEARLY ten years ago this gentleman established himself here, and has won a leading and prominent rank in dental surgery, being a practical and skillful operator in his profession. Dr. Fricke first opened an office at the corner of Chestnut and Third streets, on Jan. 1, 1876, but last February, desiring a more central location, he established himself at his present quarters. He has established a large and lucrative city and country practice, which is rapidly increasing as he is better known. He is a native of New York, and came to this city in 1857. He is a member of the State Dental Society, and was the first secretary of the Odontological Society of Milwaukee. He is a leading member of the various benevolent and co-operative insurance orders of this city; was Grand Commander of the A. L. of H. of this State, and has been the Supreme Representative of this order for a long period of years.

J. M. EVERLY,
Book and Job Printer.
298 Broadway.

"THE art preservative" has many followers in this city, and J. M. Everly, at No. 298 Broadway, is one who deserves especial mention in this particular branch, having one of the most complete offices in the city, with all new material of the very latest pattern, cylinder and job presses, and a general assortment of material such as is used in a first-class printing establishment. He is a very enterprising young man, whose business is but one year old, and consequently in its infancy, but in this short time has built up a trade that extends throughout the whole city. This is largely due to the fact that he is a practical printer and widely known as such, having had seventeen years' experience in the trade, and mastered every detail in the profession. He has been engaged in all of the principal offices in the city. A specialty is made of book and railroad work, and his facilities for this are of the very first order. A gas engine drives the machinery, which is especially adapted to the above line of work. He employs eight men, skilled in the art and standing at the head of their profession, so that the best quality of work is guaranteed in every instance.

Mr. Everly was born in Washington county, this State, in 1853, and located in this city in 1869.

JAMES CONROY,
Caterer and Confectioner.
419 and 421 Milwaukee Street.
Branch Store, Plankinton House.

ONE of the largest and most beautiful establishments of this kind in the Northwest is that of Jas. Conroy, caterer and confectioner, at Nos. 419 and 421 Milwaukee street, with a branch store in

the Plankinton House on Grand avenue. He commenced business in a small way on Grand avenue, then Spring street, in 1868. His business increasing rapidly, he moved in 1873 to Milwaukee street, near his present quarters, and a few years ago (1882) the beautiful structure, which he now occupies and owns, was erected. The space occupied covers an area of 30x120 feet, with ceilings fully 20 feet in height. A large basement of the same dimension is used for manufacturing purposes. The first floor is occupied as salesroom and ice cream parlor, the largest in the city. It is fitted in the most attractive and pleasing manner. Conroy's candies, Conroy's creams and Conroy's suppers have a reputation extending throughout the city and all over the State. He has everything necessary for the furnishing of grand suppers and dinners, which are arranged in the most artistic style. His table decorations are complete in every respect and show a superior skill in this line, which is recognized and appreciated by his many patrons. His store in the Plankinton House on Grand avenue, though smaller, is in keeping with the main establishment, both of which are ornaments and a pride to our city.

SCHRAND & WACHS,

Practical and Fashionable Harness Makers.

385 East Water Street.

ONE of the most practical and fashionable harness establishments of our city, is that of Schrand & Wachs, at No. 385 East Water street. The business was begun by the senior partner over ten years ago, while the present firm has been in existence since 1880. The reputation of this house for fine work and square, honest dealing, has won for them a large and prosperous trade, extending not only throughout the city, but all over the Northwest. They employ a force of six hands, all skilled workmen, and nothing but the best of materials is used. They manufacture harness of every description, from the heavy truck to the handsome and elaborate carriage harness; also ladies' and gentlemen's saddles of every variety; riding bridles, whips, turf goods, and articles of every description in this line of trade. They constantly keep on hand a complete stock of well-assorted goods in their line, and repairing is attended to with neatness and dispatch.

WILLIAM STRUEDER,

Manufacturer of Show Cases, Store and Office Furniture.

249 and 251 Lake Street.

THIS flourishing business was established in a small way in 1864, by Mr. Wm. Strueder, the present proprietor. The manufactory and warerooms are situated on the South Side, at Nos. 249 and 251 Lake street, and have a frontage of 50 feet, with a depth of 150 feet. Here are manufactured all kinds of show cases, store and office furniture. The material used is all first-class in every particular. The different styles of show cases are made in the best possible manner; the strongest and best shaped moldings are used, and that which is the most convenient to clean. Special attention is given to make the bottoms of every case strong, which keeps them in shape, so that there is no danger of the glass being broken in shipping. Polished French plate-glass show cases are made a specialty, and consist of the following styles: oval-front, pentagonal, square-front, and mansard. They are made of all walnut, or imitation ebony, highly polished, with metal corners and plates fitting in all the joints, which adds to the strength as well as beauty of the case. His full metal combination show cases, for cutlery and perfumery, have met with great success. Mr. Strueder has received diplomas from the various State fairs and expositions of the Northwest, for the fine quality and beauty of goods manufactured. His trade is very large and rapidly increasing, aggregating upwards of $20,000 per annum. He has just published a price list and catalogue of all styles of cases manufactured, as well as all information necessary to his business. It can be obtained free of charge, by writing, or calling at his office. Mr. Strueder is a native of Germany. He was born at Nassau, and came to Milwaukee in 1861, soon after which he established the business which has become so prominent among the industries of this city.

MASSEY & CO.,
Dealers in Crockery, Glassware, Etc.
424 Milwaukee Street.

THIS carving knife, fork and steel here represented and for sale by the above firm, is made by the celebrated Wm. Beckett, of Sheffield, England. These three articles are sold for *one dollar*. They are of the finest tempered steel and well worth five times the amount in any family, the horn handles alone being worth more than the price asked. This is a real bargain and hard to duplicate in any city, and for those who need this set it is a rare oportunity.

JONES & SON,
Dealers in Corks.
620 Poplar Street.

AN industry of no small importance to our city is that conducted by Jones & Son, cork manufacturers, at No. 620 Poplar street. This is the only factory of the kind in the city, and they turn out over 100 gross per day of all sizes, from the smallest to the largest. The machines are of the latest pattern, and are run by experienced workmen. Upwards of a dozen hands are employed during the busy season. Besides corks, they keep constantly on hand bungs, plugs and vents of all sizes and descriptions. This firm will purchase from all brewers and bottlers the old corks they may have, at a liberal price. Although this factory was only started six months ago, it has already become prominent, and the business is rapidly increasing and extending itself.

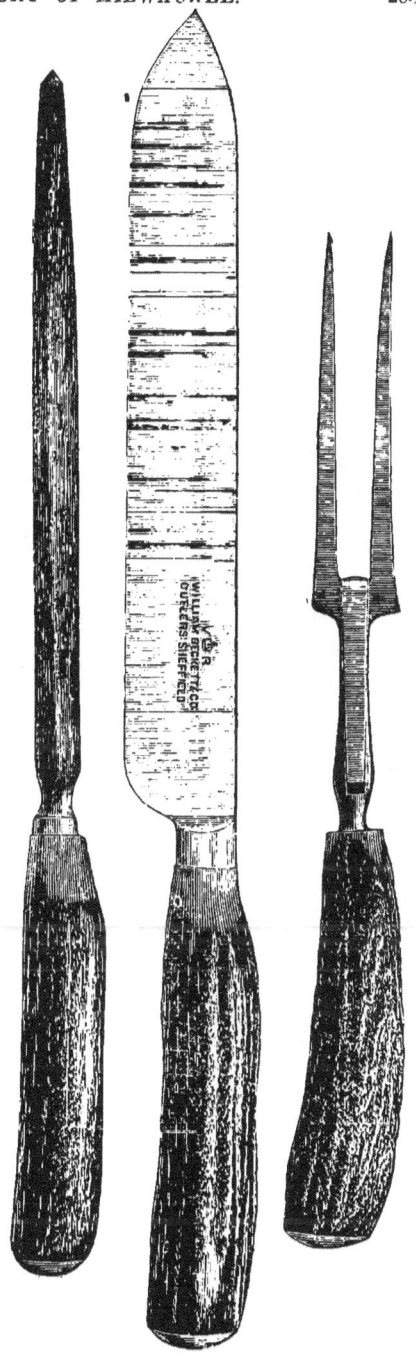

MR. Armstrong's varied experience has given him a well-merited reputation that extends beyond the confines of city or State. The attention of the intelligent public, from Maine to California, was attracted by a series of beautiful landscapes, from nature, bearing appropriate titles and published as "The real, from an ideal standpoint." These gems have received the praise of all having an eye for the beautiful, and advanced his interests by placing his genius before an admiring public. Mr. Armstrong's special feature of photography is portraiture, and in the picturing of little children he has few equals. From the Milwaukee *Sentinel* we clip the following:

"Armstrong, the artist, whose creative fancies have so happily woven the real with the ideal, and decked facts with the rosy allurements of romance, has given the possibilities of his profession a new impetus, and elevating it to a new plane, by giving rein to his genius. Three years ago this leading photographer of the Northwest came to Milwaukee with pluck and ability his only capital. He had been located in Chicago, only to awake one morning and find the savings of years gone down in the Fidelity Bank crash. Visiting this city, he thought he saw promises in the future. With him, to think was to act, and out of the humble beginning has grown a gallery second to none west of New York. The story of Armstrong's early struggle, for struggle it was, is stranger than fiction, and his advancement to prosperity can well serve as a model for emulation."

L. G. LOOMIS,
Money Loaner,
No. 452 East Water Street.

MR. Loomis is one of the first settlers in Milwaukee, having driven a team through from Detroit, Michigan, arriving here on July 25th, 1828. In 1830 he left for Toledo, Ohio, and from there for New York. Leaving there in 1836 for the East Indies, still carrying on trade in furs, he, in the course of his travels, visited the Sandwich Islands, Ceylon, Australia, Hindoostan, China, traveled in nearly all the countries of the old world, and finished by circum-navigating the globe. Returning to Milwaukee in 1843, he opened a pawnbroker's shop on East Water street, a few doors below his present stand. In 1855 he moved to 452 East Water street, and has remained there since. He can talk the English, French and Spanish languages, and several of the Indian dialects. He has translated the Lord's prayer into the latter tongue, also other portions of the Scriptures. He is now engaged in the business of pawnbroking and money lending, and does a thriving trade. He keeps on hand a fine stock of watches, clocks, jewelry, opera glasses, etc., and also sells second-hand goods of all descriptions. Mr. Loomis was born in Vermont in 1816, and is still hale and hearty, is a member of the Old Settlers' Club, and takes delight in telling his experience in the Cream City, when it was in its infant state.

The Grandest Historical Panorama Ever Placed on Exhibition.

Do Not Fail to See It when You Come to Town.

Opposite Exposition Building. Open Daily.

THIS is one of the grand sights of Milwaukee, and to those who have never seen one of these panoramas it is simply wonderful, impressing one with the reality of the scene in a marvelous way. The illusion is so perfect that we imagine ourselves in the very midst of this great battle. As a realistic scene it is incomparable.

detail to the accommodation of their numerous patrons. An elegant passenger elevator takes the visitor to every floor.

They carry a superior line of READY-MADE CLOTHING FOR MEN AND YOUNG MEN, BOYS AND CHILDREN. They make a specialty of BOYS' AND CHILDREN'S CLOTHING, and the manufacture of OVERCOATS for fall and winter wear. They also make clothing to order in the Custom Department on the second floor.

They cordially invite all their friends and customers to pay them a visit at the new store. Strangers cannot afford to leave the city before seeing this model clothing establishment.

ZIMMERMANN BROS.,
384 East Water Street,

THE leading retail clothing house in Milwaukee, was established in 1866. We may be allowed to state that this firm is enjoying the confidence of the public, and is favorably known throughout the Western States.

They have just completed their *elegant new store*, located at the old site, No. 384 East Water street. The interior of the building is furnished in substantial and modern style, and adapted in every

HALE & WILSON,
Insurance,
Chamber of Commerce.

A WELL-KNOWN and prominent insurance firm is that of Hale & Wilson, at No. 97 Michigan street, Chamber of Commerce. They represent the following leading and substantial companies: Insurance Company of North America, American Fire Insurance Company, Citizens' Insurance Company, Detroit F. & M. Insurance Company, Boatmans F. & M. Insurance Company, North American Insurance Company, and the Standard Accident Insurance Company, of Detroit, Mich. The Insurance Company of North America is not only the largest, but the *oldest* stock fire and marine insurance company in this country, being established in 1794. The Citizens' Insurance Company of New York is also eminently popular and belongs to the New York Underwriters' Agency. The Detroit Fire and Marine Insurance Company was the first company to make settlement of their losses in the Chicago fire. The Standard Accident Insurance Company of Detroit, Mich., with D. M. Ferry, president, is a strong, though recently organized company—having a list of stockholders representing as much wealth as any corporation in the West. The policies of the Standard have not only every desirable feature offered by other companies, but excel them in the following: Fifty-two weeks' indemnity. No deductions for indemnities paid for prior injuries on event of death. A world-wide, non-forfeitable policy, free from technicalities. All circulars and information regarding any of the companies mentioned above, sent free on application. Mr. P.C. Hale, the senior member of this firm, came to this city in 1842, and established the first book-store in this State. He has always been prominently connected with the commercial interests of Milwaukee, and since 1872 has been following the insurance business. Mr. Wilson is a native of New York State and came to Milwaukee about five years ago and entered into the business he still represents.

most improved machinery and appliances known to the trade. Employment is given to upwards of 150 hands, and the full capacity of the factory is taxed to meet the demands of the trade. The specialty of this firm is office and other styles of fine chairs, which have won for this house a national reputation. The motive power for the factory is supplied by a steam engine of 100 horse-power. The president of the company is Mr. John C. Spencer, who has been interested in this company since 1877, and it is entirely through his labors and judicious management that this house has been able to exert so great an influence upon this trade. Mr. Spencer is a member of the Executive Board of the Western Chair Association, also local treasurer of the Milwau-

MILWAUKEE CHAIR CO.,
Manufact'rs of Chairs and Cradles.
Office, 242 and 244 Broadway.

ONE of the large manufacturing establishments that has done much to advance the commercial standing of Milwaukee, is the "Milwaukee Chair Company." The offices and warerooms of this company are situated at 242 and 244 Broadway, while the factory is on Milwaukee street, from Nos. 233 to 243. The premises occupied consist of a spacious and commodious brick building 50x120 feet in dimensions, five stories high, which is used for a factory. Every floor is admirably arranged with all the

kee & Northern Railroad. He has been closely connected with the commercial advancement of our city's history ever since he came here.

COLUMBIA,
German Catholic Newspaper.
415 East Water Street.

THE German Catholics are ably represented through their official organ, the "Columbia," published in this city. This paper has a very large circulation throughout the Northwest, especially in Wisconsin and in our own city. The editor is J. M. A. Schultheis, formerly a professor in the St. Francis Seminary near

Milwaukee. He is known as an able and trenchant writer, and is one of the leaders in the Catholic journalistic field. Under his able direction the Columbia has gained an influential position, and under the management of Alfred Steckel it has attained a wide circulation, and such is its scope and character, that it has received recommendations and commendation from a number of bishops. The "Columbia" is published by the German Catholic Printing Society, with Monsignor J. St. Muenich as president. On account of its peculiar field of work, it reaches a class of people that cannot be reached through any other journal, and for this reason is an excellent advertising medium. It is a large seven column quarto, and the subscription price is $2.50 per year.

DIETRICH & ADAMS,
Manufacturers of Rubber Stamps, etc.
No. 4 Grand Avenue.

PROMINENT among the establishments engaged in this branch of industry is that of Dietrich & Adams, manufacturers of all kinds of rubber stamps, and dealers in amateur printing presses, types, cards, etc. They are located at No. 4 Grand avenue, and although they have but recently formed partnership, they have established a large and lucrative trade not only throughout our city, but in various parts of the State. Their entire stock is new and of the latest designs. Their specialty is in the new process of manufacturing rubber stamps, which renders them superior to others not only in design, but in the smooth printing die. They handle all the latest novelties in the rubber-stamp line, as well as rubber type, self-inking pads, seals, steel stamps, stencils, check-protectors, etc. Mr. Dietrich is an experienced and practical printer, having followed that profession, in connection with the stationery business, for a number of years. Mr. Adams has long been known to the business men of this city as solicitor and agent for the goods which he now manufactures and handles. It is this experience which has won for them a wide-spread reputation for producing the most complete and finished work in their line. This firm pay personal attention to all orders received, and are prompt in the fulfillment of them.

CARPELES, HARTMANN & CO.,
Manufacturers of and Dealers in Trunks and Traveling Bags.
Office and Salesroom, 334 & 336 East Water Street.

THIS representative firm are among the largest trunk and traveling bag

manufacturers in the Northwest. They have large and conveniently-arranged offices and salesrooms at Nos. 334 and 336 East Water Street, and a large factory at Nos. 217, 219, 221, 223 and 225 Sixth street. The business was begun in 1870 under the firm name of Carpeles, Heiser & Co., which in 1883 was changed to Carpeles, Schram & Co. The last change was made the first of the year when the present firm took charge of the business. The stock carried is the most varied and complete in the city, consisting of the best and latest styles of goods in this line. Their factory on Sixth street is a large five-story building, fitted up with machinery of the latest designs for the manufacture of trunks. The goods turned out by this firm are first-class in every respect and, having many valuable patents on trunk bottoms, cross strips, bolt and corner hinges, their goods are much sought after by the trade. A branch office has been established at No. 240 East Madison street, Chicago.

able iron castings for plows, harvesting machinery, wagons and railroad work. All their castings are made exclusively by the air-furnace process, which is greatly superior to the old method. The plant of this company is located in the Menomonee valley—on Park street, between Fourteenth and Fifteenth avenues. Their large factory is represented in the cut below, and covers an area of 150x350 feet. All the latest machinery is in use and is run by a large Corliss engine of 50 horse-power. They employ upwards of 150 men. Their facilities for supplying the trade are surpassed by none. A spur of the Chicago, Milwaukee &

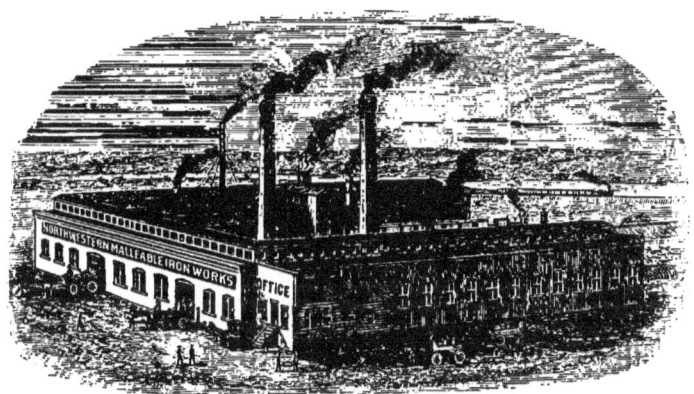

NORTHWESTERN MALLEABLE IRON CO.,

Manufacturers of Malleable Iron Castings,

Park Street, between 13th and 14th Avenues.

AMONG the active and flourishing enterprises of our city there are none whose prospects are more flattering than those of the Northwestern Malleable Iron Company. They begun business in 1882, and so rapidly has it increased that to-day their trade extends throughout the States of Michigan, Wisconsin, Minnesota, Iowa, Illinois, Indiana, Ohio, Missouri and Oregon. They are manufacturers of all forms of malle-

St. Paul Railway is run right to the foundry and is used for receiving their material and shipping their goods. The company consists of F. W. Sivyer, H. M. Wells and W. A. Draves, men of energy and progress.

HYDRAULIC POWER CO.

General Office, Cor. East Water and Wisconsin Streets.

AMONG the leading commercial industries of this country there are none more worthy of notice than that represented by the "Menominee Mining Co.," with headquarters in the Mack Block, this city, and mines in the northern part of this State and Michigan.

Some idea of the extensive operations of this company may be had, when it is stated that since their organization, in 1876, they have mined and shipped 1,151,633 tons of iron ore from their Chapin mine alone. These labors called for great power, and as steam was the only force in use, the cost for fuel was something enormous, which increased year by year as they extended their operations. With an idea of lessening this great expense, efforts were made to obtain sufficient power from water, gas and electricity, but without avail. This led to the organization of the Hydraulic Power Company, in the fall of 1882, which has developed and put into successful operation the power obtained from Quinnesec Falls. This result has been the theme of the mechanical and scientific press for the past three years, and has brought before the men of new ideas the practicability of putting in use the great power of Niagara. The enterprise, referred to above, consists of a plant of air compressors, six in number, at Quinnesec Falls, on the Menominee River, which compress air into a line of pipe leading from the Falls to Iron Mountain, three and three-fourths miles distant, where it is employed to drive the machinery of the Chapin and Ludington mines—pumping, hoisting and motive-power engines above ground, and direct-acting pumps and rock drills below ground, to the exclusion of steam. These iron pipes are twenty-four inches in diameter, laid on rollers on the surface of the ground. To overcome the expansion and contraction, which is fourteen inches every 600 feet, expansion or slip-joints are used all along the entire line of pipe. The Falls furnish a natural head of water of forty-seven-feet, but by means of a dam it is raised to fifty-four feet. The compressors are arranged in pairs, a crank being attached to each end of each compressor-shaft, and a frame attached to each pillow block. The cranks of each shaft are at right angles to one another, and this, together with the heavy gearing employed, give, so far as the eye can detect, a perfectly uniform rotary motion. Each pair of compressors stands on its own separate foundation and is supplied with its own independent turbine.

The compressors are of the Rand "Class A" type. The frames are of the Corliss pattern, with the addition of a foot under the end of the cross-head slide main bearings. Cross-head gibs and connecting rod brasses are of phosphor bronze. The main bearings are four part boxes, very large, and fitted with large steel wedges for taking up side wear. Valves are of the standard Rand poppet construction—the inlets of steel and in two pieces, and fitted with a new form of guard to avoid all possibility of falling into the cylinder. The method of absorbing the heat of compression consists of a brass-lined water-jacketed air cylinder, water-jacketed air cylinder heads, and a hollow piston supplied with water through telescoped tubes, which pass through a stuffing box in the back cylinder head, thus surrounding the air on all sides by cold metallic surfaces.

These compressors are six in number, three pairs, and arrangements are being made to put in the fourth pair at a cost of $60,000. They will be 36x60 instead of 32x60, the size of the old ones; the flume is 600 feet long, fifty feet wide and sixteen feet deep. The development of this whole matter is almost entirely due to Mr. Albert Conro, the second vice-president of the Menominee Mining Co. He has been the life and success of the enterprise, and these results are but the development and perfecting of his own ideas. Difficulties and perplexities would arise, but they were speedily overcome by his engineering skill and determination to succeed. He was ably assisted by Mr. Edward Reynolds, of E. P. Allis & Co. The *American Engineer* of December 19, 1884, Vol. 8th, No. 25, contains a full exposition and illustrations of this plant, which is now interesting scientific men all over the world.

H. M. BENJAMIN,
Coal and Pig Iron Dealer.
Cor. Juneau Ave. and River St.

MR. Benjamin, the extensive coal dealer mentioned at the head of this sketch, begun business in 1869 by

THE BELVEDERE BLOCK,
Corner Eighth street and Grand avenue.

buying out the firm of C. D. Guernsey & Co. His main yard is located at the corner of Juneau avenue and River street, but he has four others in various parts of the city, which have a total dockage of 2,000 feet. He has also an office at 146 La Salle street, and extensive rail-yards at Seventeenth street and Wentworth avenue, where the all-rail car business is distributed for the Chicago trade and the Northwest. The extensive business of this firm consists not only of the largest local trade, but extends all over the West and Northwest. Besides coal and wood, the firm deals extensively in coke, pig iron and foundry supplies. Mr. Benjamin is also engaged extensively in mining, being the president of the Norton Creek Coal and Mining Company, owning and operating mines in Vermillion county, Indiana, with a capacity of 500 tons a day, and is also largely interested in the Gogebic Iron Range, being vice-president of the Superior Iron Company, and interested in several other iron mines. He issued the first call for a meeting of the leading merchants, manufacturers and capitalists of our city to consider the project of establishing a permanent industrial exposition. This resulted in the organization of the Milwaukee Industrial Exposition Association and the erection of the beautiful structure which is represented on the front cover of this work.

WE call the special attention of our many readers to the above establishment, being what it claims to be, a Model Laundry, not only in name, but in the character of work turned out. Perfect system prevails throughout this establishment, thus avoiding vexatious delays incident to this branch of industry. Shirts, collars, cuffs, etc., are done up in a manner to give satisfaction to the most fastidious, particular attention being given to laundrying of flannels and underwear, the latter articles being done up with special care in a sanitary point of view, being subjected to great heat to drive out all moisture in all flannel or woolen garments, so they are in condition for immediate use as soon as received. So the Model Laundry is one of the sanitary institutions of the city. The motto of this establishment is "good work," which is always kept up to the same excellent standard as regards thorough washing and fine finish. Mr. and Mrs. Gause give their close personal attention to every department of the work, and with such gratifying results as to characterize the Model Laundry as one of the most perfect in the city.

HENRY BUESTRIN,

Contractor and Builder,

565 East Water Street.

HENRY BUESTRIN, the well-known contractor and builder, has his place of business and his workshop at No. 565 East Water street. The number of skilled workmen on his pay-roll is hardly ever less than fifty. The yearly business amounts to $100,000 easily.

Mr. Buestrin's specialties are the raising and moving of brick buildings, safes and heavy machinery. He raised the Reese block, a structure of 150x300 feet, a height of 16 feet. Perhaps the most remarkable feat in the moving line ever accomplished here was the job so neatly and successfully performed by Mr. Buestrin some time ago, namely, the moving of a brick smoke-stack at Sanderson's mill, 120 feet high, bodily, a distance of nearly 100 feet. The moving of the old Rindskopf homestead, a large three-story brick building from facing on Grand avenue to Eighth street, and the turning around of the large double brick residence for Hon. Edwin Hyde on Fifth street, are some of the few noted jobs of Mr. Buestrin. He also put in position the Washington monument.

As a builder, Mr. Buestrin's name is associated with the Exposition building,

ESTABLISHMENT OF RUNDLE, SPENCE & CO.,
Manufacturers of Plumbers', Steam and Gas-Fitters' Supplies,
63 and 65 Second street.   (See pages 178 and 179.)

the erection of which he superintended. He also built Immanuel church on Astor street, the Northwestern Insurance building and the block occupied by the Matthews Furniture Company. Mr. Buestrin also builds bridges, and is the inventor of a patent extension-ladder for the use of firemen.

Mr. Buestrin was born in Prussia and came to Milwaukee in 1839, when a boy only four or five years old. Mr. Buestrin takes a deep interest in Milwaukee and is closely identified with its growth and prosperity.

CREAM CITY BRUSH WORKS,

F. J. Uhlmeyer & Bro., Prop'rs,
528 East Water Street.

THE Cream City Brush Works at 528 East Water street, are among the most important of the many manufacturing establishments of Milwaukee. Mr. Uhlmeyer uses the best materials and knows how to do good work, and the natural result is that his brushes are second to none in the market. His workshop and salesroom is 30x50 in dimensions, all of the basement being used as a workshop, where the latest machinery is used. The business was established in 1881, and though begun in a small way soon grew to its present proportions. Better class goods only of all kinds are made, so if you want a cheap, shoddy article, you will have to go to some other shop. Mr. Uhlmeyer makes a great many brushes to order for factories, breweries and tanneries, and is doing, all told, a yearly business amounting to over $5,000.

Mr. Uhlmeyer was born in Watertown, this State, twenty-eight years ago, and has lived in Milwaukee about ten years. He learned his trade in this city and knows it thoroughly in all its details.

BIERBACH'S FEATHER DEPOT.

94 Oneida Street.

THE largest and most perfect feather renovating depot in the city is that of Albert G. Bierbach, at No. 94 Oneida street. He is prepared to cleanse and purify feather-beds, pillows, bolsters, etc., in the most satis-

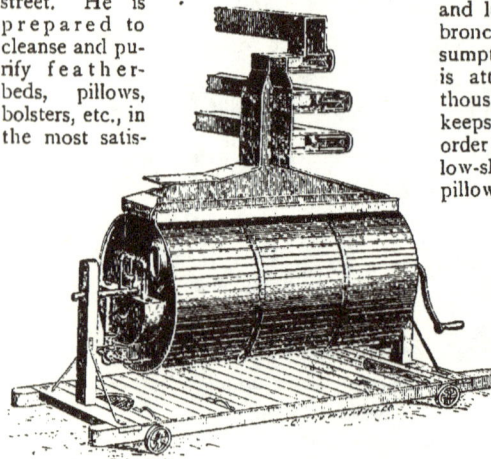

FEATHER RENOVATOR.

factory manner, by means of his patent chemical feather renovator and separator, which for perfect work is unsurpassed by anything of the kind in the world. With this machine all dirt, dust, impurity and bad smell are removed without the slightest injury to the material. In renovating the feathers, no fire comes near them, consequently there is no possibility of burning, scorching or otherwise injuring them. By this process all moths are destroyed and removed, the feathers cleansed and the fibers relieved from their matted position, giving to a bed an astonishing increase in bulk. These renovators range in price from $75 to $500.

We would call special attention to the Bierbach improved pillow, chemically treated. This pillow is composed exclusively of sponge and other yielding material, combined with a certain chemical process, which effects a permanent cure of those afflicted with nose, throat and lung diseases, such as catarrh, bronchitis, asthma and incipient consumption. The worth of this pillow is attested by the testimonials of thousands who use it. He also keeps in stock and manufactures to order quilts, comforts, bedticks, pillow-slips, mattresses, bed-springs and pillow-sham holders.

Mr. Bierbach is also the inventor of the fire escape represented in the cut below and on the inside back cover of this work, the latest patent of which was received Oct. 27th, 1885.

It consists of a permanent, movable or traveling stand-pipe, ladders and balconies, extending from the top of the building to the ground.

BIERBACH'S FIRE ESCAPE.

This escape travels in a slotted tube, which is supported by slotted brackets eight feet apart and capable of carrying from 3,000 to 5,000 pounds. The tube may run along the entire block from one corner to the other, where the buildings are all of the same height. Along the entire length of the bottom of this tube is a one-inch slot or opening, through which is passed a connecting bar, which holds and supports the apparatus below. This connecting bar is fastened to a traveling car or truck, with brass friction wheels, upon steel axles 3¾ inches in diameter, which rolls within the tube (see Figure 1, back cover). The escape can be worked by persons on the ladder, or from the ground, or from each corner. The most flattering testimonials have been received from city officials, chiefs of fire departments, architects and builders all over the country. It is placed upon the Colby & Abbot block and the Kieckhefer building of this city, and on the large "Puck" building in New York city, and other orders are rapidly coming in. He has just secured a patent for an elevated street-car railway, which is based upon the same principle as his fire escape, and which can be run by cable, electricity, or other motive power. City and State rights for sale for either his feather renovators or fire escape. All information freely given by writing or applying to Albert G. Bierbach, No 94 Oneida street.

JOHN ELSER,
Wholesale and Retail Provision and Meat Market.
483 East Water Street.

THIS house was first founded in 1840. In 1868 Mr. Elser became proprietor and has since conducted the enterprise, having steadily met with success. He occupies four floors, and has them well stocked with provisions, fresh and cured meats, sausage, etc. His business amounts to $60,000 per year, and his trade extends over the entire city. Mr. Elser is a native of Germany, and was born in 1835. He came from thence direct to Milwaukee in 1850, and has been engaged in business here ever since. His shop is always clean and neat, and his stock of meats is of the choicest and most extensive in the city. He supplies some of our largest hotels, and his shop is frequented by all classes of our citizens. Mr. Elser also does a wholesale business, and in this branch has an extensive trade throughout the State.

NEW YORK HAIR STORE,
Mrs. C. B. Kessler, Proprietress.
432 East Water Street.

FOR the past three years Mrs. C. B. Kessler has been engaged in business on the above street, and has her parlors stocked throughout with a full line of hair goods. It is a popular establishment among our ladies of fashion, who favor it with their patronage; she also has a large number of customers from outside the city. Mrs. Kessler employs two skillful artists, who are perfectly acquainted with the work, and dress ladies' hair in any style desired. Her stock of hair goods is a most select one. Having had fifteen years' experience in the old country, New York, Chicago and this city, she is thoroughly competent to perform all work placed in her hands in the highest style of the art. Her parlors are the resort of the elite of our city, among whom she is generally recognized as authority on the latest styles of hairdressing. Ladies will find her prepared at all times to attend to their wants, and any orders left with her will receive the most careful attention.

D. W. GOETZ & CO.,
Manufacturers of Hand-Knit Worsted and Silk Goods.
420 and 422 East Water Street.

THE above firm is one of the oldest and most prominent houses in Milwaukee engaged in this business, having first been established in 1857 by D. W.

Goetz. They occupy the second floor at No. 420 and 422 East Water street, which is forty by one hundred and fifty feet in area. They manufacture hand-knit worsted goods of all kinds, and employ one hundred and fifty persons in the business. They enjoy a large and increasing trade, the sales last year amounting to $40,000. They also deal in hand-knit silk goods, and strive to excel in quality of the work done. The business is now conducted by Julius Meiswinkel, who owns the entire concern. He was born in Germany in 1842, and came to Milwaukee in 1856, and has since resided here. He has held the office of clerk of the Municipal Court since 1878, and served through the civil war, being a lieutenant in the Twenty-sixth Regiment of Wisconsin Volunteers. The above firm never fails to give satisfaction.

trunks, traveling bags, tourists' outfits, etc. Their large factory is located on Tenth street, occupying the entire block between Fowler and Hibernia streets, 300 feet, and extends back fifty feet. It is of brick and four stories in height. All the latest and best machinery is in use at this establishment, and is run by an engine of fifty horse-power. Upwards of 200 hands are given employment in the various departments. They have just opened large and convenient sales-rooms at No. 114 Grand avenue, just opposite the Plankinton House, which is stocked with as full a supply of goods as can be found in the city. They begun this business five years ago, and now do a trade of nearly a quarter of a million dollars annually. Not only are the products of this establishment found thoughout the West and Northwestern States, but also

ABEL, BACH & FITZGERALD,

Manufacturers of Trunks, Traveling Bags, etc.

Tenth, Fowler and Hibernia Sts.

AMONG the important industries of our city there is no more enterprising or progressive house than that of Abel, Bach & Fitzgerald, manufacturers of in Mexico and along the Pacific Slope. The aim of this firm is always to reach the highest standard of excellence, and present the latest and best designs of goods to their many patrons. The members of this firm are representative business men, and display great energy and enterprise in the successful manner in which they conduct their large establishment, which is growing larger year by year.

GROSS BROS.,
Soap Boilers and Manufacturers of Washing Compound.
Works: 953, 955, 957, 959, 961 and 963 North Water St.

AMONG the old and representative houses of this city is that of Gross Bros., manufacturers of toilet and laundry soaps, and washing compound. The business was begun in 1866, in an old barn on Reed street, with a capacity of about 2,000 pounds per week. So rapidly did the business increase, that in one year's time they entered the wholesale trade, and in 1868 moved to their present site, where their large factory is located. It is 80x100 feet in dimensions and four stories high. They turn out over 150,000 pounds of soap per week, which requires the employment of fifty hands, five of them being traveling men. They have the largest and best purifying apparatus in use in the Union, all the fat used in making their soaps being thoroughly purified, which renders their soaps so wholesome and popular. The principal brands manufactured are the "Golden Laundry," "Electricity" and "A, B, C" Soap, which are found in almost every household in the West and Northwest. They manufacture forty other brands, besides their washing compound. They have offices established at Cleveland, Nashville, St. Louis, Kansas City, Chicago, St. Paul and Minneapolis. This firm sends out annually several millions of beautiful lithographs and oleographs of all sizes and designs, which not only serve to advertise them, but to beautify the homes of their many patrons.

J. B. KUEHLE,
Dealer in Gent's Furnishing Goods.
403 East Water Street.

THE above business was begun in 1861 by Mr. J. Bernard Kuehle, on the corner of Martin and East Water streets. He moved to the present site in 1883, where he soon established a large local and State trade. Here can be found at all times a fine line of gent's furnishing goods of every description. Here is kept constantly on hand a large stock of medium and fine goods at as reasonable prices as can be found anywhere else in the city. One of the main features of this firm's business is their custom shirts and underwear, and special attention is given to all orders received in this line. Mr. Kuehle's demise occurred one year ago, since which time the business has been ably managed by his son Henry W. Kuehle, who has had years of experience in every department of this trade.

INDEX.

Name	Page
Abel, Bach & Fitzgerald, Mnfrs. of Trunks, Traveling Bags, etc.	218
Academy (The New), Jacob Litt, Manager	194
Adler, F. P., Fine Confectionery, etc.	172
Audres, Fred. & Co., Stone Contractors	148
Andrews, C. E. & Co., Baking Powder, Spices, etc.	132
Anson Bros., Jobbers of Groceries, etc.	141
Armstrong's Broadway Gallery, Photography	206
Baird, R. S. & Co., Art Printers	135
Baugs, E. D., Photographer	134
Barber, Edward, Real Estate and Loans	162
Baumgaertner, H. J., Sign Painter	170
Beer, Richard, Livery Stable	185
Belvedere Block	213
Benjamin, H. M., Dealer in Coal and Pig Iron	212
Berthelet, H. & Co., Manufacturers of Hydraulic Cement, etc.	102
Best Brewing Co. (Philip), Mnfrs. of Beer	114
Binney, J., Platt & Co.'s Oysters	176
Blatz, Valentin, Brewer and Maltster	103
Bodden & Heith, Coffee, Spices, etc.	144
Booth, Wm., Merchant Tailor	149
Borgnis, Edw'd E., Mnfr. of Models, Dies, etc.	164
Bower, E. C., Cash Grocer	191
Boyle, Wm., Practical Horse Shoer	173
Boynton, A. L., Livery and Sale Stables	132
Bradford, James B., Piano Warerooms	137
Bradley & Metcalf, Mnfrs. of Boots and Shoes	97
Brock, W. D., Elevator Manufacturer	171
Brown Photograph Studio, Brown Bros., Prop's	141
Brown, T. H. & Co., Mnfrs. of Carriages and Buggies	143
Buell, F. R. & Co., Shippers of Coal	122
Buestrin, Henry, Contractor and Builder	214
Bunde & Upmeyer, Manufacturing Jewelers	90
Burroughs, Geo., Manufacturer of Trunks, etc.	128
Campbell Steam Laundry, H. N. Campbell, Propr.	140
Carpeles, Hartmann & Co., Manufacturers of and Dealers in Trunks and Traveling Bags	210
Carpenter & Underwood, Manufacturers of Crackers and Biscuits	183
Cassel, B., Stoves, Ranges, etc.	186
Central Warehouse, E. J. Tapping, Agent	116
City Carriage Works, R. Sherin & Co., Proprietors	122
City Steam Laundry, J. P McCarty, Proprietor	154
Chadbourne, C., Photographer	136
Chapman, T. A., Dry Goods	81
Clarke, Chas. H., Letter Cutter, Engraver, etc.	172
Clark, John, Manufacturer of Harness, etc.	157
Clements Bros., Steam Heating and Ventilating.	173
Columbia, German Catholic Newspaper	209
Conroy, James, Caterer and Confectioner	203
Continental Restaurant, etc., S. J. Eldridge, Propr.	196
Conway, Clement & Williams, Manufacturers and Dealers in Furniture	92
Cream City Brewing Co., Beer Brewers	166
Cream City Brush Works, F. J. Uhlmeyer & Bro., Proprietors	215
Cream City Preserving Works, N. M. Klein, Propr.	159
Cudworth, W. H., Dentist	140
Davis, Ira M. & Co., Gen'l Commission Merchants	106
Davis Omnibus Line, Davis & Baird, Proprietors	200
De Voe, B F., Printer and Publisher	140
Dietrich & Adams, Mnfrs. of Rubber Stamps, etc.	210
Dutcher, Collins & Smith, Jobbers of Teas	183
Ehr, Peter, Custom Tailor	175
Electro-Thermal Baths, Daniel T. Coates, Propr.	186
Ellinghausen, H. & Co., General Com. Merchants	157
Elser, John, Wholesale and Retail Provision and Meat Market	217
Elmore, R. P. & Co., Coal and Pig Iron	86
Ely, Mrs. Lydia, Artist and Art Teacher	189
Empire Fur Factory, Mnfrs. of Fur Garments	131
English Chop House, Neuman & Manasse, Proprs.	127
Erbacher, F. W. & Co., Cheese, Groceries, etc	157
Esau, Dr. Louis R., Dentist	152
Esch, John & Son, Esch's Patent Trucks	180
Everly, J. M., Book and Job Printer	203
Excelsior Business and Shorthand College, H. M. Wilmot & Co., Proprietors	99
Falk Brewing Co. (Franz), Manufacturers of Beer	146
Feather Depot, Albert G. Bierbach, Proprietor	216
Filer & Stowell Co. (Limited), The Cream City Iron Works	155
Fire Escape, Albert G. Bierbach, Proprietor	216
Fisher, D. & Co., Mnfrs. of Flavoring Extracts.	167
Flint, J. G., Star Coffee and Spice Mills	161
Flint & Pere Marquette R. R., L. C. Whitney, General Agent	180
Fox, J. M., Staple and Fancy Groceries	120
Frankfurth Hardware Co. (Limited, Wm., Wholesale Hardware	108
Fricke, Wm. A., Dentist	202
Friedmann, Julius, Restaurant and Caterer	150
Gebhardt, Geo., Confectionery Articles	201
Gerber & Gram, Musical Merchandise	190
Germania Publishing Co., Geo. Brumder, Propr.	189
Goehel, Peter, Cigars, Tobacco, Snuff, etc.	170
Goetz, D. W., & Co., Manufacturers of Hand-Knit Worsted and Silk Goods	217
Goll & Frank Co., Wholesale Dry Goods, Notions, etc.	91
Goodrich & Wagner, Wholesale Grocers	88
Goodyear Rubber Co., W. W. Wallis, Manager	147
Graf, John, Mnfr. White Beer, Soda Water, etc.	190
Grand Avenue Hotel, H. M. Merryman, Proprietor	175
Grand Central Drug Store, A. v. Trott, Proprietor	147
Grosskopf, Theo., Wine and Cigar Merchant	170
Gross Bros., Soap Boilers and Manufacturers of Washing Compound	219
Gross, Phillip, Hardware Merchant	150
Gurney Brick Machine Works, T. C. Gurney, Proprietor	176
Guy, Wm. S., Groceries, Provisions, etc.	149
Hadfield & Co., Dealers in Coal, Wood, Lime, etc.	108
Hadley, Dr. Fred S., Dentist	174
Hale & Wilson, Insurance	208
Hallaska & Co., Painters, Grainers, etc.	186
Hartmann, F. W. & Co., Distillers and Jobbers in Whiskies	118
Hassenteufel & Waechter, Lamps, Glassware, etc.	188
Hays, Geo., Planing Mill and Box Factory	172
Helming, B. H. & Co., Mnfrs. Collars, Saddles, etc.	153
Herman, Henry, Real Estate and Loans	184
Heuel & Ullmer, Artists	191
Hof, J. J., Land Office	187
Hoffman & Baur, Tin, Sheet Iron and Copper Works	169
Hoffman & Billings Manufacturing Co. (Limited), Gas, Steam and Plumbers' Supplies, etc.	89
Hydraulic Power Co.	211
Inbusch, J. D., Wholesale Grocers, etc.	132

222　INDEX.

Name	Page
Jacobi, Mrs. M., Embroideries, Fancy Goods, etc.	168
Jewett & Sherman Co., Merchants' Coffee and Spice Mills	202
Johnson, B. J. & Co., Soap Manufacturers, etc.	139
Johnson, H. R., Dentist	156
Jones & Son, Manufacturers and Dealers in Corks	205
Joseph Schlitz Bottling Works (Limited) The, Voechting, Shape & Co., Proprietors	185
Josten, S., House and Sign Painter	172
Jung & Borchert, Beer Brewers	192
Kavanaugh, Mrs. Jean, Artist and Art Teacher	186
Keogh, Edwd., Commercial Printer	107
Kieckhefer Bros. & Co., Manufacturers of Stamped and Pieced Tinware	94
Kipp Bros., Mnfrs. of Mattresses, Spring Beds,etc.	166
Knell, Wm. R., Dealer in Paper Hangings, etc.	163
Koch, H. C. & Co., Architects and Superintendents	121
Kruse & Barker, Plumbers, Steam Fitters, etc.	138
Kuchle, J. B., Dealer in Gent's Furnishing Goods	219
Kump, Mrs. B., Mattress Manufacturer	151
Lachman, Louis, Merchant Tailor	184
Landwehr, J. H. H., Dealer in Groceries, etc.	169
Langenberger, J., Contractor and Builder	174
Laverrenz, Otto & Bro., Book Binders and Paper Box Manufacturers	144
Lebeau & Schuhmann, Dentists	149
Leihammer, E., Mnfr. and Dealer in Harness	164
Little, W. H., & Co., Beet and Pork Packers	91
Litt's Milwaukee Dime Museum, Jacob Litt,propr	194
Loomis, L. G., Money Loaner	206
Luick, John, Confectioner and Caterer	128
Lydston, F. A., Artist	160
Lyon, Geo. S., Plumber, Gasfitter, etc.	105
Markham Academy, Prof. A. Markham, Propr.	200
Martin, D. A., Grain Dealer	158
Martin, H. H. & Co., Manufacturing Jewelers	168
Massey & Co., Dealers in Crockery, Glassware, etc.	205
McCanniny, M., Printing House	167
Meinecke & Co., Toys, Fancy Goods, etc.	88
Meinecke, Adolph & Son, Manufacturers of Baskets, Willow Ware, etc.	111
Mendel, Smith & Co , Wholesale Grocers	88
Miller, Fred., Brewer and Maltster	195
Milwaukee Cement Co., Manufacturers of Cement	84
Milwaukee Chair Co., Mnfrs. of Chairs and Cradles	209
Milwaukee Electropathic Institute, Dr. J. McGuffin, Proprietor	197
Milwaukee Garden, Pius Dreher, Proprietor	153
Milwaukee School of Music, J. C. Fillmore, Director	181
Milwaukee Stone Yard, Cook & Hyde, Props.	188
Milwaukee Stove Works, J. A. and P. E. Dutcher, Proprietors	145
Milwaukee Type and Electrotype Foundry, Francis Keehu, Proprietor	182
Mock, Benjamin, Livery and Boarding Stable	127
Model Laundry, C. E. Gause, Proprietor	214
Morgan, James, Dry Goods, Millinery, etc.	178
Mott, H. W., Druggist	173
Mueller & Ihardt, Wall Paper, etc.	158
Naramore, John H., Dentist	155
National Park (The), F. C. G. Brand, Proprietor.	142
Neumann, A., Merchant Tailor	152
Neumeister, Dr. A. E., Medical Institute	187
New Hampshire Block, E. D. Holton, Proprietor.	188
New York Hair Store, Mrs. C. B. Kessler, Prop'r.	217
Nichols, J. H. & Co., Jobbers in Fruits, Cigars,etc.	135
Northwestern Malleable Iron Co., Manufacturers of Malleable Iron Castings	211
Ogden, G. W. & Co., Mnfrs. of Carriages, etc.	124
Ormsby Lime Co., Mnfrs. and Jobbers of Lime	181
Packard, O. L., Machinery Depot	101
Panorama (Battle of Vicksburg)	207
Pautke, E. R. & Co., Hats, Caps and Furs	188
Parks, H. O., Bill Poster	196
Patterson, R W., Undertaker and Embalmer	106
Patton, Jas. E. & Co., Manufacturers of White Lead, Colors, etc.	147
Peacock, Sam'l F., Undertaker	168
Peters, Mrs. E.J., Dealer in Watches,Diamonds,etc	184
Podoll, G. & Co., Photographer	191
Potter, Geo. E., Livery Stables	176
Reiter, John B., Manufacturer of Soda and Mineral Waters	185
Remington Standard Typewriter, Chas. H. Welch, Manager	165
Rich, A. W. & Co., Dry Goods	123
Ringer, C. F., Architect and Superintendent	138
Rohlfing, Wm. & Co., Music and Musical Instruments	179
Rose Hill Park, Wm. Miller, Proprietor	151
Rundle, Spence & Co., Manufacturers of Brass and Iron Goods	178, 215
Saville, Butler & Co., Wooden Ware, Grocers' Sundries, etc	135
Schlitz Brewing Co. (Jos.), Manufacturers of Beer	124
Schlitz's Park	118
Schueck, F. W., House Furnisher	169
Schmidt, Peter, Stone and Marble Works	188
Schrand & Wachs, Practical Harness Makers	204
Schwalbach, Mathew, Mnfr. of Tower Clocks	150
Severance's Dancing Academy, Mr and Mrs. C. G. Severance, Proprietors	167
Seymour, F. M., Wholesale Millinery	130
Sherman, Bell & Co., Auctioneers and Commission Merchants	158
Sielaff, Loeber & Co., Wholesale Paper and Twine Dealers	113
Silber, I., Manufacturer of Suspenders, etc	184
Singer, J. E. & Co., Woolens, Tailors' Trimmings, etc	148
Singer Manufacturing Co. (The), F. W. Noyes, Agent	133
Smith, Jabez M., Confectionery, Fruits, etc	117
Spalding Bros. & Co., Publishers and Booksellers	201
Spankus, Aug., Blank Book Mnfr., Binder, etc.	152
Spence, Geo. A & Co., Fine Gas Fixtures and Plumbing	110
Spencerian Business College, Robt. C. Spencer, Proprietor	177
Standard Paper Co., Wholesale Paper Dealers	192
Stapleton, J. A., Wholesale Tobacconist	155
St. Charles Hotel, Chas. Fernekes & Bro., Proprs.	163
Stern, H., Jr. & Bro., Jobbers of Dry Goods, etc.	154
St. John, C. W., R. R. Employment Agency	174
St. Mary's Institute	197
Stout & Underwood, Patent Solicitors	143
Streckewald, G., Grass-Seeds, Bags, Twines, etc.	189
Strouneh Lumber Co., Manufacturers of Lumber and Salt	112
Strueder, Wm., Manufacturer of Show Cases, etc.	204
Sullivan, Hauf & Co., Champion Horse Shoers	171
Sutter, Harry S., Photographer	98
Thiele Bros., Pork and Beef Packers	162
Thompson, J. P. & Co., Dealers in Dye Woods, Chemicals, etc.	93
Thomas & Wentworth Manufacturing Co. (The), Manufacturers of Brass and Iron Goods	182
Trostel, Albert, Tanner and Leather Dealer	96
Tschank's Restaurant	171
Turpin & Co., 5c, 10c and 25c Store	164
Voss, Herman, Blank Book Manufacturer and Book Binder	196
Vulcan Iron Works, James Sheriff's, Proprietor	198
Wallis, J. T., Manufacturer and Dealer in Harness	175
Walters, G. W., Dealer in Groceries	170
Wechselberg, J. P., Carriage and Wagon Mnfr.	146
Weckerle, Joseph, Practical Jeweler	165
Weden, H., Dealer in Wall Paper, etc.	174
Welles, J. C., Dealer in Guns, Ammunition, etc.	160
Werner, F., Artists' Materials,Picture Frames,etc.	139
Whitehill Sewing Machine Co., The, Manufacturers of Sewing Machines	129
Williams & Brenckle, Cigar Manufacturers	184
Wisconsin Marine & Fire Ins. Co. Bank	113
Zander, Fred, Undertaker	176
Ziegler, George, Manufacturing Confectioner	137
Zimmermann Bros., Clothiers	208
Zinn, Oscar, Druggist	163
Zwengel, H., Manufacturing Jeweler	160

MILWAUKEE COMMERCIAL LIST.

JUL. GOLL.   AUG. FRANK.

GOLL & FRANK CO.,
IMPORTERS AND DEALERS IN

Dry Goods
Notions and Gent's Furnishing Goods,

COR. EAST WATER & BUFFALO STS.

See Page 91.   MILWAUKEE.

Hadfield & Co.
COAL,
LIME, CEMENT, STUCCO, LAND PLASTER, Etc.

OFFICE, 119 WEST WATER ST., MILWAUKEE.
WORKS, WAUKESHA, WIS.

See Page 108.

C. T. BRADLEY.   *Established 1843.*
W. H. METCALF.

BRADLEY & METCALF,
MANUFACTURERS AND JOBBERS IN

Boots and Shoes,
389, 391 & 393 East Water St.

See Page 97.   MILWAUKEE

Milwaukee Cement Co.
OFFICE, 154 WEST WATER ST.

DIRECTORS.

ALEX. MITCHELL,   HENRY BERTHELET,
GEO. H. PAUL,   JOHN JOHNSTON,
D. J. WHITTEMORE,   THOS. A. GREENE,
SAMUEL MARSHALL.

See Page 84.

— THE —
Wisconsin Marine and Fire Insurance Co.
BANK.
Established 1839.

ALEXANDER MITCHELL, President.
DAVID FERGUSON, Cashier.
JOHN JOHNSTON, Assistant Cashier.

The stockholders are individually liable without limit for all the debts of the Bank.

See Page 113.

O. L. PACKARD,
MACHINERY,
ENGINES, BOILERS,
Tools and Supplies,

85 and 87 WEST WATER ST.,

See Page 101.   MILWAUKEE.

Wm. Frankfurth Hardware Co.
JOBBERS OF
HARDWARE,
CUTLERY, REVOLVERS, METALS,

MECHANICS AND EDGE TOOLS OF ANY DESCRIPTION, FARMING TOOLS, SAWS, AXES, ETC.

See Page 108.   116 and 118 Clybourn St., MILWAUKEE.

GEO. S. LYON,
(LATE OF SPENCE & LYON),

Practical Plumber,
FINE GAS FIXTURES AND PLUMBING MATERIAL,

410 Grand Avenue, Library Block.

See Page 105.   MILWAUKEE.

J. A. & P. E. DUTCHER,
MILWAUKEE STOVE WORKS.

670 Kinnickinnic Avenue,

See Page 145.   MILWAUKEE.

Jas. E. Patton & Co.,
MANUFACTURERS OF
White Lead, Zinc, Colors and Varnishes,
AND DEALERS IN

Linseed and Lubricating Oils, Putty, Window Glass, Brushes, Artists' Materials.

NOS. 268, 270 & 272 EAST WATER ST.

See Page 147.   MILWAUKEE.

MILWAUKEE COMMERCIAL LIST.

Sutter's Studio,
128 WISCONSIN ST.

Finest Cabinet Photographs reduced to $4 per dozen.

Artistic Water Colors, Crayons or India Ink of the finest finish, from life, or copied from any picture, at the lowest prices.

BRANCH, GRAND CENTRAL STUDIO,

See Page 98.   Corner Oneida Street Bridge.

Dutcher, Collins & Smith,
IMPORTERS AND TEAS JOBBERS OF

A SPECIALTY.

See Page 133.   Milwaukee, Wis.

F. W. HARTMANN.   H. SCHOENFELD.

F. W. HARTMANN & CO.,
DISTILLERS AND JOBBERS IN

Fine Whiskies
IMPORTERS OF
WINES AND LIQUORS,

See Page 118.   206 and 208 WEST WATER ST.

Mendel, Smith & Co.,
IMPORTERS AND
WHOLESALE GROCERS,
East Water and Huron Sts.,

HENRY M. MENDEL.   MILWAUKEE.
IRA B. SMITH.

See Page 88.

VAL. BLATZ,
BREWER AND MALTSTER
MILWAUKEE.

See Page 103.

Geo. Ziegler,
MANUFACTURING
CONFECTIONER,
235, 237 & 239 E. Water St.

SPECIALTIES:
Fine Creams, Chocolate Creams and Jelly Goods.

See Page 137.

Annual Capacity, 500,000 Barrels.

Jos. Schlitz
BREWING COMPANY,
Manufacturers of Standard Brands of Lager Beer.

HENRY UIHLEIN, Pres't.
ALFRED UIHLEIN, Sup't.   MILWAUKEE.
AUG. UIHLEIN, Sec'y.

See Page 124.

THE FILER & STOWELL CO. (LIMITED),
Cor. Clinton and Florida Sts.

MILWAUKEE, WIS.

SPECIALTIES:
Steam Engines, Steam Pumps,
Circular Saw Mills,
Steam Feed Works,
Rope Feed Works,
Gang Edgers,
Gang Bolters,
Gang Lath and Picket Mills,
Shingle Mills,
Patent Head Blocks,
"Boss" Dogs,
Timber Gauges,
Bracket Supports,
Patent Saw Guides.

See Page 155.

ESTABLISHED 1851.

IRA M. DAVIS & CO.
General Commission Merchants,

For the sale of BUTTER, EGGS, CHEESE, APPLES, ORANGES, LEMONS, SEEDS, Etc.,

165 & 167 West Water St., Milwaukee.

Liberal Cash Advances on Consignments.

See Page 106.

KRUSE & BARKER,

Steam Heating and Ventilating

ENGINEERS.

Sole Agents for WALKER & PRATT SAFETY SECTIONAL BOILER.

Correspondence Solicited. **450 East Water St.**

See Page 138.

F. W. SCHNECK,
General House Furnisher,

—DEALER IN—

FURNITURE, STOVES, CARPETS, OIL CLOTHS, CROCKERY, GLASSWARE,

New and Second Hand,

Nos. 255 & 257 THIRD ST.,

See Page 169. MILWAUKEE.

H. C. KOCH. H. P. SCHNETZKY.

H. C. Koch & Co.,

ARCHITECTS AND SUPERINTENDENTS,

PFISTER'S BLOCK,

COR WISCONSIN ST. AND BROADWAY.

See Page 121. MILWAUKEE.

G. H. Brown & Co.,

MANUFACTURERS OF FINE

◁ CARRIAGES, BUGGIES, PHAETONS, ▷

ROAD CARTS—Brown's Patent,

Sleighs, Cutters, Delivery Wagons, Etc.,

182 & 184 THIRD STREET,

See Page 143. MILWAUKEE.

J. E. SINGER & CO.,
WOOLENS

AND TAILORS' TRIMMINGS.

372 and 374 Broadway,

See Page 148. MILWAUKEE.

CLEMENTS BROS.,

PRACTICAL

Steam-Heating and Ventilating

ENGINEERS,

445 Jefferson Street.

See Page 173. Telephone 873.

G. STRECKEWALD,

DEALER IN

GRASS SEEDS,

BAGS, TWINES, ETC.

{ Bags Loaned to Shippers. } **37 West Water St.**

See Page 139.

For Ladies and Gents. On the European Plan.

NEUMAN'S

English Chop House,

120 GRAND AVENUE,

NEUMAN & MANASSE, Proprietors. Opposite Plankinton House.

See Page 127.

Sam'l F. Peacock,

UNDERTAKER.

A full line of METALLIC, CLOTH and WOOD CASKETS, COFFINS, ROBES, Etc., and everything in the Undertaker's line, kept constantly on hand.

Orders Promptly Attended by Night or Day.

See Page 168. **431 BROADWAY.**

W. D. BROCK'S ELEVATOR WORKS,

MANUFACTURER OF

∷ Steam, Hand and Hydraulic ∷

ELEVATORS,

Shafting, Pulleys, Hangers, Etc.,

219, 221 & 223 CLYBOURN ST.,

See Page 171. MILWAUKEE.

MILWAUKEE COMMERCIAL LIST.

F. Werner,
DEALER IN
ARTISTS' MATERIALS,
Manufacturer of Picture Frames,
No. 436 BROADWAY,
See Page 139. MILWAUKEE.

THEODORE GROSSKOPF,
IMPORTING
Wine and Spirit Merchant,
Importer of Havana Cigars.
No. 107 GRAND AVENUE,
See Page 170. MILWAUKEE.

Portraits, Views, Landscapes, Etc.
Northwestern View Co.
Headquarters—333 THIRD ST., MILWAUKEE.

All orders should be directed to
GUSTAVE PODOLL, General Manager.
See Page 191.

SULLIVAN, HAUF & CO.,
CHAMPION
HORSE SHOERS,
112 Clybourn St., Milwaukee.

Corns, Quitters and Sand Cracks properly treated.
Horses stopped from interfering and forging.
See Page 171.

JOHN ESCH & SON,
Manufacturers of every Description of
TRUCKS and WAGONS,
Shop, 58 & 60 Second St.,
See Page 180. MILWAUKEE.

AUGUST SPANKUS,
Blank Book Manufacturer,
BINDER AND RULER,
234 West Water Street, MILWAUKEE.

Art Binding a Specialty.
See Page 152.

E. R. PANTKE & CO.,
MANUFACTURERS AND DEALERS IN
HATS AND CAPS,
LADIES' AND GENT'S FURS,
390 East Water St., below Wisconsin, MILWAUKEE.
Silk and Cassimere Hats made to Order.
See Page 188.

J. P. WECHSELBERG,
MANUFACTURER OF
CARRIAGES AND WAGONS,
218 and 220 Wells Street,
MILWAUKEE.
See Page 146. Repairing Done.

JAMES LEIGH,
LEIGH HOUSE
Dining Rooms,
414 to 418 Broadway,
Milwaukee, Wis.

OTTO LAVERRENZ. CHAS. LAVERRENZ.
OTTO LAVERRENZ & BRO.,
MANUFACTURERS OF
PAPER BOXES
BOOKBINDING
Of Every Description.
428 East Water St., Milwaukee.
See Page 144. Telephone No. 633.

J. B. KUEHLE,

— DEALER IN —

Gent's Furnishing Goods,

And Manufacturer of

CUSTOM SHIRTS AND UNDERWEAR.

403 East Water St., Milwaukee.

See Page 219.

William Boyle,

PRACTICAL

HORSESHOER,

49 Second St., Milwaukee.

Shoes made to Order and Horses Shod as Desired.

See Page 173.

F. W. Erbacher & Co.,

WHOLESALE

Cheese and Fancy Groceries,

Canned Goods, Fish, Etc.

83 West Water St., Milwaukee.

See Page 157.   Telephone No. 802.

A. Meinecke, Sr.   A. Meinecke, Jr.   C. Penshorn.   F. Goetz.

MEINECKE & CO.,

Importers and Jobbers of

Toys, Fancy Goods, Notions,

BOHEMIAN GLASS AND CHINA WARE,

Druggists' Sundries, Bird Cages, Fishing Tackle, Masks,

CHILDREN'S CARRIAGES,

Wooden and Willow Ware,

348 and 350 East Water St., Milwaukee.

See Page 88.

Model Laundry,
C. E. GAUSE, PROP'R,
No. 440 MILWAUKEE ST.
[TRADE MARK.]

See Page 314.

www.ingramcontent.com/pod-product-compliance
Lightning Source LLC
Chambersburg PA
CBHW021834230426
43669CB00008B/970